CLASSIC DOLOMITE C

UIAA	UK Traditional	Yosemite
II–III-	H Diff – V Difficult	5.2
III+	Hard V. Difficult	5.3
IV–	Mild Severe 3b / 4a	5.4
IV	Severe 4a	5.5
IV+	Hard Severe 4b	5.5 / 5.6
V-	Mild VS 4b	5.6
V	Very Severe 4c	5.6 / 5.7
V+	Very Severe 5a	5.7 / 5.8
VI–	Hard VS 5a	5.8 / 5.9
VI	Hard VS 5b	5.9 / 5.10a
VI+	E1 5b	5.10a
VII–	E2 5c	5.10b/c

Emilio Comici making the sensational bridging move (VI −) across the gap between Torre Leo and Torre del Diavolo (Rt. 57), first done by Hans Dülfer in 1913. *Photo: Archivo Società Alpina della Guide*

Anette Köhler
Norbert Memmel

Classic
DOLOMITE
Climbs

102 high quality rock-climbs
between the UIAA grades III and VII

Adapted from a translation by Tim Carruthers

BÂTON WICKS • LONDON

Position and Access. This is a translation of a popular German guidebook describing a selection of classic rock-climbs in the Dolomites. This challenging and beautiful range of steep limestone peaks is situated south of the Austrian/Italian border, stretching 50 miles (80 kms) east from the main Brenner Pass Autostrada where it passes Bolzano. The slightly detached Brenta group is west of the Autostrada, north of Lake Garda. The nearest main line rail stations are at Bolzano and Venice. Road approaches are best made from Bolzano to the west or from the south via Venice and Belluno. The most convenient international airports are Venice and Verona to the south and Munich and Salzburg to the north. This is a holiday area, well-served by hotels, guest houses and campsites. The mountain huts of the Italian Alpine Club offer concessionary rates to members of other affiliated alpine clubs. As a semi-alpine region the climbs are high, and thus exposed to changeable weather.

First published in Germany in 1993. Reprinted and revised in 1998.
© 1998 by Bergverlag Rother, Ottobrun. © in maps by Freytag and Berndt, Vienna.

The English-language edition was first published in 1999 in Great Britain and America
© in English translation by Bâton Wicks, London

Reprinted and revised in 2008 by Bâton Wicks, London

Trade enquiries: Cordee, 3a DeMontfort Street, Leicester LE1 7HD

British Library and Cataloguing in Publication Data
A catalogue record for this book exists in the British Library
ISBN (10 figure) 1-898573-34-4 (13 figure) 9781-898573-34-0

Printed in Spain by GraphyCems, Navarro

Photographic Credits: Archivio Siocietà Alpina delle Giullie of Trieste 2, Richard Goedeke 11, 70, 73, 131, 140, 150, 157, 159; Thomas Heinze 56, 57; Thomas Holzmann 193, back cover; Heinz Mariacher 54, 72, 74, 78; Werner Neumayer 80; Foto Pedrotti 178; Rudolf Rother 16; Edwin Schmitt 144, 162; Rolo Steffens 35, 196; Heinz Steinkötter 198, 202, 207, 210; Bernd Wendt 152. Of the 28 colour illustrations added to the English language edition: Tom Prentice flaps, front cover and three others, F.Hauleitner, Werner Neumayer, Siegfried Lechner, H.Andergassen, Rollo Steffens and Rudi Lindner are acknowledged with their photographs.
In addition, valuable editorial help was given by those credited at the foot of page 216.

PREFACE

For many years we have spent almost every spare minute in the Dolomites, hunting down the classics and the little-known gems. We have made old dreams come true and have discovered more of the stuff of which new ones are made. 'Fun climbing' was the watchword as, gradually, the idea evolved for a new climbing guidebook. The more summits we sat on sketching our topos, the more the reality of the whole project began to become apparent. In the evenings we sat over spaghetti and red wine, reviewing pitch by pitch the day's haul, discussing, grading and characterising; finding this too easy and that too hard, too short, too long, too demanding. Then deciding at some point simply to take things as they were – highly subjective, rich and varied in character.

It is now five years since the idea became a book. The first edition of *Dolomiten Genussklettern* (here titled *Classic Dolomite Climbs*) appeared in 1993, with 66 selected routes, yet the matter could not and cannot rest there. A second edition soon followed with a total of 101 routes. And now this new topo guide, with more than 100 routes from the whole of the Dolomites. Just as in the first book, you will find here long alpine routes next to short sport climbs, new bolts and quietly rusting pitons, classic routes and routes in the modern idiom, sun-kissed faces and walls deep in shadows, towering mountains both remote and next to the road. All have one thing in common: we reckoned they were really good. This evaluation does presuppose, however, that the rock quality fulfils our high expectations, that reasonable belays can be found and that the climber is not required to stare too bravely into the cold eye of objective danger. The fact that many famous routes are to be found here – the 'classics' – should be obvious.

When making our selection we have attempted both to illustrate the various areas by means of representative routes (perhaps one might once have spoken of the 'best' routes) and to do justice to as wide a variety of tastes and requirements as possible, with regard to difficulty and alpine ambience.* The parameters thus extend from grade III to grade VII on the UIAA scale, with an emphasis on routes in the V to VI range. Many of the more difficult routes can be 'technically outwitted' with a few A0 passages. Although the descriptions and characterisation of the routes are bound to be subjective, we have tried to make them honest and hope they allow you to prepare as well as possible for the situations you are likely to encounter on them. One thing is certain: climbing in the high mountains is to be enjoyed most when the difficulties (and not just those of a technical nature) are well within one's capabilities and the mind is free to explore things on a deeper level. The fact that this volume concludes with the "Via della Soddisfazione" needs also to be understood in context – we wish you always a safe return and that you top out with all the inner satisfaction that can be found when climbing in the Dolomites.

Anette Köhler and Norbert Memmel

* See page 216 for notes for the English language edition.

CONTENTS

NUVOLAU CRODA DA LAGO

POMAGAGNON CRISTALLO CADINSPITZEN

DREI ZINNEN

BOSCONERO MEZZODI

MOIAZZA CIVETTA

PALA

BRENTA

A GUIDE TO THE TOPOS

All the essential information necessary for an independent ascent of a route is represented in the topos. Where necessary and when possible, sketches have also been included for the descent routes. These topographical route descriptions, with information condensed down to the basics, replace the more usual written route descriptions. They are supported by cliff photographs which are intended to give a first impression of the mountain and the line of the route.

The topos are intended as an aid to orientation when climbing independently and not as a pre-programmed route description with every last move and detail faithfully recorded. When consulting the sketches please note the following:

Lengths quoted are approximate and pitch lengths may be rounded up or down by + or − 5m. On some routes, pitch lengths were dispensed with entirely.

The grading of difficulty always refer to pure free climbing (other possibilities are mentioned in brackets) and to the technical crux section of a pitch, although no separate mention is made of this.

The belays depicted on the topos are to be understood as possible belays only (the ones we used) and are not obligatory. Not all of the belays shown are equipped with pitons or the like. It may be necessary to set up your own belay using threads, nuts or camming devices.

Belay bolts are always marked on the topo, normal pitons are shown in some cases, additional pitons are never shown.

As a general rule, the starting point for each route is given as the nearest hut or, where no convenient hut is available, the nearest parking place. Strong walkers wishing to dispense with overnight hut accommodation can approach almost all of the objectives described from the valley base.

The suggested times are also only approximations and arose from a kind of consensus agreement between the usual times quoted in the guidebooks (generally very tight) and our own times (generally considerably longer!).

Directions (right and left) refer to the direction in which the climber is facing (i.e. facing in when ascending or facing out when descending).

A set of nuts/cams and a selection of slings should always be carried as basic alpine equipment, even when this is not specifically stated under the heading 'protection'.

Keys to the symbols used on the topos:

☒ FIRST ASCENT PARTY	ℙ NEAREST PARKING	↗ ROUTE APPROACH	ℝ ROUTE SUMMARY
⚙ PROTECTION (in-situ and needed)	⌂ HUT APPROACH	🄴 DETAILED START OF CLIMB	↘ DESCENT DESCRIPTION

The following symbols are used in the route descriptions:

Route:

− − − −	Line of Route
············	Line of Route (hidden from view)
−·−·−	Variation
	Abseil point (abseil length in metres)
	Coming from the other side
	Leading around to the other side
mA	Abseil length in metres
expo	Exposed and/or bold

Protection:

⌒	Piton
✕	Bolt
SU	Sling
⊖	Belay

Terrain:

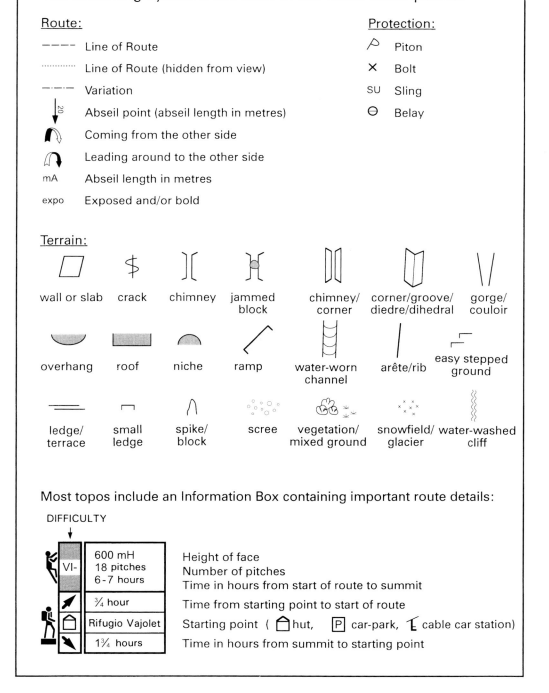

wall or slab   crack   chimney   jammed block   chimney/corner   corner/groove/diedre/dihedral   gorge/couloir

overhang   roof   niche   ramp   water-worn channel   arête/rib   easy stepped ground

ledge/terrace   small ledge   spike/block   scree   vegetation/mixed ground   snowfield/glacier   water-washed cliff

Most topos include an Information Box containing important route details:

DIFFICULTY

Height of face	600 mH
Number of pitches	18 pitches
Time in hours from start of route to summit	6-7 hours

VI-

¾ hour	Time from starting point to start of route
Rifugio Vajolet	Starting point (⌂ hut, P car-park, ☂ cable car station)
1¾ hours	Time in hours from summit to starting point

LANGKOFEL (SASSOLUNGO)
SELLA / PUEZ / STEVIA

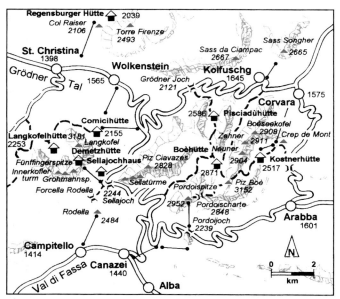

The Sassolungo (Langkofel) and the Sella groups are the two areas of the Dolomites which are the quickest to reach when approaching from the north via the Brenner Pass and thence along Val Gardena. Separated only by the Sella Pass, they are nevertheless two completely different climbing areas. Whereas the south-facing Sella routes – on the Sella Towers or Piz Ciavazes, for example – have something of the character of low-lying crags, the Sassolungo group has an alpine seriousness and even a certain air of savagery about it. Neither the Sassolungo nor the Grohmannspitze (Sasso Levante) or Innerkofler Tower (Punta Pian de Sass) are far from the bustle of the Sella Pass, yet one climbs here in totally different, primitive world. The "Sella scene" conjures up images of sundrenched faces, short approaches and easy descents; of relaxed climbing on well-protected routes that are not too long. These expectations are also taken into account in the selection of routes. However, one should not expect the solitary mountain experience here – a tip that is equally valid for the Fünffingerspitze (Punta delle Cinque Dita). For those with similar expectations of sun, rock quality and short approaches who wish to experience a different Sella to that found around the Sella Pass, the Vallon corries high above Corvara are to be warmly recommended.

Also readily accessible from Val Gardena are the Puez and the Stevia groups, whose seemingly loose rock quality has undermined their reputation amongst climbers. Despite this image, here too, we discovered some fine routes – the North-West Ridge of Torre Firenze and above all the 'Old South Face' route on Sass da Ciampac leave no desire unfulfilled.

All of the routes described in this chapter can be done as single day undertakings from the valley base. In principle, any of the villages in Val Gardena (St. Ulrich, St. Christina, Wolkenstein) are suitable starting points. Canazei, in the Fassa Valley, has a campsite and is recommended as a base for the routes on the Pordoispitze. The Sella Towers and Piz Ciavazes can be reached equally easily from either Canazei or the Val Gardena. For the Ciampac and Vallon corries, Colfuschg (campsite) or Corvara are the most suitable valley bases.

1 LANGKOFEL   3181m
SASSOLUNGO

North Ridge (Pichl/Waizer) IV+

The Langkofel towers above Val Gardena like a huge, cast iron monolith – a torn and twisted world of ridges, pinnacles and gullies. The North Ridge of the Langkofel – actually, the words 'North' and 'Ridge' tell only half the story since most of the route follows the East Face, only emerging onto the ridge after the notch of the "Pichlscharte" – is a great route on a great mountain. It is not only a wonderful climb, it is also serious and big and long. There are some splendid sections – the relatively easy, slightly greasy lower slabs which catch the morning sun and the pitch after the Pichlscharte which

hugs the crest of the ridge. Other sections of the route are more demanding – there are a few less solid bits in the upper part and the last 300 metres take in some exposed and broken terrain. On the difficult pitches, superb bridging and chimneying predominate. The descent is long and requires full concentration on the job in hand, although the tiny bivouac shelter below the summit does detract slightly from the seriousness of the situation. All in all, this is not a route for a quick bit of fun but a great traverse of a majestic mountain – and an unforgettable experience.

⚔ Eduard Pichl, Rolf Waizer. August 1918.

🏳 Very few in-situ pitons up the the Pichlscharte, thereafter numerous belay and protection pegs. Selection of nuts and slings required.

🅿 Sellajochhaus (2176m).

↗ From Sellajochhaus follow the flat path to the Comici Hut. Shortly before the hut (drag lift station), head up diagonally across steep meadows to the foot of the obvious grey slabs of the East Face Pillar.

🄴 The route starts at the foot of a chimney system, grassy in its lower part, which slants up rightwards. A faint path leads to this point.

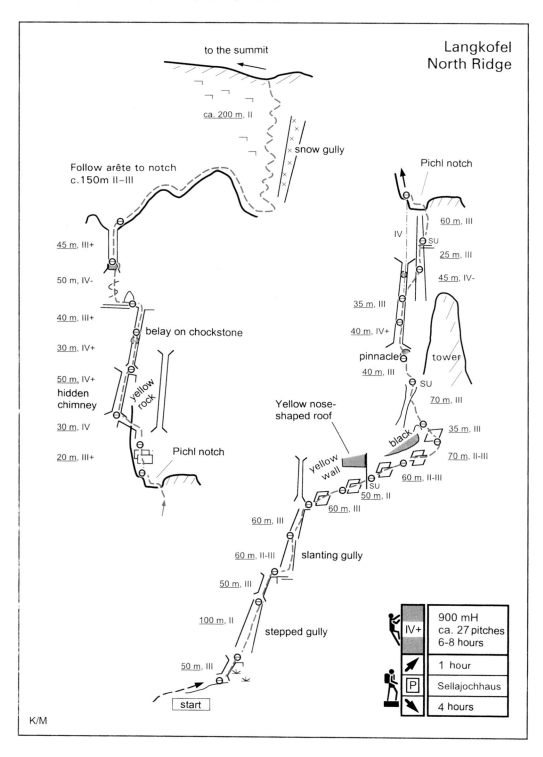

to the summit

Langkofel
North Ridge

ca. 200 m, II

× snow gully

Pichl notch

Follow arête to notch
c.150m II–III

60 m, III

IV   SU

45 m, III+

25 m, III

50 m, IV-

45 m, IV-

40 m, III+

35 m, III

belay on chockstone

40 m, IV+

30 m, IV+

pinnacle   tower

40 m, III

50 m, IV+
hidden
chimney

yellow
rock

SU

70 m, III

30 m, IV

Yellow nose-
shaped roof

black   35 m, III

20 m, III+

Pichl notch

yellow
wall

70 m, II-III

60 m, II-III

SU
50 m, II

60 m, III

60 m, III

60 m, II-III   slanting gully

50 m, III

100 m, II   stepped gully

50 m, III

start

IV+	900 mH ca. 27 pitches 6-8 hours
↗	1 hour
P	Sellajochhaus
↘	4 hours

K/M

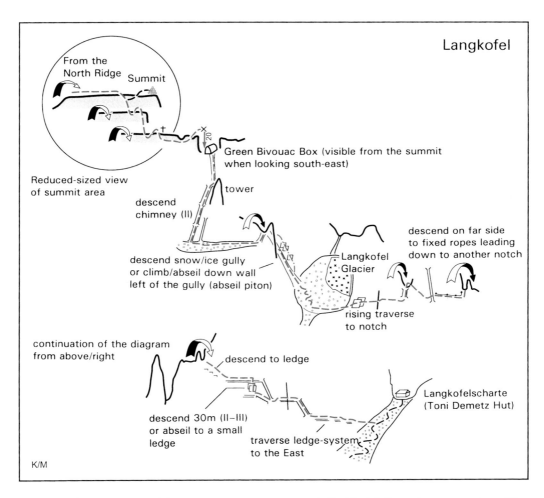

From the North Ridge

Summit

Reduced-sized view of summit area

Green Bivouac Box (visible from the summit when looking south-east)

tower

descend chimney (II)

descend snow/ice gully or climb/abseil down wall left of the gully (abseil piton)

descend on far side to fixed ropes leading down to another notch

Langkofel Glacier

rising traverse to notch

continuation of the diagram from above/right

descend to ledge

Langkofelscharte (Toni Demetz Hut)

descend 30m (II–III) or abseil to a small ledge

traverse ledge-system to the East

Langkofel

K/M

The lower section of the route (some 500 metres of climbing) follows the upper edge of the grey slabs diagonally rightwards to a chimney system which is bounded on its right hand side by a conspicuous tower and leads up into the "Pichlscharte". From this notch, first follow crest of the ridge and then go left into a hidden chimney system which leads up to easier angled ground. Now follow the ridge itself onto the North Tower. Finally, descend the gap between the North Tower and the summit (exposed in places) and continue to the top without further difficulty.

From the summit, descend to the south-east to the bivi shelter (visible from the summit). From here, the descent to the Langkofelscharte (about 3½ hours) is via the south-west side of the mountain and is marked in places by cairns and red paint. Long and demanding.

2 FÜNFFINGERSPITZEN 2996m
PUNTA DELLE CINQUE DITA

Traverse (Huter/Jahn/Merlet) IV

The traverse of the Fünffinger-spitzen, the peak which pops up so cheekily out of the Lang-kofelscharte between the Lang-kofel and the Grohmannspitze (Sasso Levante), has many fine qualities. The disadvantage is that many people are well aware of this! From Sellajochhaus, the lift deposits you almost at the start of the route; a hot tip is to grab the first gondola if you want to be first on the route! The climbing is on solid rock, covered in holds, and excitingly exposed, particularly on the "Thumb". Here, the real diffi-culties end and many climbers descend from the top of this pinnacle, directly over the 'ball of the thumb' (abseils). The continuation traverse takes in some interesting climbing, however, and offers magnificent and unique views across to the white peaks of the main Alpine chain.

Hans Huter, Gustav Jahn, Erwin Merlet.   Summer 1917.

Belay pitons in-situ. On the "Thumb" there are also adequate pitons for protection.

Sellajochhaus (2176m), valley station of the lift to the Langkofelscharte.

From Sellajochhaus, take the lift to the Langkofelscharte (Demetz Hut, about 1 hour on foot). Follow the path and scree up and left. Roughly in the fall line of the prominent notch in the ridge is the start of a chimney/ramp slanting up to the right.

Either climb the ramp and move left shortly before it ends or, better, climb the slabs to the right to a scree basin and up to the notch.

Climb the North Ridge direct to the top of the Thumb. Climb down about 40m to the south to an abseil point. Abseil into the notch (possible descent to the Langkofelscharte from this point). Climb out of the notch onto the 'Index Finger'. Traverse its East Face and go up to the top of the "Middle Finger". Climb down/abseil to the notch between the Middle Finger and the "Ring Finger". Traverse the West side of the Ring Finger and descend to the notch at the base of the "Little Finger". Turn this on its west side and abseil into a little notch. Descend stepped rocks on the west side and finally the West Ridge, to a ramp leading into the Fünffingerscharte gully.

Descend from the Fünffingerscharte down a scree gully on the east to Sellajochhaus.

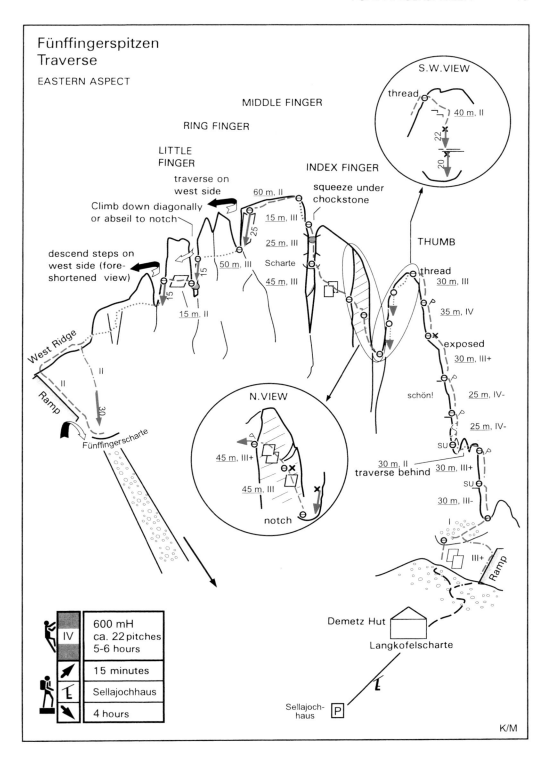

Fünffingerspitzen Traverse

EASTERN ASPECT

MIDDLE FINGER

RING FINGER

LITTLE FINGER

INDEX FINGER

S.W.VIEW

thread

40 m, II

22

20

traverse on west side

60 m, II

Climb down diagonally or abseil to notch

15 m, III

25

25 m, III

THUMB

squeeze under chockstone

descend steps on west side (fore-shortened view)

50 m, III   Scharte

45 m, III

thread
30 m, III

35 m, IV

15

15

15

15 m, II

exposed
30 m, III+

West Ridge

schön!

25 m, IV-

II

II

N.VIEW

25 m, IV-

Ramp

30

45 m, III+

SU

Fünffingerscharte

45 m, III

30 m, II
traverse behind

30 m, III+

notch

SU

30 m, III-

I

III+

Ramp

Demetz Hut

Langkofelscharte

IV (gray)	600 mH ca. 22 pitches 5-6 hours
↗	15 minutes
↰	Sellajochhaus
↘	4 hours

Sellajoch-haus P

K/M

3 GROHMANNSPITZE 3126m
SASSO LEVANTE

South Face, "Dimai/Eötvös" (Dimai/Eötvös/Summermatter) IV

The mighty South Face of the Grohmann-spitze cannot be seen from the Sella Pass. So, despite the relatively short approach, solitude is the norm. The first party to succeed in climbing this huge face were an adventurous pair of Hungarian baronesses, Ilona and Rolanda Eötvös, guided by Antonio Dimai*, the team that had made the notable first ascent of the South Face of Tofana di Rozes. In comparison with the Tofana route, the Grohmannspitze route has a cleaner line and has a more consistent difficulty and rock quality; it is, of course, shorter too, despite the arduous descent. The rock is very solid and scoured by the frequent torrents of water which cascade over it. On the lower, slabbier sections the line of the route is rather arbitrary. Seemingly unpleasant sections like the chimney or the gully on the upper wall prove to be just as amenable as the rest of the route on closer acquaintance. The descent route is exposed, difficult to follow and requires concentration, particularly on the abseils.

* Dimai had first attempted this route in 1890 but failed at the overhanging section to the left of the gully, which was subsequently turned by a traverse to the right (see topo) *A.J.* Vol 24 , 1909, p443.

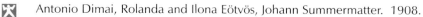

Antonio Dimai, Rolanda and Ilona Eötvös, Johann Summermatter. 1908.

On the lower section of the face, some belays equipped with ring bolts. On the upper section only a few in-situ belay and protection pegs. Take slings for threads!

Sellajochhaus (2176m).

From Sellajochhaus, first head for Rifugio Valentini (parking); 5 minutes on foot. Follow the road up into Forcella di Rodella and then a path off to the right, along an erosion scarred spur, to the foot of the South-East Arête. Easy (I–II) scrambling up and slightly left over broken ground leads to a rubble covered terrace below the steeper face.

E From the rubble terrace, traverse left to a water-worn (and often wet) gully. Just to the right of this gully is the first equipped belay.

R The gully widens and becomes more prominent in its upper reaches. The route keeps to the left of the gully, venturing onto its left edge at the start of the major difficulties.

Descend by the North-East Ridge, climbing (sections of II, cairns, red markers) and abseiling (ring bolts in-situ) into the Fünffingerscharte and thence down to the Sellajochhaus.

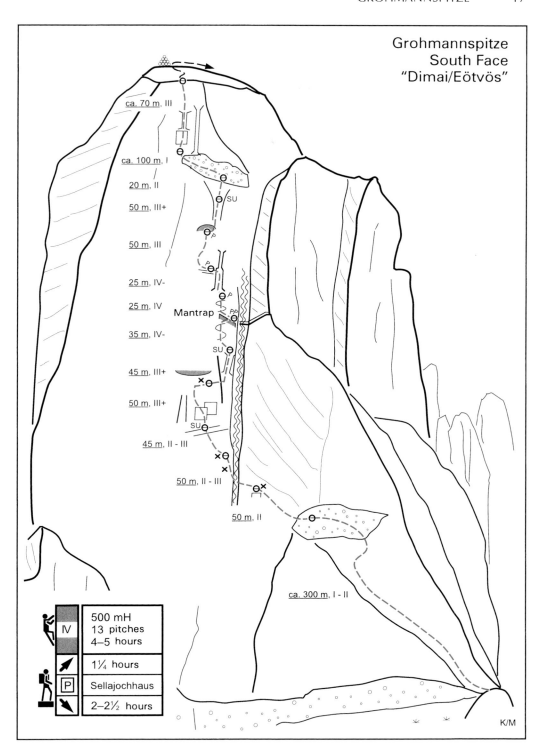

Grohmannspitze
South Face
"Dimai/Eötvös"

ca. 70 m, III

ca. 100 m, I

20 m, II

50 m, III+

SU

P

50 m, III

P

25 m, IV-

P

25 m, IV

Mantrap   PA

35 m, IV-

SU

45 m, III+

50 m, III+

SU

45 m, II - III

50 m, II - III

50 m, II

ca. 300 m, I - II

	IV	500 mH 13 pitches 4–5 hours
	↗	1¼ hours
	P	Sellajochhaus
	↘	2–2½ hours

K/M

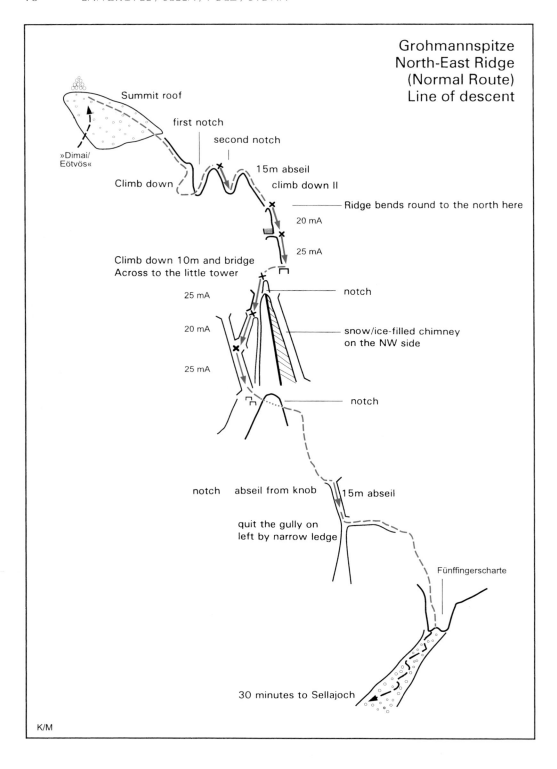

Grohmannspitze
North-East Ridge
(Normal Route)
Line of descent

Summit roof

first notch

second notch

»Dimai/
Eötvös«

Climb down

15m abseil
climb down II

Ridge bends round to the north here

20 mA

25 mA

Climb down 10m and bridge
Across to the little tower

25 mA

notch

20 mA

snow/ice-filled chimney
on the NW side

25 mA

notch

notch   abseil from knob   15m abseil

quit the gully on
left by narrow ledge

Fünffingerscharte

30 minutes to Sellajoch

K/M

4 INNERKOFLER TOWER   3081m
PUNTA PIAN DE SASS

South Face, "Via del Calice" (Maffei/Steghel) VII

"Calice" means "chalice" and with a little imagination the shape of a drinking vessel can actually just be made out in the structure of the rocks to the left of the prominent "Rizzi Chimney". It is filled with a pretty potent brew, for the "Via del Calice" gives a demanding free climb at a consistent level of difficulty. Make sure you are really up to it, because almost all the protection has to be hand-placed on the lead and although the mountain is only a few hundred metres from the hectic goings-on of the Sella Pass, here you are usually on your own. The excitement is maintained right up to the end since the last pitch is also the crux and here of all places the usually sound rock quality stupidly takes a turn for the worse. Those intending to free this pitch will need to be prepared for grade VII climbing. Grabbing the odd piece of protection reduces the standard to about VI+.

Graziano Maffei, Guiliano Steghel. September 1977.

Few belay pegs in-situ. You will need to place your own protection.

Sellajochhaus (2176m).

Take the Sellajochhaus/Rif. Valentini road to Forcella di Rodella, then follow a path to the right, along an eroded spur, to the South-East Arête of the Grohmannspitze and thence below the Grohmannspitze and Innerkofler Tower to the start.

The route starts below a yellow niche, to the left of the "Rizzi Chimney".

Through the narrow rock chalice just left of the "Rizzi Chimney". See topo p.20.

From the summit, first climb down to the south-west and then slightly left, descending chimney/grooves (optional 20m abseil). Descend a short groove and continue down, keeping generally to the right crossing several ribs and groove systems to reach an abseil station. Make two 20m abseils and continue the down rightwards into a basin of loose rocks. Follow the spur down to the point at which it breaks off before the "Zahnscharte" (notch). Climb leftwards down the rocky spur until a steep descent to the left towards the notch gains an abseil station next to a mud- and ice-filled couloir. Abseil 45m into the niche. 1½ hours to this point. Descend to the south and back to the start of the route.

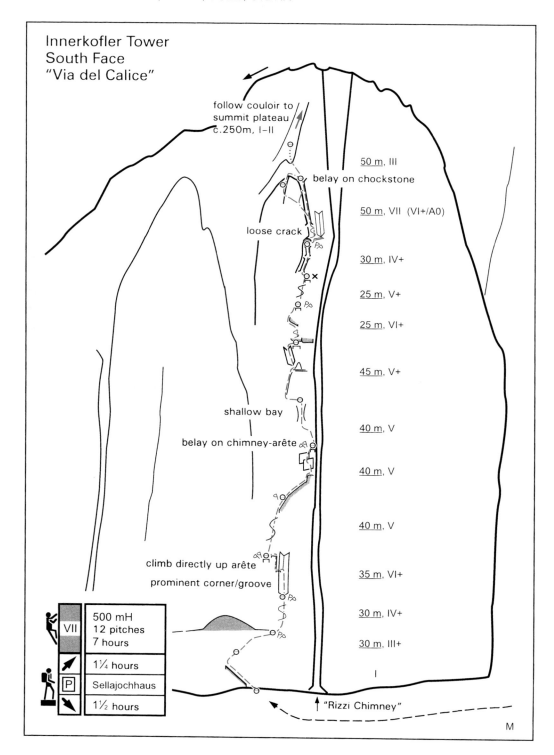

Innerkofler Tower
South Face
"Via del Calice"

follow couloir to
summit plateau
c.250m, I–II

50 m, III

belay on chockstone

50 m, VII (VI+/A0)

loose crack

30 m, IV+

25 m, V+

25 m, VI+

45 m, V+

shallow bay

40 m, V

belay on chimney-arête

40 m, V

40 m, V

climb directly up arête

prominent corner/groove

35 m, VI+

30 m, IV+

30 m, III+

I

	500 mH
VII	12 pitches
	7 hours
	1¼ hours
P	Sellajochhaus
	1½ hours

"Rizzi Chimney"

M

5 THE SELLA TOWERS

Traverse IV+

The traverse of the first three Sella Towers combines the most worthwhile of the easier routes on the towers to give an itinerary which is both long and demanding. In the high season, however, it is often hopelessly overcrowded. Descending from the top of the First and Second Towers is not difficult, but in less certain weather these well-known escape options may have a disturbing feel about them. The descent from the Third Tower should certainly not be underestimated. Better to follow the 'First Prussian Law of Descent' and make sure you are happy down-climbing grade II and III pitches before you set out!

FIRST SELLA TOWER   2533m

North-West Arête, "Steger" (Steger/Holzner) IV+

Entertaining crack and chimney climbing – and polished to a high sheen. Get there early if possible, if only to avoid the irritating two-way traffic (abseil descent follows the same line)!

Hans Steger, Ernst Holzner. 30 June 1928.

Sufficient belay and protection pegs in-situ.

Sellajoch (2244m).

From the Sella Pass a well-trodden path leads to the start of the route.

The route begins in the notch between the "Locomotive" (small rock tower) and the First Sella Tower, beneath a shattered looking wall.

The line is to the right of the actual arête, joining the arête at the third stance before heading off rightwards again. The rest of the route is simply a matter of following the numerous other climbers – or the trail left by them! 1–2 hours. To reach the Second Sella Tower, descend from the summit of the First into the notch between the two towers (easy). From this point, there is also an easy and well-trodden descent to the south to the base of the face (about 30 minutes; topo p.23).

SECOND SELLA TOWER   2597m
South-West Face, "Kostner" (Kostner/Gabloner) III+

Unfortunately the route consists of only three pitches – although the groove pitch is superb – and is only really worthwhile as a link in the complete traverse of the three towers.

Franz Kostner, Maria Gabloner. 1905.

Belay pegs in-situ but a selection of nuts would be very useful.

From the notch between the First and Second Towers, traverse left about 30m along a ledge to a large block.

The short South-West Face is split by three grooves. The route takes the left-hand of these short grooves (allow 1 hour).

To reach the Third Sella Tower, descend from the summit of the Second Tower to the east. Keep just below (south side of) the connecting ridge between the Second Sella Tower and Piz Ciavazes, heading for the notch which separates them. The first abseil ring is located on the northern side of the ridge before the notch, but is not very easy to find. Make two abseils (15m, 20m) into the gully between the Second and Third Towers. The lower section of the "Jahnweg" climbs this gully. Climb up and right to reach the "Spiral Terrace" of the Third Sella Tower.

If neither time nor inclination permit an ascent of the 'Jahnweg', descend from the top of the Second Sella Tower in an easterly direction via a faint path leading to the gully which runs southwards and divides the Second Tower from Piz Ciavazes. Junction with the descent from the routes on the South Face of Piz Ciavazes via the "Gamsband" (Chamois Terrace). Scramble down the gully following a small well-marked path (grade II in places) to the foot of the face and back to the Sellajoch; ¾ hour.

THIRD SELLA TOWER   2688m
South-West Face, "Jahnweg" (Jahn/Merlet/Dyhrenfurth) IV

The upper part of the 'Jahnweg' offers fun climbing on juggy, solid rock with a welcome lack of polish. This provides the best section of the whole traverse.

Gustav Jahn, Erwin Merlet, Günther Oscar Dyhrenfurth. 11 August 1918.

All necessary belay and protection pegs in place. Numerous threads.

Start on the "Spiral Terrace", about 30m left of the gully, at an obvious crack/ramp.

The route follows a line to the right of the vague South-West Arête; 2 hours.

From the summit, descend a few metres towards Piz Ciavazes (well marked). Move left to a ring bolt and make a 25m abseil. Follow the red markers, keeping left, and descend to the "Spiral Terrace" (II–III, exposed in places). Follow the terrace back to the start of the route and the gully. Climb down the gully for about 100m (sections of II–III) to where it steepens. A narrow ledge leads out of the gully to the left. From the end of this ledge, climb down about 5m (exposed) to an abseil ring. Three abseils (15m, 20m, 20m) land you at the bottom of the wall. Follow the vague track back to the Sella Pass; 1¼ hours.

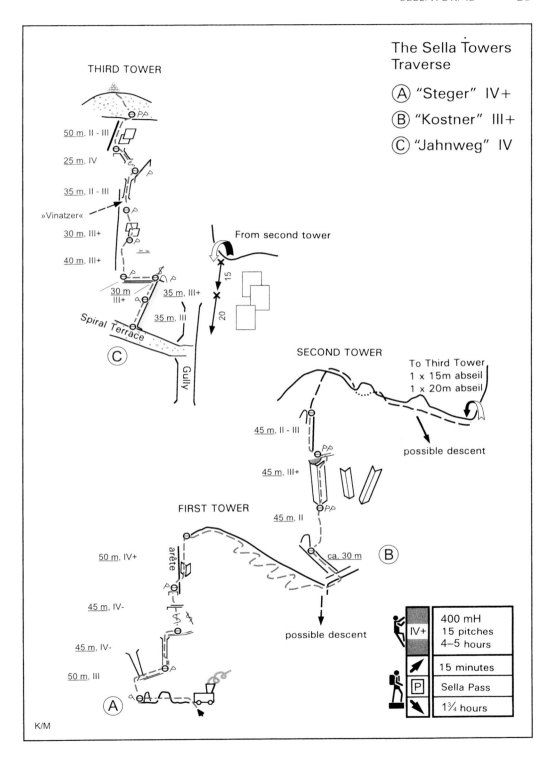

THIRD TOWER

50 m, II - III

25 m, IV

35 m, II - III

»Vinatzer«

30 m, III+

40 m, III+

30 m III+   35 m, III+

35 m, III

Spiral Terrace

Gully

(C)

From second tower

15

20

The Sella Towers Traverse

(A) "Steger" IV+

(B) "Kostner" III+

(C) "Jahnweg" IV

SECOND TOWER

To Third Tower
1 × 15m abseil
1 × 20m abseil

possible descent

45 m, II - III

45 m, III+

45 m, II

FIRST TOWER

50 m, IV+

arête

45 m, IV-

45 m, IV-

50 m, III

(A)

ca. 30 m   (B)

possible descent

IV+	400 mH 15 pitches 4–5 hours
	15 minutes
P	Sella Pass
	1¾ hours

K/M

6 FIRST SELLA TOWER 2533m

South-West Corner, "Trenker" (Trenker/Pescota) V−

It is famous, overrun and polished and yet it remains a legend. There is evidently no escaping the prodigal son of the mountains, Luis Trenker, and thus, at some time or another, every Sella Towers pilgrim will find himself roping up at the foot of the "Trenker Crack". After all, this big groove is the most prominent line on the face, the rock is good and the climbing is very nice, too. And there is only one really difficult pitch − the polished Trenker Crack itself. And even this has an elegant solution − bridge up it! Only those who weasel inside it will lose style points.

▢ Luis Trenker, Hans Pescota. 1913.

▢ The belays are generally equipped with cemented-in pegs or bolts. Protection pegs are there when you need them, but a rack of nuts will not go amiss.

P Sellajoch (2244m).

▢ From the top of the Sella Pass, follow a track upwards, passing beneath the south side of the "Locomotive", to the South-West Face of the First Sella Tower. Continue until below a prominent corner system to the right of the glaringly obvious South Face.

E Scramble up rock steps to the foot of the prominent corner/crack which gives the route.

R Follow the corner all the way to a ledge which leads rightward to the finish.

▢ Climb down into the notch between the First and Second Sella Towers. On the Second Tower, traverse right and descend grooves (II) (well marked). Finally climb down diagonally rightwards to the path which runs beneath the South Face. Follow this back to the Sellajoch.

First Sella Tower
South-West Corner
"Trenker"

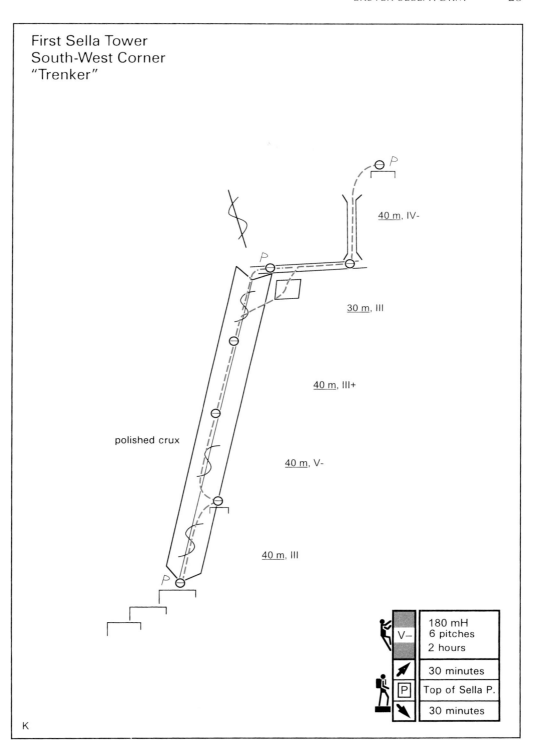

P

40 m, IV-

P

30 m, III

40 m, III+

polished crux

40 m, V-

40 m, III

P

	180 mH 6 pitches 2 hours
V-	
	30 minutes
P	Top of Sella P.
	30 minutes

K

7   FIRST SELLA TOWER   2533m

W.S.W. Arête, "Tissi" (Tissi/Guglielmini/Masè Dari/Ascheiri) VI

Attilio Tissi and his compatriots were the first climbers who dared venture onto the smooth South Face of the First Sella Tower and the "Tissi Route" is one of the great classics of the Towers. The legacy of its popularity is felt particularly keenly on the first two pitches in particular, where an unpleasant polish to the awkward wide crack gives the whole experience a rather sardonic appeal. By way of contrast, the steep, white wall of the upper section is really beautiful, although caution does need to be exercised – do not be tempted by the line of loose pegs placed by mistake in the crack system to the right.

Attilio Tissi, Mariola Guglielmini, Giorgio Masè Dari, C. Ascheiri. 1936.

Pitons in place for belays and protection.

Sellajoch (2244m).

From the top of the Sella Pass, follow the climbers' path, passing beneath the south side of the "Locomotive" to reach the South-West Face of the First Sella Tower.

Start at the foot of a crack to the right of a tower-like pillar.

On the lower section, follow the crack line and continuation corner to a ledge. Follow cracks above and right which split the wall to the summit.

There are two possible descents. Either (a) abseil down the West Arête (cemented-in abseil pitons) or (b) climb down the Normal Route.
(a) After topping out, follow a faint path to the left (when looking in) until above the West Arête. Climb down 10m to the first cemented-in abseil peg. Make five 20m abseils. Descend to the south, back to the foot of the face (II).
(b) From the summit, scramble down into the gap between the First and Second Sella Towers. Traverse right along a ledge on the Second Tower and follow the well marked descent down gullies (II). Finally, climb down diagonally rightwards to the path leading along the base of the South Face and back to the Sellajoch.

First Sella Tower
West-South-West Arête
"Tissi"

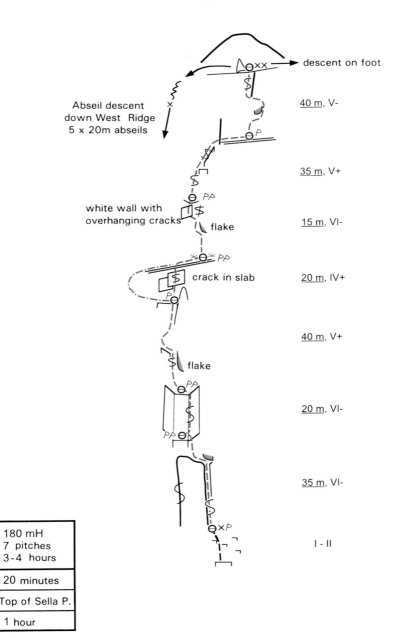

descent on foot

40 m, V-

Abseil descent
down West Ridge
5 x 20m abseils

35 m, V+

white wall with
overhanging cracks

flake

15 m, VI-

crack in slab

20 m, IV+

40 m, V+

flake

20 m, VI-

35 m, VI-

I - II

VI-	180 mH 7 pitches 3-4 hours	
	20 minutes	
P	Top of Sella P.	
	1 hour	

K/M

8 SECOND SELLA TOWER 2597m

North-West Arête, "Kasnakoff" (Zelger/von Kasnakoff) V+ (VI+)

The "Kasnakoff" route is one of the best-known and most popular of the mid-grade Sella classics.* It offers exposed face and corner climbing on solid rock plastered with good holds. Unfortunately, the rock is no longer in the pristine, rough state it once was. From the point of view of difficulty, the climb is often underestimated. Firstly, there are numerous variations on the route, some of them considerably harder than the classic route. Secondly the crux comes at the start of the fifth pitch and is distinctly more difficult than the rest of the route. Even if you accept the pegs as handholds, it can be a bit gripping, particularly if rope drag or similar chicanery conspire to spoil the moment.

*Frau von Kasnakoff came from Tiflis, Georgia.

Anton Zelger, Frau Baronin von Kasnakoff. 1913.

All belay pegs and sufficient protection pegs are in-situ.

Sellajoch (2244m).

Head towards the Pössneckersteig and thence to below the Second Tower's North Face.

Start at a conspicuous memorial plaque.

Climb up, keeping to the left of the arête bounding the North Face at first. Continue directly up the arête, with occasional brief excursions onto the North and West Faces.

(a) Follow a faint path east and into the gully leading south between the Second Sella Tower and Piz Ciavazes. Descend the gully (II) to the foot of the face and the Sellajoch; 1 hour.
(b) Those wishing to return directly to the start of the route can abseil down the gully between the Second and Third Sella Towers. From the summit, walk down to the east following the faint path. Keep slightly below (south) of the connecting ridge between the Second Tower and Piz Ciavazes, heading for the notch between the two. On the northern side of the ridge is the first abseil ring (not easy to find). Abseils of 15m and 20m lead down the gully between the Second and Third Sella Towers. Climb down the gully ("Jahnweg") for about 100m (sections of II–III) to where it suddenly steepens. A narrow ledge leads out of the gully to the left. From the end of this ledge, climb down about 5m (exposed) to an abseil ring. Three abseils (15m, 20m, 20m) land you at the bottom of the wall. Follow the vague track back to the Sella Pass.

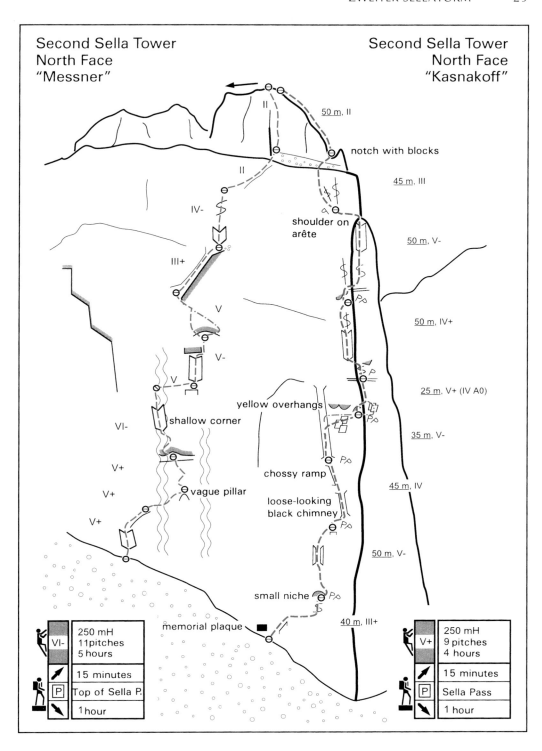

Second Sella Tower
North Face
"Messner"

Second Sella Tower
North Face
"Kasnakoff"

50 m, II

notch with blocks

II

45 m, III

II

IV-

shoulder on
arête

50 m, V-

III+

V

50 m, IV+

V-

V

25 m, V+ (IV A0)

yellow overhangs

VI-   shallow corner

35 m, V-

V+

chossy ramp

V+   vague pillar

loose-looking
black chimney

45 m, IV

V+

50 m, V-

small niche

memorial plaque

40 m, III+

	250 mH
VI-	11 pitches
	5 hours
↗	15 minutes
P	Top of Sella P.
↘	1 hour

	250 mH
V+	9 pitches
	4 hours
↗	15 minutes
P	Sella Pass
↘	1 hour

9   SECOND SELLA TOWER   2597m

North Face, "Messner" VI

Reinhold Messner and his brother Günther climbed the line of the black water streak on the North Face of the Second Sella Tower, giving the Sella climbing community an elegant and object lesson in free-climbing. On this route, you can learn all over again what it is to climb grade VI! The rock is uniquely solid and covered in holds, the wall steep and exposed, the climbing strenuous, continually hard and as free as a bird. A fantastic climbing experience, but only for those with an absolute mastery of this standard of climbing.

Günther and Reinhold Messner. August 1968.

Belay pegs and some protection pegs in place. Take slings for threads and a selection of nuts, especially in the medium size range.

Sellajoch (2244m).

From the Sellajoch, follow the path towards the Pössneckersteig and continue up the climbers' path to beneath the North Face of the Second Tower and a point roughly level with the foot of the face of the Third Tower.

Start to the left of the water streak in the middle of the wall below and slightly left of a groove leading into a rightward facing ramp.

The route is based around the black water streak roughly in the middle of the wall. It is gained from the left and quitted on the right on the easier upper pitches; see topo p.29.

Either: follow a faint climbers' path east and into the gully leading south between the Second Sella Tower and Piz Ciavazes. Descend the gully (II) to the foot of the face and return to the Sellajoch. Or: abseil down the gully between the Second and Third Sella Towers (for details see p.28).

10 THIRD SELLA TOWER   2688m

West Face, "Vinatzer" (Vinatzer/Peristi) V+

The Third Sella Tower is both the highest and the most impressive. Through the central part of the steep West Face, one of the most popular routes in the Sella area threads its way – this is the "Vinatzer" route. At rush hour, the line of the climb can be traced from the queues of parties, lined up like pearls on a necklace. The crux pitch after the Spiral Terrace – a finger crack leading into an overhang – is a tough nut to crack. Done totally free, the route may seem undergraded at its official V– (hence our grade). In general, lovely, demanding corner and groove climbing on which solid rock predominates.

☒ Giovanni Battista (Hans) Vinatzer, Vicenzo Peristi. 23 June 1935.

↗ Belay and protection pegs in-situ. Carry a selection of nuts in addition.

P Sellajoch (2244m).

↗ Follow the path towards the Pössneckersteig and continue up the climbers' path beneath the North Face of the Second Tower to the gully between the Second and Third Towers.

E Start to left of the gully, to the left of and below a black and yellow niche.

R The route follows a crack and groove system up the middle of the wall, reached by climbing in from the right. The upper section of the route joins up with the "Jahnweg" (topo p.32).

↘ From the summit, descend a few metres towards Piz Ciavazes (well marked). Move left to a ring bolt and make a 25m abseil. Follow the red markers, keeping left, and descend to the Spiral Terrace (II–III, exposed in places). Follow the terrace back to the start of the "Jahnweg" and the gully. Climb down the gully for about 100m (sections of II–III) to where it steepens abruptly. A narrow ledge leads out of the gully to the left. From the end of this ledge, climb down about 5m (exposed) to an abseil ring. Three abseils (15m, 20m, 20m) land you at the bottom of the wall. Follow the vague track back to the Sella Pass.

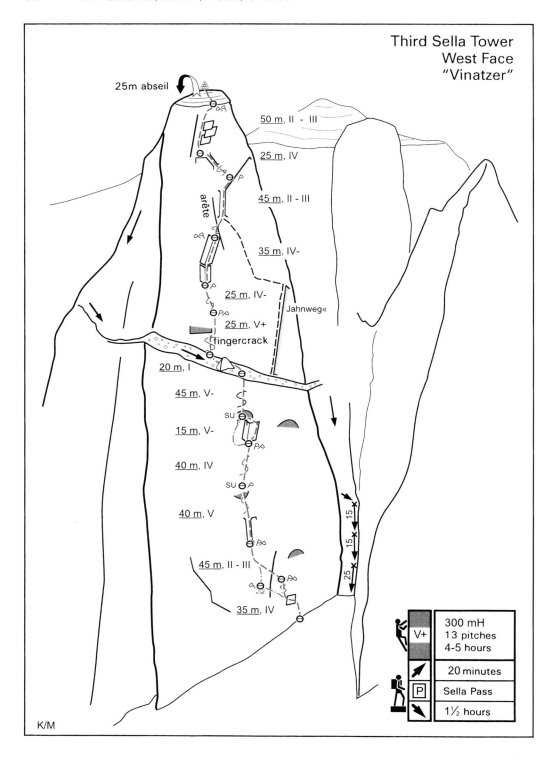

Third Sella Tower
West Face
"Vinatzer"

25m abseil

50 m, II - III

25 m, IV

45 m, II - III

arête

35 m, IV-

25 m, IV-

Jahnweg«

25 m, V+

fingercrack

20 m, I

45 m, V-

SU

15 m, V-

40 m, IV

SU

40 m, V

45 m, II - III

35 m, IV

15

15

25

V+	300 mH 13 pitches 4-5 hours	
	20 minutes	
P	Sella Pass	
	1½ hours	

K/M

11 PIZ CIAVAZES   2828m

South Face, "Little Micheluzzi" (Micheluzzi/Rogers/Slocovich) IV+

To the right of the prominent gully that splits the South Face of Piz Ciavazes more or less straight down the middle is the zig-zag line of the route known as the "Little Micheluzzi". "Little" because here – in contrast to the "Big Micheluzzi" – the first ascent team were quite happy just to tackle the lower section of the face, pushing the route only as far as the "Gamsband" (Chamois Terrace). The climbing difficulties are not great yet the pleasure derived is considerable albeit a little short lived. The three central pitches weave their way up a steep, juggy wall and provided you pick the right line it is hard to believe that the climbing is actually no more than 'good IV'. Yet the good holds, the feeling of exposure and the often unobvious route-finding make the route so exciting and full of surprises that even those climbers capable of much more are guaranteed their fun.

🏠 Luigi Micheluzzi, William Rogers, Piero Slocovich. 14 August 1928.

🔑 Cemented-in pitons on all belays. Adequate protection pegs.

🅿 Sella Pass road. Park at the level of the South Face of Piz Ciavazes (just head for the throng of spectators).

↗ From the parking space, follow an obvious path to below the South Face.

🅴 Start to the right of the obvious chimney/gully splitting the South Face.

🆁 The route zig-zags its way up the face to the right of the gully in two right-left doglegs. The line is obvious, taking ramps to start and finishing up the steep wall; topo see p.34, photo p.35.

↘ To descend, traverse left (west) along the Gamsband to the gully between Piz Ciavazes and the Second Sella Tower where easy climbing (II) and scrambling leads down to the road.

Piz Ciavazes
South Face
"Little Micheluzzi"

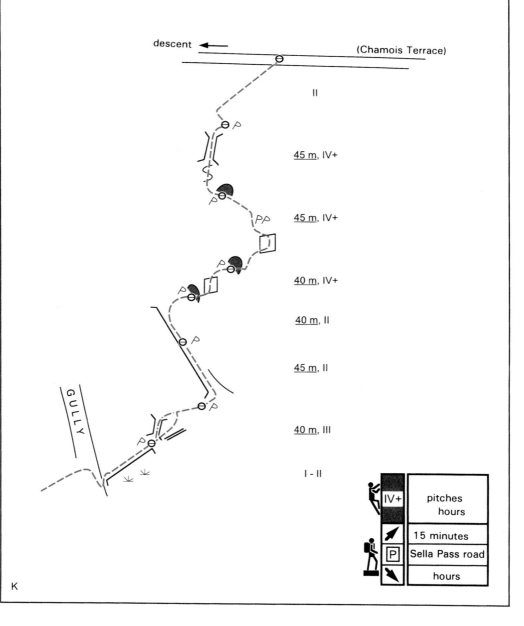

descent ← (Chamois Terrace)

II

45 m, IV+

45 m, IV+

40 m, IV+

40 m, II

45 m, II

40 m, III

I - II

GULLY

IV+	pitches hours
	15 minutes
P	Sella Pass road
	hours

K

12 PIZ CIAVAZES   2828m

South Face, "Big Micheluzzi" (Micheluzzi/Castiglioni) VI

The "Gamsband" (Chamois Terrace) splits the huge South Face of the Piz Ciavazes almost exactly at half-height and also represents a kind of demarcation line between fun climbing and the true Alpine experience, for while the lower section of the face will spoil you with wonderfully solid rock (if a little polished in places), the upper part is said to be grim and occasionally pretty loose. The complete route from bottom to top of the face is also long and demanding, while by contrast the lower section is the perfect length for an enjoyable outing. Thus it is that when climbers talk of the "Big

Micheluzzi", they are, by convention, referring to the lower part of the face only. Its climax is the impressive and exposed rightwards traverse, where a splendid little pocket seems always to materialise in the nick of time, just as things are looking desperate. A route worth queuing for!

Luigi Micheluzzi, Ettore Castiglioni. 26 September 1935.

All belays as far as the big traverse equipped with expansion bolts. Normal peg belays thereafter. Adequate protection pegs.

Sella Pass road. Park at the level of the South Face of Piz Ciavazes (just head for the throng of spectators).

From the parking space, follow an obvious path to below the South Face.

Idiot-proof start (with a route name crassly 'inscribed' at the foot of the climb)!

The route starts direct, but after four pitches traverses far over to the right below the central part of the steep yellow area of the cliff and finally gains the "Gamsband" (Chamois Terrace) via a right-left dogleg (topo p.36).

To descend, traverse left (west) along the Gamsband to the gully between Piz Ciavazes and the Second Sella Tower where easy climbing (II) and scrambling leads down to the road.

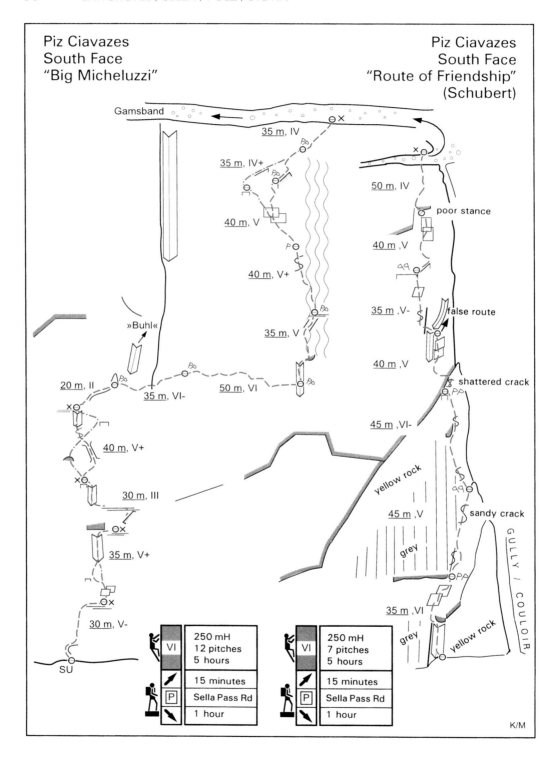

Piz Ciavazes
South Face
"Big Micheluzzi"

Piz Ciavazes
South Face
"Route of Friendship"
(Schubert)

Gamsband

35 m, IV

35 m, IV+

50 m, IV

poor stance

40 m, V

40 m ,V

»Buhl«

40 m, V+

35 m ,V-   false route

35 m, V

40 m ,V

shattered crack

20 m, II

50 m, VI

35 m, VI-

45 m ,VI-

40 m, V+

yellow rock

30 m, III

45 m ,V   sandy crack

grey

35 m, V+

35 m ,VI

grey   yellow rock

GULLY / COULOIR

30 m, V-

SU

VI	250 mH 12 pitches 5 hours
	15 minutes
P	Sella Pass Rd
	1 hour

VI	250 mH 7 pitches 5 hours
	15 minutes
P	Sella Pass Rd
	1 hour

K/M

13 PIZ CIAVAZES   2828m

South Face, "Route of Friendship" (Schubert/Matthies) VI

Just a little bit to the right of the "Big Micheluzzi", and left of the prominent left edge of the gully, is the line of the "Weg der Freundschaft" (Route of Friendship); a splendid line, with continuously difficult and very airy and exposed climbing, especially in its upper reaches. Even on the first few moves you soon start to appreciate the atmosphere of the climb as the initial corner crack is much more than a simple warm-up and stretch routine. The theme of the lower section is demanding crack and groove climbing, while further up you climb wonderfully solid and compact grey slabs. Control is the watchword here – the route demands a clean technique and good nerves, with a healthy shot of adrenaline included for good measure. So, could it be improved in any way? Well, maybe "Safety Pit"* could be enticed back to perform another act of friendship and place a few new belay pegs.

Pit Schubert, Karl Heinz Matthies. 26 May 1967.

On the lower section of the route all belay pegs are in-situ and there are adequate protection pegs. The higher you get, the sparser they get!

Sella Pass road. Park at the level of the South Face of Piz Ciavazes (just head for the throng of spectators).

From the parking space, follow an obvious path to below the South Face.

Start at a yellow corner about 30m left of the big gully that bisects the South Face.

The route follows a line just left of the edge of the gully, taking in the solid, grey area of rock in its upper reaches.

To descend, climb up and right from the last belay bolt, then traverse left (west) along the Gamsband to the gully between Piz Ciavazes and the Second Sella Tower where easy climbing (II) and scrambling leads down to the road.

(* Publisher's Note: Pit Schubert's programme of replacing and adding fixed equipment to alpine rock routes, under the aegis of the Safety Committees of the DAV and the UIAA, is now well-known. It has been questioned by some for both safety and environmental reasons – though superficially worthy it is far from clear whether this official fixed-gear policy is wise, though the authors of this guidebook clearly support it.)

14 PIZ CIAVAZES   2828m

South Face, "Zeni Corner" (Zeni/Trottner) VII–

On the left-hand side of the Ciavazes lower wall the steep yellow cliff to the left of the jagged roofs on the arête of the "Via Italia" provides a typical Dolomite face. Here the Zeni/Trottner route, though of short duration, gives a wonderful sampling of the 'total Dolomite experience'. The first difficult pitch is intimidatingly loose followed by an exposed and rather frightening hanging belay. A pleasant and unexpected surprise follows in the shape of a lovely crack pitch, leading into a joyous corner system. And finally, after turning the final roof, you arrive in climbers' seventh heaven, the purgatorial sufferings on the loose rock below now long forgotten.

Donato Zeni, Lino Trottner. 1960.

Average 'alpine-quality' belay and protection pegs.

Sella Pass road. Park at the level of the South Face of Piz Ciavazes (just head for the throng of spectators).

From the parking space on the Sella Pass road, follow an obvious path, keeping left to below the left hand section of the South Face.

Start at the debris cone about 80m left of the impressive roofs of the 'Via Italia', the left edge of the gully bounding the face on the right. Scramble up to the top of the cone. A small leaning pillar indicates the start of the route.

Gain the yellow wall by a right-to-left dogleg and climb up to reach a corner system which slices through the roofs at their extreme left hand end. Climb the corner and go over the roof to reach the 'Gamsband'.

To descend, traverse left (west) along the "Gamsband" (Chamois Terrace) to the gully between Piz Ciavazes and the Second Sella Tower where easy climbing (II) and scrambling leads down to the Sella Pass road.

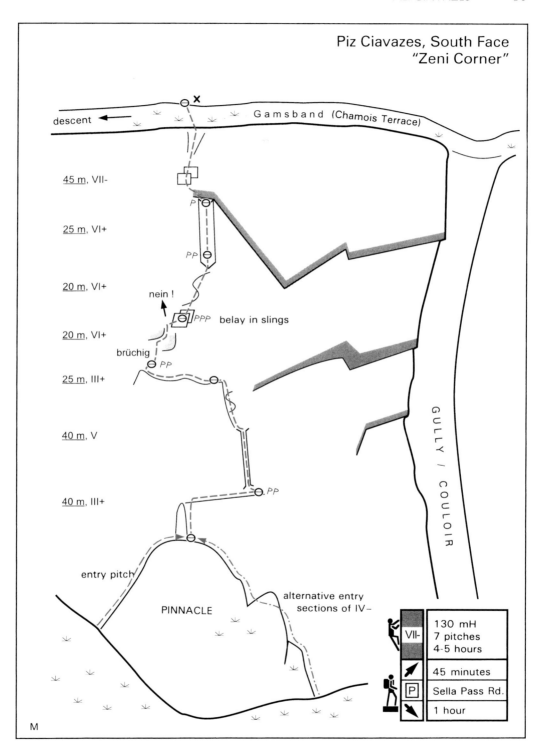

Piz Ciavazes, South Face
"Zeni Corner"

descent ← Gamsband (Chamois Terrace)

45 m, VII-

25 m, VI+

20 m, VI+

nein !

20 m, VI+   belay in slings

brüchig

25 m, III+

40 m, V

40 m, III+

entry pitch

PINNACLE

alternative entry
sections of IV–

GULLY / COULOIR

VII-		130 mH 7 pitches 4-5 hours
		45 minutes
	P	Sella Pass Rd.
		1 hour

M

15 PORDOISPITZE 2952m
PIZ PORDOI

North-West Face, "Fedele" (Bernard/Masè Dari) IV+

With unbelievable skill, the first ascentionists managed to find a route up the big, black water streak on this seemingly unfriendly face. The water, which often runs down the face, has in fact made the rock gloriously solid and covered in holds. The fact that the pitches below the large terrace are often streaming with water even after extended periods of fine weather is more than made up for by the extravagant profusion of good holds. If time is pressing, escape can be made by scuttling off along the terrace to the right. But really you should not forgo the pleasures of the upper section. After all, the stature and quality of the route is as much dependent on the size of the face as on anything else. And this is one of the finest long routes of its grade in the Dolomites.

Fedele Bernard, Giorgio Masè Dari. 1 August 1929. The exit pitches follow the Dibona Route climbed by Angelo Dibona, Guido & Max Mayer, Luigi Rizzi. 8 August 1910.

Belay pegs and some protection pegs in-situ. Take a selection of nuts and slings in addition.

Pian Schiavaneis (1877m), an inn on the Canazei/Sellajoch road.

200m above Pian Schiavaneis on the Sella Pass road is the start of the footpath into Val Lasties. Leave this path at the foot of the face, below a large boulder on the wide terrace.

Start below a U-shaped depression. Climb up rightwards to a protruding knob just left of a small leaning pillar.

To the right of the large perched block on the wide terrace above is a black water streak running the entire height of the face. The route follows the right hand edge of this streak. The summit wall is climbed by a crack and chimney system slanting up from left to right.

To descend, first head up towards the Pordoischarte and then follow the long trench down into Val Lasties (waymarked) and back to the base of the wall.

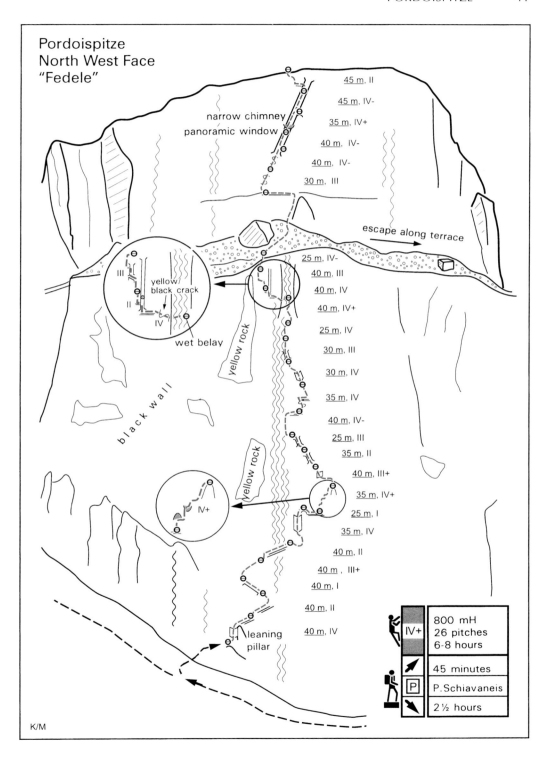

Pordoispitze
North West Face
"Fedele"

45 m, II

45 m, IV-

narrow chimney — 35 m, IV+
panoramic window

40 m, IV-

40 m, IV-

30 m, III

escape along terrace

25 m, IV-

40 m, III

yellow/
black crack — 40 m, IV

III

II — 40 m, IV+

IV — 25 m, IV

wet belay

30 m, III

yellow rock — 30 m, IV

35 m, IV

black wall

40 m, IV-

25 m, III

35 m, II

40 m, III+

yellow rock

IV+ — 35 m, IV+

25 m, I

35 m, IV

40 m, II

40 m, III+

40 m, I

40 m, II

leaning — 40 m, IV
pillar

K/M

IV+ | 800 mH
26 pitches
6-8 hours

45 minutes

P | P.Schiavaneis

2 ½ hours

16 PORDOISPITZE
PIZ PORDOI
2952m

South Pillar, "Mariakante" (Piaz/Dezulian) IV+

The "Mariakante" is one of the most popular routes on the Pordoispitze. Consequently, the frequency of traffic can be rather tiresome but there is a by-product of this popularity in the shape of drilled ring bolts on (almost all) the belays. The uncomplicated approach and descent and the sunny position make the route additionally attractive. The rock is sound and astonishingly free of polish, the climbing varied and at times elegantly exposed. The line of the route is not quite as obvious on the upper section, while the first pitch after the notch does place increased demands on the moral fibre of the leader.

Giovanni Battista (Tita) Piaz, Virginio Dezulian. 1932.

Mainly bolt belays; sufficient protection pegs in-situ.

Pordoijoch (2250m); ski-lift and parking.

From the Pordoijoch, follow a marked path in the direction of the Pordoischarte, ascending to just beneath the South Face. Traverse left across the scree below the cliff (climbers' path) until almost at the end of the South-East Face.

Start at the foot of the gully between the main face and the tower (pegs).

The South-East Face of Piz Pordoi is bounded on its left by a tower which tops out a good half way up the Face and is separated from it by a chimney/gully. The route begins at the foot of this gully and follows the vague arête of the tower to join the right edge of a large yellow roof before crossing the gully onto the South Face itself. The easier summit ground is reached by keeping to the left of the upper arête all the way.

To descend with knees intact, use the ski-lift. Alternatively, follow a marked path via the Pordoischarte back to the Pordoijoch.

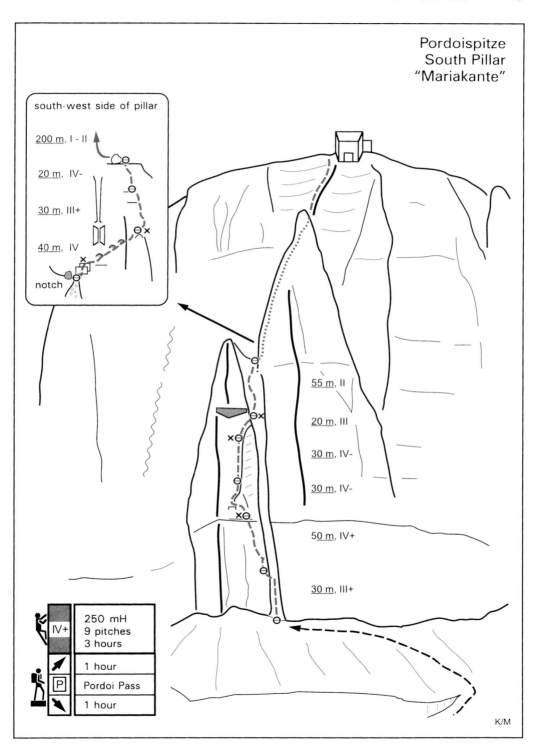

Pordoispitze
South Pillar
"Mariakante"

south-west side of pillar

200 m, I - II

20 m, IV-

30 m, III+

40 m, IV

notch

55 m, II

20 m, III

30 m, IV-

30 m, IV-

50 m, IV+

30 m, III+

IV+ | 250 mH
9 pitches
3 hours

1 hour

P | Pordoi Pass

1 hour

K/M

17 NEUNER   2904m

South-East Face, "Castiglioni/Detassis" V

The "Neuner" (nine o'clock face) is the southernmost of the 'hands of the clock' in the Vallon corrie, and is separated from the "Zehner" by a deep, narrow rift. The East Face is split by several chimney lines running the whole height of the wall, with the chimney on the far right being the most prominent. This obvious line is the one Castiglioni and Detassis made their own on one of their Sella outings. The climber who views this route expecting endless bridging and off-width thrutching will be surprised. In fact, the chimney is in places more like a couloir and so wide and flat that it almost gives face climbing. The rock is sound and well supplied with holds, even if at first sight the initial pitch does not look like it. The frequent streams of water coursing down the route compels the climber to proceed in an orderly manner, but without neoprene in your armoury you would be well-advised to await a dry spell in late summer and even then climb only after a few rain-free days.

☒ Ettore Castiglioni, Bruno Detassis. 10 July 1935.

🗡 A few pegs in-situ. Definitely take nuts and lots of slings.

P Corvara (1575m).

↗ From Corvara, take the Boè lift to Crep de Mont, then the Vallon chair lift (or on foot from Corvara using paths 639 and 638 to the Kostner Hut, involving a 985m height gain). From the top station of the lift follow a marked path below the Boèseekofel and then past the Zehner to the foot of the East Face of the Neuner.

E Start at the foot of the prominent chimney system which splits the wall from bottom to top.

R Follow the prominent chimney system up and right all the way.

↘ To descend, first scramble up and left to join a rib of scree and boulders. Follow this down left (south) into a cleft with a little pool (cairns). From here go left and descend the via ferrata (bridge and waterfall traverse!) back into the Vallon corrie and on down to the lift station.

! Those who wish to stay a while longer in the Vallon corrie will find Rifugio Kostner, situated near the top lift station, an ideal base.

Neuner
East Face
"Castiglioni/Detassis"

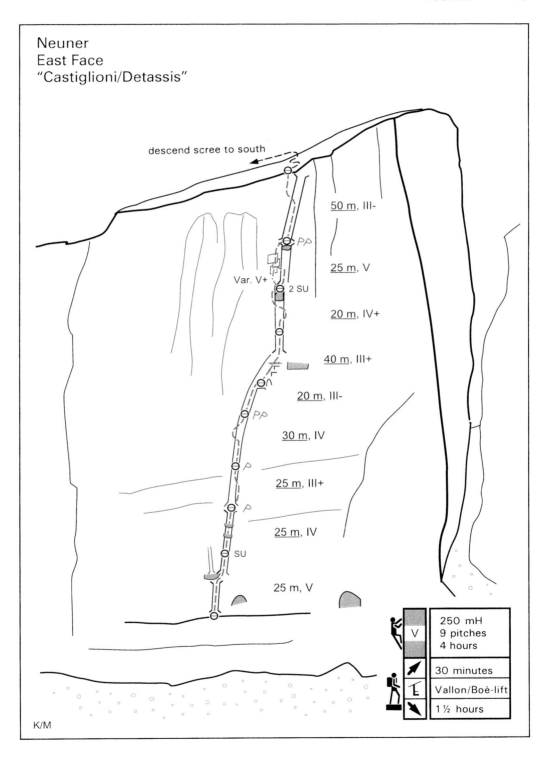

descend scree to south

50 m, III-

PP

25 m, V

Var. V+

2 SU

20 m, IV+

40 m, III+

20 m, III-

PP

30 m, IV

P

25 m, III+

P

25 m, IV

SU

25 m, V

	250 mH 9 pitches 4 hours
V	
↗	30 minutes
↙	Vallon/Boè-lift
↘	1 ½ hours

K/M

18   BOÈSEEKOFEL   2908m

South-East Face, "Castiglioni/Detassis" IV+

The Vallon corrie is one of the secrets hiding over on the less well-known 'other side' of the Sella massif. A great, boulder-strewn amphitheatre surrounded by steep walls which glow golden in the morning and midday sun. Up there, there are indeed some very worthwhile climbing objectives; above all the South-East Face of the Boèseekofel, split right down its middle by a large corner/chimney system. The walls of this chimney are solid and covered with holds, making it a pleasure to climb. The fact that the start of the route lies a mere fifteen minutes walk from the top station of the Vallon chair lift also makes the whole thing a pretty relaxed affair. Those wishing to do several routes will find the Franz Kostner Hut an ideal base for their untertakings. It is reached in ten minutes from the top station. If the route is to be experienced in dry conditions, it should not be approached too early in the year and then only after a longer period of fine weather.

- ⚔   Ettore Castiglioni, Bruno Detassis. 10 July 1935.
- 🗝   A few pegs in-situ; plenty of natural protection – take a rack.
- 🅿   Corvara (1575m).
- ↗   From Corvara, take the Boè lift to Crep de Mont, then the Vallon chair lift (or on foot from Corvara via marked paths 639 and 638 to the Kostner Hut involving a 985m height gain). From the top station of the lift follow a marked path below the face and scramble up easy-angled rocks to a grassy terrace at the foot of the wall.
- 🄴   Start directly below a chimney system running up and diagonally rightwards.
- 🅁   Approach the chimney system splitting the South-East Face by climbing in from the right. Follow this line to the summit.
- ↘   Descend by a marked path to the via ferrata on the East Rib. Climb down this (exposed in places).

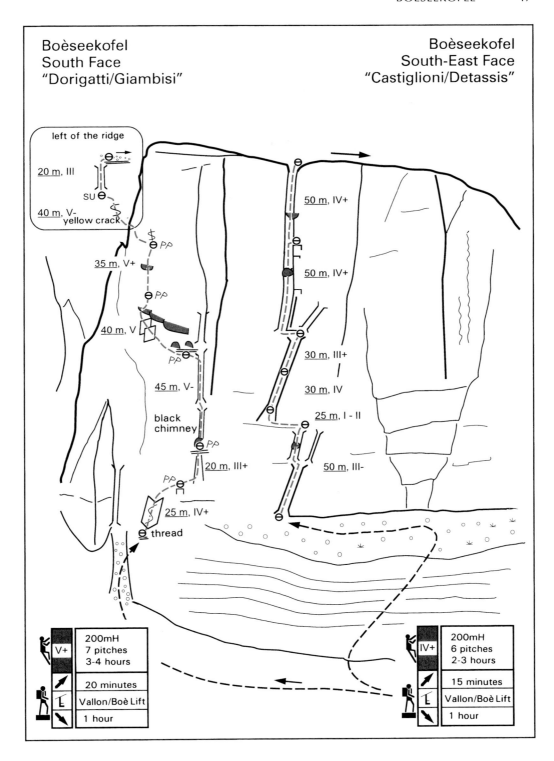

Boèseekofel
South Face
"Dorigatti/Giambisi"

Boèseekofel
South-East Face
"Castiglioni/Detassis"

left of the ridge

20 m, III

SU

40 m, V–
yellow crack

35 m, V+

PP

PP

40 m, V

PP

45 m, V–

black
chimney

PP

20 m, III+

PP

25 m, IV+

thread

50 m, IV+

50 m, IV+

30 m, III+

30 m, IV

25 m, I - II

50 m, III–

V+	200mH 7 pitches 3-4 hours
	20 minutes
	Vallon/Boè Lift
	1 hour

IV+	200mH 6 pitches 2-3 hours
	15 minutes
	Vallon/Boè Lift
	1 hour

19 BOÈSEEKOFEL   2908m

South-East Face, "Dorigatti/Giambisi" IV+

The "Dorigatti/Giambisi", on the left-hand sector of the South Face of the Boèseekofel, is, like the "Castiglioni/Detassis" up the middle of the face, one of those ideal routes which lie hidden in the sunny Vallon corrie. The approach and descent are both short and simple (always presuming one is not too proud to use the Boè lift and the Vallon chair lift), the route is on the side that catches the sun and the climbing is very varied and on best quality rock. On the pitches up to the prominent yellow band of overhangs in the middle part of this route, the water which frequently runs over the rock has dyed it black, removed the loose stuff and scoured out a splendid assortment of good holds. As a result, even the potential horrors of a tight squeeze chimney rapidly diminish. On the two crux pitches through the yellow band of overhangs the trick is to be brave and enjoy the steep, exposed and gymnastic climbing.

⚑   Alberto Dorigatti, Almo Giambisi. 19 August 1973.

⚷   A few pegs in-situ; plenty of natural protection – take a rack.

Ⓟ   Corvara (1575m).

↗   From Corvara, take the Boè lift to Crep de Mont, then the Vallon chair lift (or on foot from Corvara via marked paths 639 and 638 to the Kostner Hut involving a 985m height gain). From the top station of the lift follow a marked path, keeping beneath the South Face until almost at its end, where a scree shoot rises up to the right. Climb this and traverse right along a narrow ledge to the start of the route.

Ⓔ   Start at the foot of a yellow and black crack/ groove (thread), about 20m right of the gully.

Ⓡ   Follow the black chimney to beneath the prominent yellow band of overhangs at roughly half height. Traverse left below the overhangs and pull through at the weakest point. Continue up, finally moving left round the arête to reach the summit rocks (topo p.47).

↘   Descend by a marked path to the *via ferrata* on the East Rib. Climb down this (exposed in places).

20 TORRE FIRENZE   2493m

North-West Arête IV+

High above the Val Gardena, the Geisler and Stevia group is an area not normally celebrated as a top climbing paradise. Thus it is all the more surprising to find here such an utterly good-natured route as the North-West Arête of Torre Firenze, remarkable for its beautiful line, varied and pleasant climbing and solid, juggy rock. The second nice surprise is that the belays are equipped with expansion bolts.   Not all of them, it must be said, but nevertheless! The most difficult and technically interesting pitches come right at the start of the route: the funny traverse round the rib and the subsequent wall where you have to hang on pretty hard. Pure enjoyment follows on the upper pitches, directly up the solid, juggy arête. The descent crosses some impressive ground, too, over the sterile stone desert of the Stevia plateau and down to the alpine meadows at the Schuatsch Hut.

In early summer, these meadows are a carpet of flowers – a nice bonus for a nice route.

⚔ First ascent details unknown

🔑 Some belays equipped with bolts. On the easier pitches it will be necessary to set up your own belays. Some protection pegs in place.

🅿 St. Christina (1570m) in the Val Gardena, valley station of the Col Raiser lift.

↗ Follow a waymarked path to the Regensburg Hut. After about 45 minutes (at a water pipe and large boulder) leave this path, turning off right and continuing up through a copse of pine trees to emerge on the boulder and scree slopes at the foot of the North-West Arête.

🄴 The start of the route is located approx. 50m left of the arête and left of a reddish groove, at the foot of a ramp leading out to the arête.

🆁 Approach the arête from the left. Climb it direct, with occasional excursions to the right.

↘ From the summit, scramble down a short way into a notch and climb a gully to the Stevia plateau. Descend the crest, keeping right, until a leftwards curve allows you to join a walkers' path. Go right into a notch (junction of paths). Follow a marked path down and right to the Schuatsch Hut (1 hour to here) and continue to join the approach path to the Regensburg Hut. Follow this path back to the starting point.

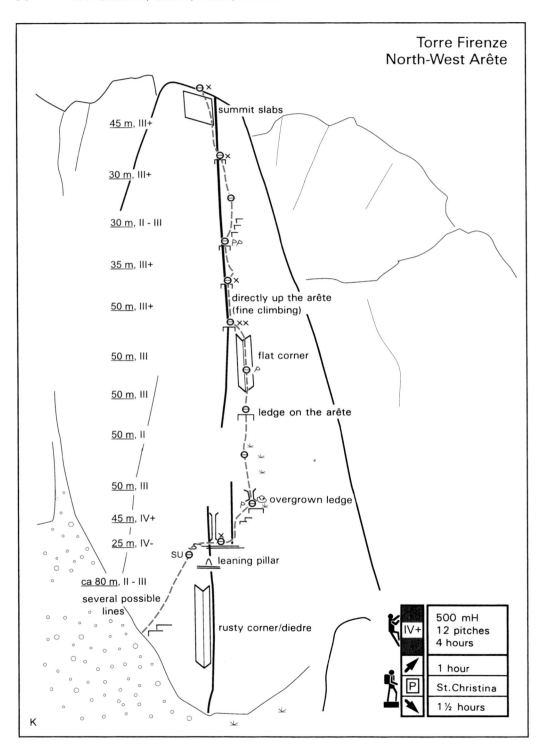

Torre Firenze
North-West Arête

45 m, III+

summit slabs

30 m, III+

30 m, II - III

35 m, III+

50 m, III+

directly up the arête
(fine climbing)

50 m, III

flat corner

50 m, III

ledge on the arête

50 m, II

50 m, III

overgrown ledge

45 m, IV+

25 m, IV-

SU

leaning pillar

ca 80 m, II - III

several possible
lines

rusty corner/diedre

IV+   500 mH
       12 pitches
       4 hours

       1 hour

P   St.Christina

       1 ½ hours

K

21 SASS DA CIAMPAC   2667m

"Old South Face" (Pospischil/Adang/Nogler) V

The mighty South Face of Sass da Ciampac rises from the green carpet of the Val Gardena Col like a true Dolomite ideal; uncompromisingly steep and marked with a row of buttresses, some more prominent than others. The "Old South Face" route takes a line up the grey pillar at the right-hand end of the face, its obvious rounded rib rising ramp-like up the wall. It offers splendid climbing, particularly in the upper two thirds, on

solid, often rough, rock covered in good holds. Add a pleasant approach over a soft, springy alpine meadow and a descent devoid of dangers and you have a route not to be missed!

- ⚔ Franz Pospischil, Josef Adang, Josef Nagler. 21 August 1903.

- 🗝 Relatively few belay and protection pegs in-situ. Rack of nuts and slings necessary. Maybe a few pegs to back up the belays, too.

- **P** Val Gardena Col (Grödner Joch) (2125m)

- ↗ From the Col, follow the road downhill towards Corvara for a little way, before branching off to follow the (almost horizontal) marked footpath to Colfuschg. Below the South Faces of Sass di Ciampac, turn off the path and strike directly up the slope to the foot of the face (several possible routes). An obvious grassy ledge leads back left onto the face from the start of the extreme right-hand pillar.

- **E** Start at the end of the grassy ledge at the foot of a crack leading into a ramp slanting up diagonally to the right.

- **R** Follow the ramp-like pillar. On the upper section keep to the right of a conspicuous crack and groove system (topo p.52).

- ↘ Descend to the west by a well-marked path along the summit ridge to the Crespeina col and back to the Val Gardena col.

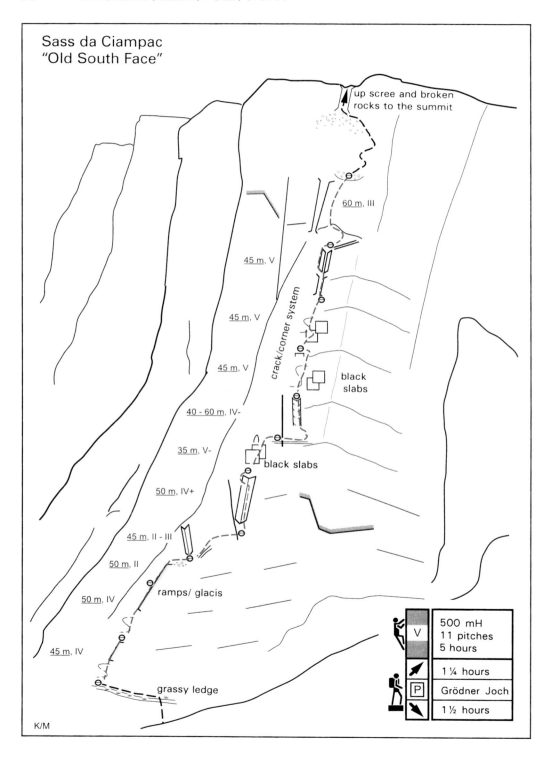

Sass da Ciampac
"Old South Face"

up scree and broken
rocks to the summit

60 m, III

45 m, V

45 m, V

crack/corner system

45 m, V

black
slabs

40 - 60 m, IV-

35 m, V-

black slabs

50 m, IV+

45 m, II - III

50 m, II

ramps/ glacis

50 m, IV

45 m, IV

grassy ledge

500 mH
11 pitches
5 hours

1 ¼ hours

Grödner Joch

1 ½ hours

K/M

ROSENGARTEN
CATINACCIO GROUP

The group with the poetic name ("rose garden") is the most westerly part of the real Dolomites. At its heart lies the area around the "Gartl" (a deep gorge) – the mighty Rosengartenspitze (Cima Catinaccio) itself and, of course, the Vajolet Towers. In summer this area is hopelessly overrun by tourists. Legend has it that somewhere in the Gartl was the entrance to the kingdom of King Laurin; small wonder, then, that the latter-day knights of leisure should choose to spend some time here. Those climbers wishing to pick more than a single rose from King Laurin's garden are advised to set up court at the Vajolet Hut (2243m). From Gardeccia, it is reached in a fast and easy

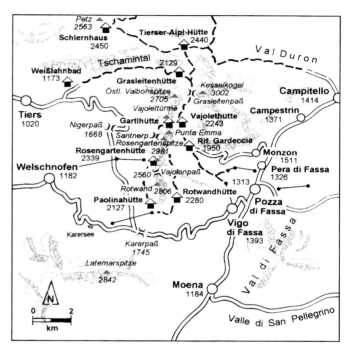

45-minute walk. A bus/taxi runs daily from 7.30am to 7.00pm along the road to Rifugio Gardeccia (road close to normal traffic after Monzon). From the bus turning point it is then only a matter of 20 minutes more to the hut. The bus stop is located at Pera, in the Val di Fassa, where the little road to Monzon branches off. From Monzon itself (no parking spaces) it is a 90 minute walk to Rifugio Gardeccia.

The huge Rotwand (Roda di Vael), which dominates the Karer Pass, may also be reached quickly and easily by the Karer Pass chairlift, enabling the party to do without a hut stop. On a cautionary note, the Rotwand recently reminded us that mountains do not stand forever when part of the famous "Buhlweg" fell victim to a massive rockfall. The Valbonspitze is situated in the remotest corner of the Group. It is reached from Weisslahnbad in the Tiers valley, but only after a walk involving a height gain of 1000m! Yet the slog up to the Grasleiten Hut (Rifugio Bergamo) is worth it for the outdoor experience alone and the cosy hut, almost right at the start of the Valbon Arête, reminds of times long past – its tiled stove and wooden tables darkened by age.

The most important valley bases for the Rosengarten Group are all in Val di Fassa – Vigo di Fassa (campsite), Pozza di Fassa, Pera, Campitello (campsite) and Canazei (campsite). For the Valbon Arête we recommend Tiers, in the valley of the same name.

22 EAST VALONSPITZE 2705m
CIMA ORIENTALE DI VAL BONA

N.W. Arête, "Valbonkante" (Dülfer/Schaarschmidt/Schroffenegger) V

The "Valbonkante" lies slightly away from the well-known climbing areas of the Rosengarten Group in the scenically lovely and, unlike the Vajolet Valley, relatively unspoiled Tschamintal. It rises impressively straight up behind the cosy little Grasleiten Hut (Rif. Bergamo). In spite of the short approach and the uncomplicated descent the route has an something of an air of austerity and seriousness about it. This has much to do with the dark, shaded aspect of the wall and the immediate proximity of the narrow cleft, almost like a canyon, which falls away to the right of the arête. The start of the route, up a slabby tower, is ill-defined and from the flat, scree-strewn shoulder which marks the start of the summit arête itself the rock is shattered and, in parts, loose. For those who feel confident enough to do so, it is better to coil the ropes after the last difficult pitch and solo to the top. By contrast, the meat of the route gives solid climbing on rough rock. There are several delightful and varied pitches that are steep and exposed.

Hans Dülfer, Werner Schaarschmidt, Franz Schroffenegger. August 1912.

No pegs on the lower slabby section to join the arête. On the actual arête, most of the belay and protection pegs are in-situ. There are some thread belays (take slings!)

Grasleiten Hut or Rif. Bergamo (2129m). Reached on foot in 3 hours (1000m of ascent) from the Tschaminschwaige in Weisslahnbad in the Tiers Valley, via a scenically beautiful path. The hut can also be reached from Rif. Vajolet by crossing the Grasleiten Pass (2½ hours).

Walk up the Grasleiten Pass path for a few minutes before turning off right along a path that crosses a stream to arrive at the foot of the slabby tower guarding the approach to the arête.

Pick your own line up and right (II–III) to an obvious ledge directly beneath a steepening on the arête. Start up a shattered looking crack left of the arête.

Follow the arête to a ledge. Continue easily up the ridge (30 minutes) to the top.

Just below the summit there is a little notch (abseil peg) which is the key to the descent into the Valbon notch. Make two abseils (25m, 15m) down a gully, traverse left along a rubble ledge and abseil 25m (pegs) into the Eastern Valbon notch. Scramble down a scree gully (heading south) to the Grasleiten basin and follow the marked path back to the hut.

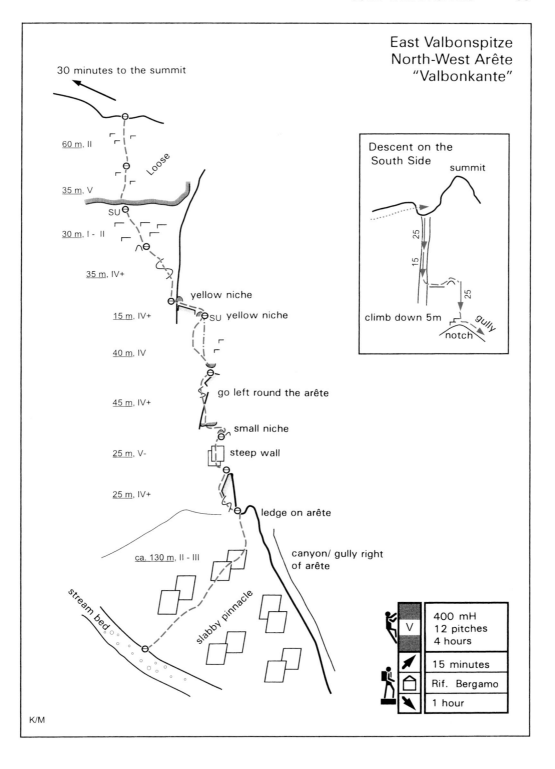

East Valbonspitze
North-West Arête
"Valbonkante"

30 minutes to the summit

60 m, II

Loose

35 m, V

SU

30 m, I - II

35 m, IV+

yellow niche

15 m, IV+   SU yellow niche

40 m, IV

go left round the arête

45 m, IV+

small niche

25 m, V-   steep wall

25 m, IV+

ledge on arête

canyon/ gully right
of arête

ca. 130 m, II - III

stream bed

slabby pinnacle

Descent on the
South Side   summit

25

15

25

climb down 5m   gully

notch

V   400 mH
     12 pitches
     4 hours

     15 minutes

     Rif. Bergamo

     1 hour

K/M

23 ROTWAND
RODA DI VAEL

2806m

West Face, "Dibona" (Dibona/Broome/Verzi/Corning) V–

The West Face of the Rotwand rises like a vertical shield above the Karer Pass. In the past this was considered to be one of the last great unclimbed walls of the Dolomites. The first to solve the problem was the Ampezzo mountain guide Angelo Dibona*, who in 1908 led a strong party up a line on the right-hand part of the face – without recourse to a single piton! The climb has since become a classic nowadays sporting a dozen or more pegs. The only unpleasant feature is the loose, and poorly protected rock on the easy initial section. The route is therefore best attempted only by climbers competent at moving on 'alpine' grade III terrain without causing stonefall. Once the real difficulties begin, the rock becomes pretty solid.

*Though credited to Dibona, Edward Broome deserves equal recognition for this advanced climb. In his account (A.J. Vol 24, p.465) he notes 'I had long set my affections on this ancient virgin wall … and discussed her weak points, written secret letters to guides about her, and indeed had almost said too much for our men got so keen that they began, on off days, to make explorations before we were ready for the assault..' It is clear from the account that the route-finding high on the route owed much to careful advanced study. *Editor's note.*

🏔 Angelo Dibona, Edward Broome, Angelo Verzi, Hanson Kelly Corning. 21 August 1908.

🪝 No pegs for belays or protection on the initial chossy pitches.

🅿 Rifugio Paolina (2127m), top station of the Karer Pass chairlift. Valley station and parking near the Hotel on Lake Karer.

↗ From Rifugio Paolina, head first for the Rosengarten Hut (Rifugio Coronelle) then in the direction of the Vajolon Pass, heading uphill until beneath the face. Scramble along scree and boulders at the base of the wall to the start of the route.

🅴 Start about 10m–20m right of the corner formed by the junction of the main wall and the easier-angled rocks of the initial pillar.

🆁 The first few pitches of the route, as far as the boulder ledge, are not clearly defined. Pick your own line. Thereafter, the climb follows a crack and chimney system between the true West Face and the right hand bounding pillar.

↘ From the summit, scramble along the North Ridge (safety ropes) to the Vajolon notch and an easy descent back to Rifugio Paolina.

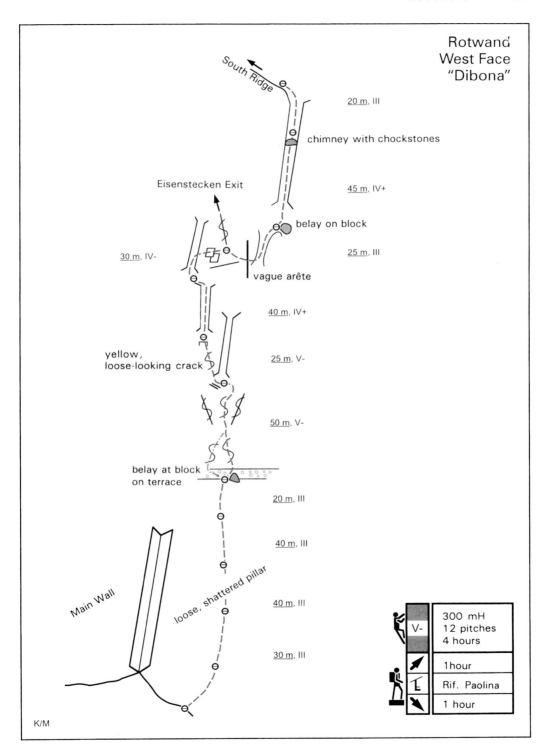

Rotwand
West Face
"Dibona"

South Ridge

20 m, III

chimney with chockstones

45 m, IV+

Eisenstecken Exit

belay on block

30 m, IV-

25 m, III

vague arête

40 m, IV+

yellow,
loose-looking crack

25 m, V-

50 m, V-

belay at block
on terrace

20 m, III

40 m, III

Main Wall

loose, shattered pillar

40 m, III

30 m, III

	300 mH
V-	12 pitches
	4 hours
↗	1 hour
☷	Rif. Paolina
↘	1 hour

K/M

24 ROTWAND
RODA DI VAEL

2806m

W. Face, "Eisenstecken" (Eisenstecken/Rabanser/Oberrauch) VI

Otto Eisenstecken and his companions made this impressive route (using very few pitons) up a crack system on the left-hand side of the West Face. It took two days to complete. Eisenstecken and Erich Abram pointed Hermann Buhl at the climb for the second ascent which was thus speedily completed in a day (again with little recourse to pitons). Even today, this strenuous, classic chimney and crack climb is no gift, even if nuts and Friends do make the protection both easier and safer. The crux in particular, an impending chimney-crack and slippery as an eel, has to be fought for. The rock is predominantly solid, although there are parts of the lower section which give a contrary impression. The upper pitches of the route provide the payback for the toil and trouble down below, with solid, enjoyable slab climbing. A route of considerable character!

🍴   Otto Eisenstecken, Florian Rabanser, Luitfried (Luis) Oberrauch. 1947.

🪝   Belay and protection pegs of varying quality in-situ. Nuts and Friends a must!

P   Rifugio Paolina (2127m), top station of the Karer Pass chairlift. Valley station and parking near the Hotel on Lake Karer.

↗   From Rifugio Paolina, head first for the Rosengarten Hut (Rifugio Coronelle or Rifugio Fronza) then in the direction of the Vajolon Pass, heading uphill until beneath the face. Scramble along the base of the wall to the start of the route.

E   Start at the foot of the prominent corner system in the left hand part of the West Face, at two parallel cracks.

R   Follow the obvious corner system, passing to the left of a large black overhang roughly at the mid point of the Face. The route joins the ridge, from where scrambling remains to the summit.

↘   From the summit, scramble along the North Ridge (safety ropes) to the Vajolon notch and an easy descent back to Rifugio Paolina.

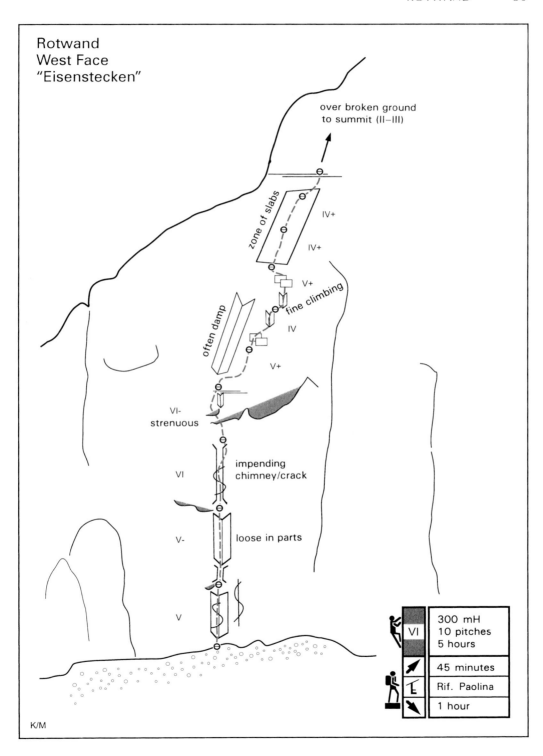

Rotwand
West Face
"Eisenstecken"

over broken ground
to summit (II–III)

zone of slabs

IV+

IV+

V+

fine climbing

often damp

IV

V+

VI-
strenuous

VI

impending
chimney/crack

V-

loose in parts

V

300 mH
10 pitches
5 hours

VI

45 minutes

Rif. Paolina

1 hour

K/M

25 ROSENGARTENSPITZE 2981m
CIMA CATINACCIO

East Face, "Steger" (Steger/Wiesinger/Masè Dari/Lechner) VI–

The walk up from Rifugio Gardeccia to Rifugio Vajolet is dominated by the broad and mighty presence of the East Face of the Rosengartenspitze. Twin col-like shoulders frame the Face, reducing the height of the wall on the extreme left and right hand sides and thus accentuating the big central lines all the more clearly. Hans Steger and Paula Wiesinger, the Dolomite first ascent couple of the 1920s, managed to climb the line of the wall: their route follows the parallel cracks splitting the East Face in the direct fall line from the summit of the mountain. This long – and thus strenuous and sustained – route offers plenty of great, varied climbing, from the steep corner right at the start to the tricky yellow wall on the upper part of the Face. The rock is solid and those sections that traditionally have not always been too sound have cleaned up nicely over the years.

Hans Steger, Paula Wiesinger, Fred Masè Dari, Siegfried Lechner. August 1929.

Belay and protection pegs in-situ on the difficult pitches. 50m ropes needed.

Rifugio Vajolet (2243m). Reached on foot in 45 minutes from Rifugio Gardeccia (bus taxi from Pera di Fassa, see p.53) via a waymarked track.

Descend a short distance from the Rifugio Vajolet to a point where a signposted path branches off right to the Tschagerjoch. This leads under the East Face of the Rosengartenspitze. 45 minutes from Rifugio Vajolet; 1¼ hours from Gardeccia.

E The left hand of the two obvious cracks in the direct fall line from the summit starts life as a corner. It is reached from the left by scrambling over broken slabby ground.

R Follow the left hand corner and crack system at first. After the 7th pitch, the route swops over to the right hand crack system. Do not miss the turning (a crack branching off to the right)!

From the summit, descend the North Ridge to a notch; ring peg. Either climb down (II-III) or make three abseils (20m, 50m, 50m) out of the notch to the west and continue down to the Santner Pass. From here, a path leads via Rifugio Alberto (Gartl Hut) to Rifugio Vajolet.

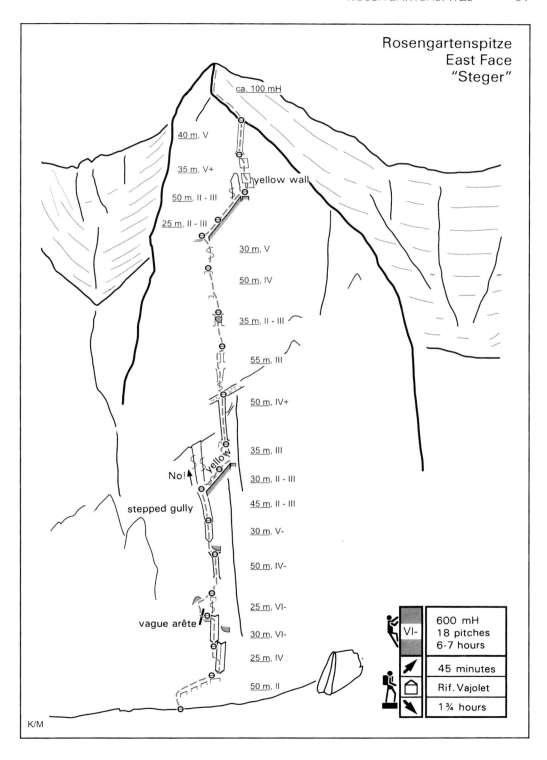

Rosengartenspitze
East Face
"Steger"

ca. 100 mH

40 m, V

35 m, V+

yellow wall

50 m, II - III

25 m, II - III

30 m, V

50 m, IV

35 m, II - III

55 m, III

50 m, IV+

35 m, III

No!   yellow

30 m, II - III

stepped gully

45 m, II - III

30 m, V-

50 m, IV-

25 m, VI-

vague arête

30 m, VI-

25 m, IV

50 m, II

VI-	600 mH 18 pitches 6-7 hours
	45 minutes
	Rif. Vajolet
	1 ¾ hours

K/M

26 PUNTA EMMA   2617m

East Face, "Piaz Crack" V–

Tita Piaz, the first ascentionist of the Punta Emma, was also the first to climb the striking corner line on its East Face, a remarkable feat in the history of alpinism when one pauses to consider that he did the route in the year 1900, solo! Nowadays the route is amongst the most popular in the entire group, due not least to the short approach walk. The difficulties in the corner system are concentrated into the second and third pitches. The impending chimney crack of the third pitch calls for a certain spiritedness and commitment; rucksack wearers seldom give a good account of themselves here! On the difficult pitches the rock is solid, although polished by the sweat of fear on the crux itself.

🍴 Giovanni Battista (Tita) Piaz. 1900.

🔑 On the difficult pitches, all necessary belay and protection pegs are in place. It is advisable to carry a selection of slings and a few nuts in addition.

🏠 Rifugio Vajolet (2243m). Reached on foot in ¾ hour from the Rifugio Gardeccia (bus taxi from Pera di Fassa, see p.53) via a waymarked track.

↗ From Rifugio Vajolet, follow the path towards Rifugio Alberto/Gartl Hut until it is possible to traverse across debris on an ill-defined terrace to the foot of the obvious corner crack.

🄴 Start at the obvious corner system just to the right of the fall line.

🅁 Follow the corner system, exiting left onto a flat shoulder.

↘ Go west along the summit ridge and descend a gully between Punta Emma and the Rosengartenspitze to the "Gartl" path (two abseils). For more detail, see route 27, p.64.

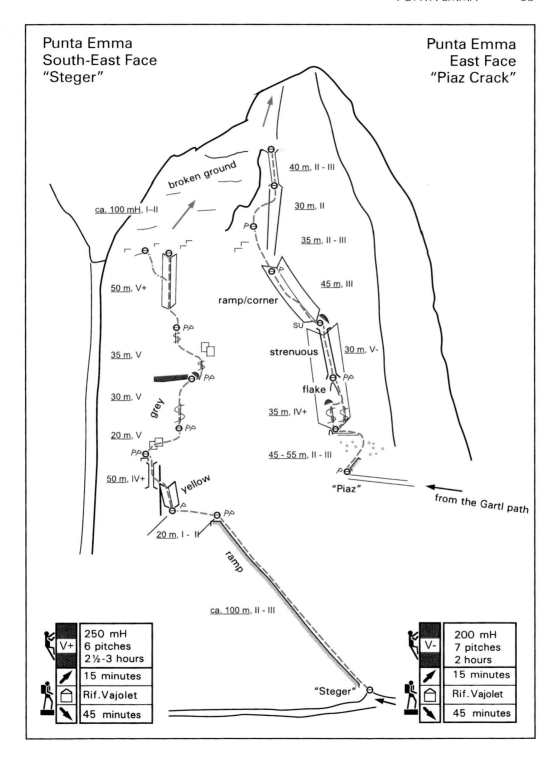

Punta Emma
South-East Face
"Steger"

Punta Emma
East Face
"Piaz Crack"

broken ground

ca. 100 mH, I–II

40 m, II - III

30 m, II

35 m, II - III

50 m, V+

ramp/corner

45 m, III

SU

35 m, V

strenuous

30 m, V-

grey

flake

30 m, V

35 m, IV+

20 m, V

45 - 55 m, II - III

50 m, IV+

yellow

"Piaz"

from the Gartl path

20 m, I - II

ramp

ca. 100 m, II - III

"Steger"

V+	250 mH
	6 pitches
	2½-3 hours
	15 minutes
	Rif. Vajolet
	45 minutes

V-	200 mH
	7 pitches
	2 hours
	15 minutes
	Rif. Vajolet
	45 minutes

27 PUNTA EMMA   2617m

South-East Face, "Steger" (Steger/Wiesinger) V+

The Punta Emma was named after Emma della Giacomo who, with Tita Piaz, was the first to reach the summit of this peak in 1899 via the modern day descent route. The Punta Emma is a favorite climbers' objective, due in no small part to the short approach and the uncomplicated descent. The route described here offers lovely and at times exposed climbing on solid rock. From the top of the first pillar the difficulties are continuous; however, the routefinding is not always immediately apparent.

☒ Hans Steger, Paula Wiesinger. July 1929.

⚲ All necessary belay pegs and many protection pegs in-situ.

⌂ Rifugio Vajolet (2243m). Reached on foot in ¾ hour from the Rifugio Gardeccia (bus taxi from Pera di Fassa, see p.53) via a waymarked track.

↗ From the Punta Emma, traverse across to an obvious ramp line.

Ⓔ Start at the obvious ramp running up leftwards.

Ⓡ Follow the ramp to its end and move left into a corner. Climb the corner to the top of a vague pillar. The obvious roof above is turned on the right. Climb a crack and corner system to join easier-angled rocks leading to the summit. Topo p.63.

◣ From the summit, descend the ridge to the west for about 40m (well trodden). Before the wall steepens, go left round the arête at a little terrace (cairn) and climb down and left – exposed – for a little way to reach a niche with a cemented-in abseil ring. Make one 25m abseil into the notch between Punta Emma and the Rosengartenspitze. Descend the right hand edge of the gully (full of snow, even in early summer) to the Gartl path (30 minutes).

28 THE VAJOLET TOWERS

Much vaunted and the subject of so much kitsch, yet a fascinating group of cliffs nonetheless, this has become the klettergarten of the area, thanks to the short approaches and – on the popular routes at least – bolted belays and abseil 'pistes'. The climber should therefore not come to the Vajolet Towers expecting peace and solitude. The routes described here can be linked and done in one day as an intégrale, since the descent from the one tower invariably deposits you at the start of the next. The Steger Route on the South Face of Winklerturm is the odd one out here in terms of difficulty and is only recommended to those who have warmed up nicely on the other routes.

🏠 Rifugio Alberto / Gartl Hut (2621m). Reached in 1¾ hours on foot from the Rifugio Gardeccia, via the Rifugio Vajolet and the Gartl path. Waymarked. The bus taxi from Pera di Fassa stops just short of the Rif. Gardeccia; see p.53.

DELAGO TOWER   2790m

South-West Arête "Delagokante" (Piaz/Jori/Glaser) IV+

The "Delagokante" is one of the most celebrated of all Alpine climbs. As a result it is very popular – on summer days every stance is occupied. If this human route-finding system should fail, just follow the polished holds. Despite its popularity, with such a magnificent position the climbing on the arête on little edges and flakes, cannot fail to inspire, from the first moves right up to the summit of the tower.

 Giovanni Battista (Tita) Piaz, Francesco Jori, Irma Glaser, August 1911

 Cemented-in belay bolts, lots of protection pegs (some cemented-in).

↗ From the hut, a path leads round the Piaz Tower to the South Face of the Delago Tower.

E Scramble up rock steps on the far side of the little notch between the Piaz and Delago Towers to reach a terrace leading to a ledge directly on the arête.

R Follow the arête, first on the right then (on pitch two) on the left. Pitch three starts on the left before moving round to the right again and continuing to the top (100m, 90 minutes).

↘ To descend, two 20m abseils give access to the notch between the Delago and the Stabeler Towers (large jammed block). Four more 20m abseils lead down the gully to the south to reach the flatter terrain at the foot of the wall. Cemented-in abseil rings – allow 45 minutes.

STABELER TOWER   2809m

South Face, "Fehrmann" (Fehrmann/Perry-Smith) IV+

With their ascent of the corner system on the South Face of the Stabeler Tower, the two Saxony Sandstone pioneers Rudolf Fehrmann and Oliver Perry-Smith made the most strikingly obvious line on the wall their very own. As part of the intégrale, this route forms the logical continuation to the "Delagokante" – the last abseil point from the Delago Tower is almost directly at the start of the Fehrmann/Smith. However, do not expect too much after your experience of the Delago – in terms of elegance, the Fehrmann does not even come close.

☒ Rudolf Fehrmann, Oliver Perry-Smith. August 1908.

⚲ All necessary belay and protection pegs in-situ. Double ropes useful on the descent.

↗ Approach as for the Delagokante as far as the terrace. Traverse this to the right to the Delago/Stabeler Gully. Alternatively start after the abseil descent from the Delago Tower.

E The start of the route is at the last abseil station (ring peg) in the Delago/Stabeler Gully. From here, climb up diagonally rightwards to the start of the corner system.

R The route follows the obvious corner system of the South Face (120m, allow 90 minutes).

↘ From the summit (cemented-in ring) abseil 25m to a ledge (ring). Abseil over the south-east flank into the gully between the Stabeler and Winkler Towers (20m, 20m, 30m, 25m – cemented-in rings). Climb down easily over broken ground to the Gartl path; 1 hour. Those wishing to continue up the Winkler Tower will need to take a stance on the ledge at the last abseil ring.

WINKLER TOWER   2800m

South-East Face, "Winkler Crack" IV+

In 1887(!), Georg Winkler set off alone into the vertical world of this then totally unclimbed (and very bold) rock tower. He climbed the crack that bears his name, solo, and then soloed back down it again, an event in the history of alpinism equalled by very few others. Even applying modern criteria, this is a very worthwhile and – when one considers the date of the first ascent – surprisingly steep piece of climbing. The rock is good, the line obvious and the climbing very varied, changing from chimney to crack to face climbing. The route is an absolute must for the 'alpine historian' and is an ideal third part to the intégrale.

The Valojet Towers

Ⓐ "Delagokante" IV+
Ⓑ "Fehrmann" IV+
Ⓒ "Winkler Crack" IV
Ⓓ "Steger" VI

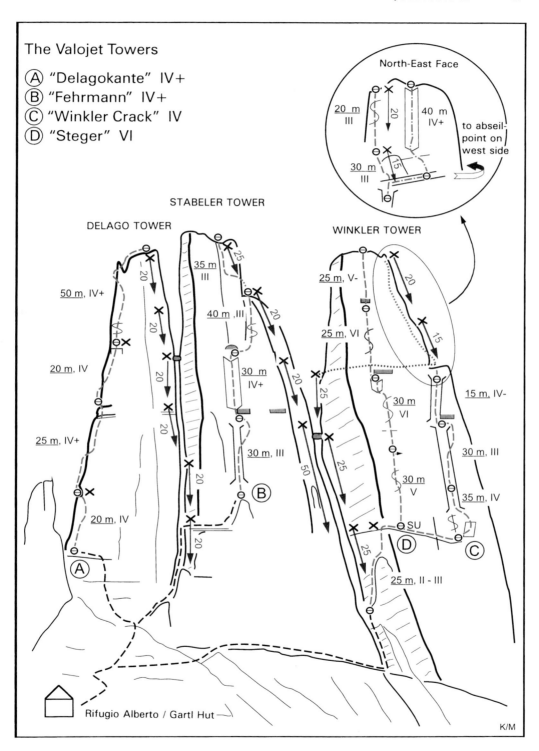

North-East Face

20 m
III

20

40 m
IV+

to abseil-
point on
west side

30 m
III

15

STABELER TOWER

DELAGO TOWER

WINKLER TOWER

35 m
III

50 m, IV+

20

20

25 m, V-

20

20

25

25 m, VI

40 m ,III

20

15

20 m, IV

20

30 m
IV+

20

15 m, IV-

30 m
VI

25 m, IV+

20

50

30 m, III

25

30 m
III

20 m, IV

20

50

25

30 m
V

35 m, IV

SU

Ⓑ

Ⓓ

Ⓒ

Ⓐ

25

25 m, II - III

Rifugio Alberto / Gartl Hut

K/M

⚔ Georg Winkler. 1887.

🗝 Many belay and protection pegs in-situ.

↗ From the Rifugio Alberto, follow the Delagokante approach to the South Face and traverse right across ledges and broken ground to the Stabeler/Winkler Gully; 20 mins. Alternatively, if descending from the Stabeler Tower, abseil to the ledge leading right to the start.

E Start at a chimney between the Stabeler and Winkler Towers. Follow this for about 50m (II–III) to a ledge with a cemented ring peg (junction with the abseil 'piste' from the Stabeler Tower). Follow the ledge round to the right (c. 50m, exposed) to the foot of the Winkler Crack.

R The route uses the obvious South Face crack and chimney system to begin with. From the shoulder there are two possible variations: either climb the South-East Arête direct (the original, and easier, route) or the corner/groove system round on the East Face (more difficult); 120m, allow 90 minutes (topo page 67).

↘ From the summit, climb down 10–15m to the south-east to the ledge with the cemented-in peg on the original route. Abseil 20 m and then 15 m. Traverse west along a ledge on the north side – one short exposed section – to reach a further abseil ring. Abseil 25m into the notch between the Winkler and Stabeler Towers. A further 25m abseil will deposit you on the ledge which marks the start of the route. From here, abseil down to easier ground. Allow 45 minutes; all abseil rings cemented-in.

WINKLER TOWER   2800m

South Face, "Steger" (Steger/Wiesinger/Masè Dari/Paluselli) VI

Only four pitches in length, yet in those four pitches Hans Steger and Paula Wiesinger needed to draw on their entire repertoire of climbing skills. The first pitch awaits with lovely, steep face climbing on grey limestone. On the second, things get considerably more demanding: strenuous, vertical crack and face climbing on rock which is rather shattered in places. The third pitch is a classic 'wooden wedge' crack; well equipped with a few Friends or Hexentrics, it is an absolute joy for crack climbers.

⚔ Hans Steger, Paula Wiesinger, Fred Masè Dari, A. Paluselli. September 1929.

🗝 Plenty of belay and protection pitons. Take a selection of medium-size Friends or Hexentrics.

↗ From Rifugio Alberto (Gartl Hut), follow the Delagokante approach to the South Face of the Vajolet Towers and traverse right across ledges and broken ground to the gully between the Stabeler and Winkler Towers (20 minutes). Climb the gully to the ledge at the start of the climbing proper. Alternatively, if descending from the Stabeler or Winkler Tower, abseil to the last abseil point on the ledge leading rightwards to the start of the route.

E Start on the ledge which runs rightwards out of the gully between the Stabeler and Winkler Towers at a thread between two cemented-in ring pegs.

R Climb cracks straight up the South Face (100m, 2 hours, topo p.67).

↘ Descend as for the 'Winkler Crack' (see above).

MARMOLADA

The Marmolada, the highest mountain in the Dolomites, presents two very different faces to the observer. When viewed from the north, the only real snowy mountain of the area warrants her claim to the title of "the Queen of the Dolomites". To the south, she breaks off into an impressive 800m-high and three kilometers wide wall famous for its splendid, solid-plated limestone. On this monstrous wall many chapters in the history of climbing in the Dolomites have been written. The trio of routes described here are not only amongst the finest on the South Face, they also reflect important stages in the history of exploratory climbing. The "Via Classica" (Zagonel/

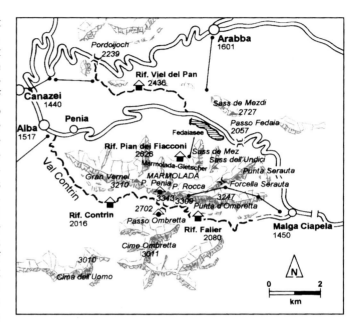

Tomasson/Bettega) was the first climb of any importance to tackle this face; the "Vinatzer/ Castiglioni" was at the time considered to be the the most difficult route in the Dolomites (and later had its direct finish added by Reinhold Messner, climbing solo at the height of his rock climbing powers); finally, "Don Quixote" (Schiestl/Mariacher) is representative of the age when sport-climbing ideas began to have an influence on the big alpine faces.

All of the climbs are long and the summit is high; for these reasons a bivouac bag should be taken on every climbing trip. The ideal base for all of the South Face routes is the beautifully situated Rifugio Falier, reached by a ninety-minute hike from Malga Ciapela. A campsite may also be found at the end of this little village on the Fedaia Pass road, together with the valley station of the Marmolada cable car. The days when the climbers could use the cable car to glide back down into the comfort of the valley free of charge are finally over, seemingly as the cable car company's reply to the protests of the environmental organisation "Mountain Wilderness". Nowadays, descent of the mountain by this method means spending lots of lire. Even then one must, in addition, have completed the route and reached the top station by about 4 pm for the last lift down to the valley – easier said than done. On the long descent on foot to the Fedaia Pass, the Marmolada shows her second, icy face – she is, after all, the only mountain in the Dolomites where you get a real glacier under your feet. A pair of instep crampons can be a real help here, especially in late summer. Lightweight boots and gaitors are advisable, in training shoes or similar, you will quickly get cold feet. And there are crevasses to contend with as well!

29 MARMOLADA DI PENIA 3343m

South Face, "Via Classica" (Zagonel/Tomasson/Bettega) V–

The first route to find a way up this mighty face was opened up in 1901 by Beatrice Tomasson* with her guides Bettega and Zagonel. For that time, it was a huge undertaking, particularly for a woman, for the route is both long and demanding in an alpine sense, and also has difficult sections especially on the first series of chimneys. Indeed chimney climbing predominates, sometimes tight work with a rucksack and elsewhere calling for wide bridging. The route, not always easy to find, demands alpine urgency because of its length. This is the highest peak in the Dolomites and exposed to the weather. It is best not to get caught by a storm in these chimneys and gullies – nor, indeed, on the descent of the *via ferrata* ladders and cables. Due to their close proximity to the big gully, the pitches above the First Terrace are exposed to stonefall. The rock is good to the Second Terrace but thereafter deteriorates yet remains of acceptable quality to both leader and second. A route for people who seek both pure climbing pleasure and the experience of tackling a big face on a big mountain.

* The client initiated the expedition. In September 1900 Beatrice Tomasson (who was English, though erroneously noted elsewhere as American or Scottish) hired Luigi Rizzi to reconnoitre the face. While Tomasson watched from the Passo Ombretta, Rizzi climbed 150m up chimneys to the first ledge and then descended. In June 1901 she hired two more guides who investigated another line, with little success. Tomasson (42) returned with the experienced Bettega (47) and Zagonel (33) and, using the Rizzi line, completed the climb during which they were caught by bad weather   continued on page 72

🍴 Michele Bettega, Miss Beatrice Tomasson, Bortolo Zagonel. 1 July 1901.

🪛 Most necessary belay and protection pegs in-situ. From the Second Terrace, protection becomes rather sparse. A few pegs in addition to nuts and slings will increase the safety margin.

🏠 Rifugio Falier (2080m) or Rifugio Contrin (2016m). Rifugio Falier can be reached from Malga Ciapela via the road which branches off the main road at the valley station of the Marmolada cable car. Go past the campsite to the end of the road (parking). Follow a waymarked path to the hut (90 minutes).Rifigop Contrin is best approached along a signposted path from

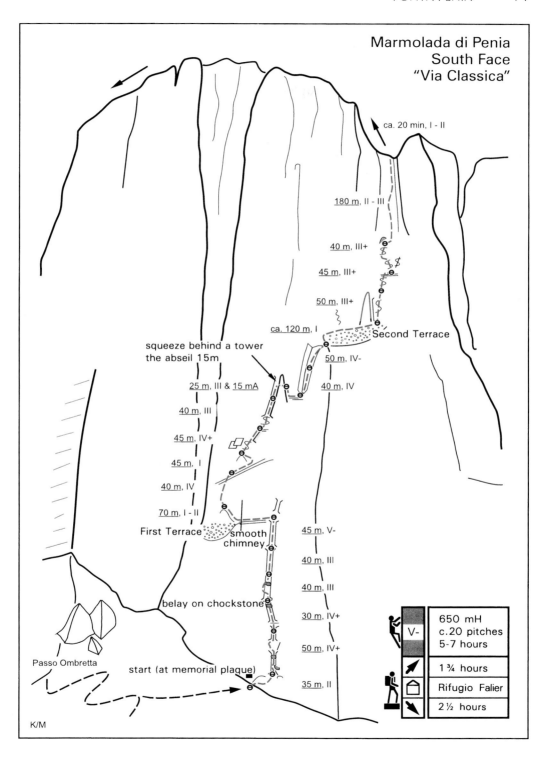

Marmolada di Penia
South Face
"Via Classica"

ca. 20 min, I - II

180 m, II - III

40 m, III+

45 m, III+

50 m, III+

ca. 120 m, I

Second Terrace

squeeze behind a tower
the abseil 15m

50 m, IV-

25 m, III & 15 mA

40 m, IV

40 m, III

45 m, IV+

45 m, I

40 m, IV

70 m, I - II

First Terrace

smooth chimney

45 m, V-

40 m, III

40 m, III

belay on chockstone

30 m, IV+

50 m, IV+

Passo Ombretta

start (at memorial plaque)

35 m, II

K/M

	650 mH c.20 pitches 5-7 hours
V-	
	1 ¾ hours
	Rifugio Falier
	2 ½ hours

Canazei (2 hours). There is also a bivouac box on the Ombretta Pass (south of the top of the pass, on the ridge).

From either hut, follow a waymarked path to the Ombretta Pass. On the east side, below the top of the pass, traverse across scree on the climbers' path to reach the foot of the route. About 2 hours from either hut.

To the right of the big gully which drops down from the summit of Punta Penia is a compact pillar which ends at the first terrace. The pillar is bounded on its right hand side by two chimney lines.The start of the route is located to the left of these chimneys at a memorial plaque. Scramble up rightwards to reach the left-hand of the two chimneys which leads to a ledge level with the first terrace.

Follow the series of chimneys to reach a ledge leading leftwards to the first rubble terrace. Up and right of the terrace is the start of a further chimney and corner system leading to the second terrace. Traverse right along the terrace and duck behind a split pillar to reach another line of cracks. Finally, climb up to the left of a big gully to arrive on the East Ridge. Climb the ridge to the summit and the hut (food, drink and custodian in situ!).

Descend from the summit to the West Ridge and follow this down to the *via ferrata* (impossible to miss) and thence to the Marmolada Notch; 1 hour. From the notch, descend to the south to Rifugio Contrin. Alternatively, follow an ill-defined path traversing below the South-West Face, eventually regaining the Ombretta Pass and the path to Rifugio Falier.

continued from page 70
– Zagonel being praised by Tomasson in his *führerbuch* for fine leading in snowy conditions. Here then was an important historical event – one of the biggest rock climbs of the period that has been compared to the North Face of the Dru – albeit rather easier. A 650m route of sustained Grade IV with some V– on a major, and quite serious unclimbed face, completed in a day – a major landmark in both alpine and women's climbing. Also of note is Rizzi's initial solo climb and descent. Pitons were placed to half height, seemingly as a retreat precaution. (Research: Hermann Reisach and Mirella Tenderini.)

30 MARMOLADA DI ROCCA 3309m

South Face, "Vinatzer/Castiglioni" with "Messner" finish VI+

For many years after its first ascent, the "Vinatzer/Castiglioni" was rated as one of the most difficult routes in the Dolomites but after the post-war period of inflationary 'dangle and whack' pitoning its original difficulties were emasculated. Heinz Mariacher reminded us that on the 1936 first ascent Hans Vinatzer had in all probability free-climbed sections of grade VI and also that the completely free version of the route is no harder than hard VI. Nowadays, the "Vinatzer/Castiglioni" – together with the Messner Finish – is one of the most popular classics on the South Face of the Marmolada. On the original route, with just a few exceptions (notably on pitch 7), the rock is very sound and rough in texture; the fact that even in summer several of the chimneys are often still running with water in no way detracts from the pleasure of the climbing where elegant chimney and corner work predominates.

In 1969, after the first solo ascent of the lower part of the "Vinatzer/Castigioni", Reinhold Messner avoided the upper chimneys by a new line on the wall to their left. This certainly counts as one of his greatest rock-climbing achievements. Perched on the plentiful little solution pockets on the steep exposed slabs of the middle section of the route one can hardly help feeling respectful for the man. The crux of the route comes right at the top and is not as pleasant an experience as the rest, taking a steep, shattered crack bristling with pegs.

Giovanni Battista (Hans) Vinatzer, Ettore Castiglioni. 2–3 September 1936; Reinhold Messner. 16–17 August.1969

All necessary belay and protection pegs in-situ on the lower section but protection is sparser on the Messner Finish. The possibility of retreat should also be considered on a face of this nature – in addition to a rack of nuts and slings, a few pegs and a hammer should be taken.

Rifugio Falier (2080m) reached from Malga Ciapela via the road which branches off the main road at the valley station of the Marmolada cable car. Go past the campsite to the end of the road (parking). Follow a waymarked path to the hut (90 minutes).

From Rifugio Falier, follow a waymarked path into the Ombretta Pass, finally traversing across scree below the face of the Marmolada di Rocca, right of the fall line from the summit and left of the fall line of an obvious chimney which starts below the ledge.

Start below a prominent series of chimneys and cracks. The bottom of the chimney forms a reddish niche at the base of the wall.

As far as the ledge, the route generally follows the line of the chimney and cracks systems, slanting up and leftwards like a huge, steep ramp. To reach the start of the Messner Finish, traverse right on gaining the ledge. Climb to the right of a collection of niches and pull over an overhang to reach easier ground. The Messner route now takes a line roughly up the middle of the face, eventually moving right at a little ramp on the upper section of the face and climbing a steep, pillar-like feature to reach the ridge leading to the summit.

The easiest descent is by a 20-minute walk east along the ridge to the cable car station (visible from the top of the route) and a relaxing ride down to the valley at Malga Ciapela. Alternatively, descend the Normal Route to the Fedaia Pass. From the cable car station, descend to the north-east along the ski piste, heading down the glacier towards the Forcella Serauta lift station. Two rocky ribs are clearly visible on the glacier – to the right (when descending) is Sass delle Undici, to the left Sass de Mez. Depending on the conditions, two possibilities now present themselves. Either descend the glacier to the north-west (watch out for crevasses!) to the Pian dei Forcella lift situated to the left of Sass de Mez. From here a path leads down to the Fedaia Lake. Alternatively descend to a point just short of the Forcella Serauta station and then directly down the glacier to the right of Sass delle Undici to reach a debris-strewn area levelled by the piste grooming machinery. From here, a towing path leads down to the Fedaia Pass (3 hours).

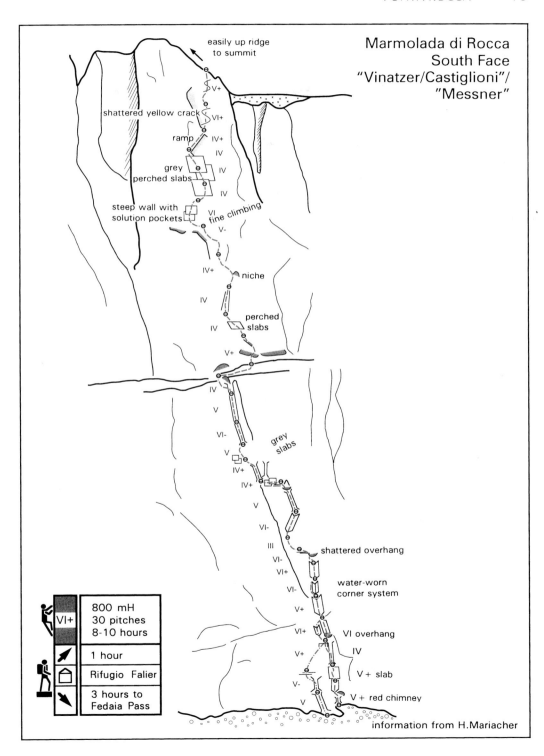

Marmolada di Rocca
South Face
"Vinatzer/Castiglioni"/
"Messner"

easily up ridge
to summit

V+

shattered yellow crack   VI+

ramp   IV+

IV

grey   IV
perched slabs

IV

steep wall with   VI
solution pockets   fine climbing
V-

IV+   niche

IV

IV   perched
slabs

V+

IV

V

VI-

V   grey
slabs
IV+

IV+

V

VI-

III

VI-   shattered overhang
VI+

VI-   water-worn
corner system

V+

VI+   VI overhang

V+   IV

V + slab

V-

V + red chimney

V

800 mH
VI+   30 pitches
8-10 hours

1 hour

Rifugio Falier

3 hours to
Fedaia Pass

information from H.Mariacher

31 MARMOLADA D'OMRETTA 3247m

South Face, "Don Quixote" (Schiestl/Mariacher) VI

One of the most amenable modern routes on Marmolada's South Face, "Don Quixote" has now become a classic. The fun starts early; just looking at the line up the edge of the big, evenly proportioned buttress, like a white bird with wings outstretched, is a pleasurable experience in itself. The easier and rather average quality lower section of the climb is really just a lead-in to the second part, where the real fun is to be had. Solid, water-worn plate limestone awaits, with some outstanding pitches, amongst them the overhanging yet lavishly pocketed face-climbing on the third pitch above the ledge. From then on, airy and enjoyable slab-climbing predominates. The crux comes at the start of the curving crack splitting the upper wall. This can be avoided on the left by bold climbing up very exposed slabs (VI) or climbed direct (strenuous VI+, but very well protected), following the fine crack all the way. As cracks and chimneys are avoided (with the exception of the entry pitches and the crux variation), with a corresponding lack of seepage, ice or snow, it is climbable early in the year.

☒ Reinhard Schiestl, Heinz Mariacher, 24 June 1979.

◩ Though most belay and protection pegs are in-situ, for routes on this face, a small selection of pegs, in addition to a rack of nuts, is almost obligatory.

⌂ Rifugio Falier (2080m) reached from Malga Ciapela via the road which branches off the main road at the valley station of the Marmolada cable car. Go past the campsite to the end of the road (parking). Follow a waymarked path to the hut (90 minutes).

⬈ From Rifugio Falier, follow a waymarked path in the direction of Passo Ombretta, branching off after about 30 minutes to climb up diagonally rightwards over steep grass and finally along a chossy ramp which starts to the right of an ill-defined scree basin and leads up and right to the top of the tower marking the start of the route.

▣ Start about 50m below the highest point of the tower, from where a system of ramps and cracks leads up diagonally leftwards.

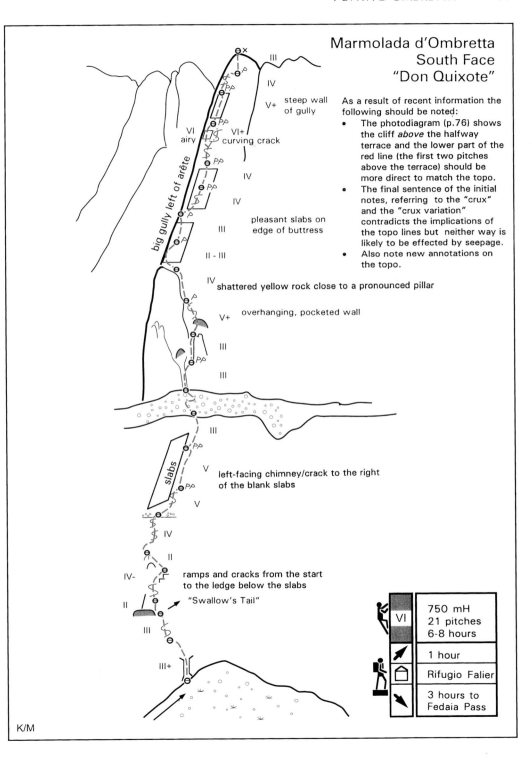

Marmolada d'Ombretta
South Face
"Don Quixote"

III

IV

V+ steep wall
    of gully

VI   VI+
airy curving crack

IV

IV

III

II - III

IV shattered yellow rock close to a pronounced pillar

V+ overhanging, pocketed wall

III

III

III

V left-facing chimney/crack to the right
   of the blank slabs

V

IV

II

IV- ramps and cracks from the start
     to the ledge below the slabs

II   "Swallow's Tail"

III

III+

pleasant slabs on
edge of buttress

big gully left of arête

slabs

As a result of recent information the
following should be noted:

- The photodiagram (p.76) shows
  the cliff *above* the halfway
  terrace and the lower part of the
  red line (the first two pitches
  above the terrace) should be
  more direct to match the topo.
- The final sentence of the initial
  notes, referring to the "crux"
  and the "crux variation"
  contradicts the implications of
  the topo lines but neither way is
  likely to be effected by seepage.
- Also note new annotations on
  the topo.

	750 mH 21 pitches 6-8 hours
	1 hour
	Rifugio Falier
	3 hours to Fedaia Pass

VI

K/M

R Follow this ramp/crack system to a little ledge below a zone of compact slabs. Climb a crack to the right of the slabs to the large ledge in the middle of the face. On the upper section of the face (see photo p.76) the route generally takes a line just to the right (on the upper third to the left) of the edge of the buttress. This is reached from the right.

From the summit, descend diagonally rightwards over easy rocks (climb down and abseil) heading north-east to the glacier. From the last abseil station on the lowest rocky spur, abseil 50m to a point beyond the bergschrund. In late summer and autumn the rocks above the bergschrund are often iced up. Walk along the glacier ski run to the cable-car station and a nice ride down to the valley. Alternatively, descend the glacier to the Fedaia Lake. From the cable-car station, descend to the north east along the ski piste, heading down the glacier towards the Forcella Serauta lift station. Two rocky ribs are clearly visible on the glacier – to the right (when descending) is Sass delle Undici, to the left Sass de Mez. Depending on the conditions, two possibilities now present themselves. Either descend the glacier to the north-west (watch out for crevasses!) to the Pian dei Forcella lift situated to the left of the Sass de Mez. From here a path leads down to the Fedaia Lake. Or descend to a point just short of the Forcella Serauta station and then directly down the glacier to the right of Sass delle Undici to reach a debris-strewn area levelled by the piste grooming machinery. From here, a towing path leads on down to the Fedaia Pass. About 3 hours.

FANES and TOFANA

The Fanes Group is a large and extensive area, consequently the selected routes included here are also scattered. The region around the Falzarego Pass is the core area for enjoyable, middle-grade climbing with a wealth of short objectives offering everything one could wish for: south-facing crags; short, easy approaches and uncomplicated descents; solid rock and nice, well-protected routes. Here, too, is the Hexen-stein, just a short distance away from the Falzarego Pass. Further into the back country of the Fanes and far away from the hustle and bustle of the Falzarego lie a few greater challenges. They can be tackled as single day outings starting either from the valley base or from the beautifully situated

Scotoni Hut, according to personal taste, and include the impressive faces of the Cima del Lago, the Cima Scotoni and the Lagazuoi North. St. Kassian, below the Valparola Pass, has a campsite and is the most convenient point of departure for all of the routes in the region around the Valparola Pass and the Scotoni Hut.

From the point of view of both its geographical location and the character of its climbing, the South Face slab of the Neunerspitze is something of an outsider here. Yet its phenomenally different nature and position, amidst a landscape so unique yet so typical for the Fanes, mean it would be unthinkable to leave it out. Also in the heartland of the Fanes, nestling in the Fanes Valley far from the outside world, is the big face of Spalti di Col Bechei. First climbed only as late as the 1980s by a team from Ampezzo, the routes there are very much in the modern idiom, despite the long approach march.

For Spalti di Col Bechei, Cortina d'Ampezzo (campsite) is the best point of departure. The routes in the Falzarego Pass itself are similarly easily reached from Cortina. Those bound for the slabs of the Neunerspitze generally start from St. Vigil in the Gader Valley.

In contrast to the aforementioned disparate collection the mighty Tofana di Rozes (3225m) offers a tight group of several worthwhile routes of all grades. These have the advantage of a short, easy approach and enjoy a south-facing aspect, fine panoramic views and splendidly solid rock. A real three-star mountain! In principle, all of these Tofana routes are possible as one-day expeditions starting from the valley base, since it is possible to drive right up to the Rifugio Dibona. Comfortable accommodation is also available at the Rifugio for those parties seeking a strategic base.

32 NEUNERSPITZE   2968m
SASSO NOVE

South Face, "Messner" (Messner/Lottesberger) V

The pale, symmetrical slab which forms the South Face of the Neunerspitze, perched above the fabled landscape of the Fanes alpine pastures, is so uncompromisingly devoid of features that it has an almost weird feel to it. In any event, it fails spectacularly to conform to the usual Dolomite crag norm. The same goes for the route, too: pure friction climbing, smearing up splendid waterworn slabs of quality limestone. Once accustomed to this style of climbing and trusting in the friction of your boot rubber, you will wish only that the pleasure were not over so quickly.

🍴 Reinhold and Günther Messner, Hermine Lottesberger. 1965

🔑 Well-spaced protection pegs on the lower section (particularly noticeable for those unused to such slab climbing). Hardly any other means of protection.

🏠 Rifugio la Varella (2038m). From the Gader Valley, head for St. Vigil in the Rau Valley and continue to Pederü. From here, a jeep taxi runs to the hut. On foot, follow the same road to the hut in about 2 hours.

↗ From Rifugio la Varella take Path 7 to the high pastures of the Fanes alp. From here, head north-west (no path) to the face.

E Start on a ledge at the foot of the black water stripe, reached from the right.

R The lower section of the route follows the black water stripe leading to an obvious dark 'cut out' in the direct fall line from the summit. From here, either move right to reach a corner and follow this to the top or exit leftwards via the Diagonal Route.

↘ Head down to the east over a chossy spur (sections of II) to a rocky rib (cairns). Descend to the south down an obvious boulder gully.

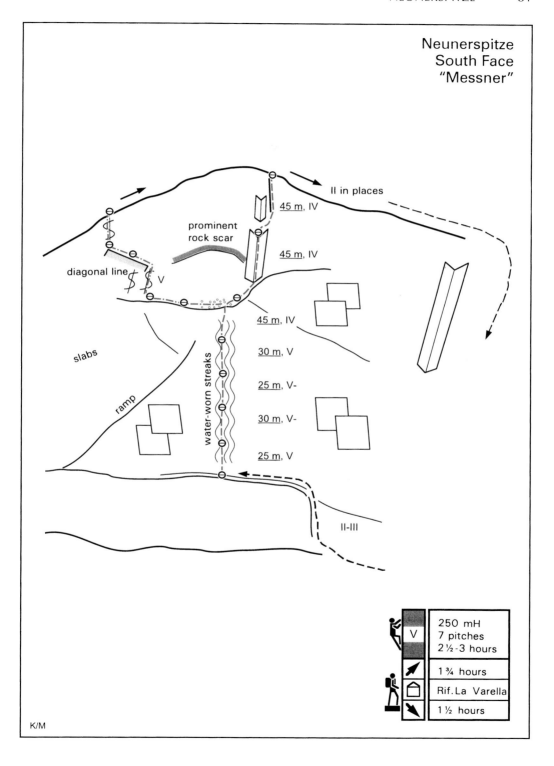

Neunerspitze
South Face
"Messner"

II in places

45 m, IV

prominent
rock scar

45 m, IV

diagonal line

V

45 m, IV

slabs

water-worn streaks

30 m, V

25 m, V-

ramp

30 m, V-

25 m, V

II-III

	V	250 mH 7 pitches 2½-3 hours
		1¾ hours
		Rif. La Varella
		1½ hours

K/M

33 SPALTI DI COL BECCHEI

South Face, "Via Los Angeles '84" (Bellodis/Dibona) VI+

The wonderfully solid climbs on the south-facing Spalti di Col Becchei were only developed in the last ten years or so, by a group of Ampezzo climbers known as the "Scoiattoli". At VI+, the "Via Los Angeles '84" is one of the easiest of this modern crop of routes and also one of the most obvious lines. The lower part of the climb is obvious and characterised by a clear, no-compromise corner/groove system with athletic climbing more reminiscent of granite. A little bit of Yosemite in the wild and romantic Fanes Valley! Admittedly, the approach to this little piece of paradise is unpleasantly long but up there one really does have peace and quiet.

P. Bellodis, Mario Dibona. 24 August 1984

The belays are equipped partly with normal pegs and partly with a mixture of bolts and pegs. Nuts and Friends are highly recommended for protection.

The road up to the 'Fanestal' parking place branches off left shortly before the big bend on the Cortina d'Ampezzo – Schluderbach road.

Take Path 10 into the Fanes Valley to a point at about 1750m. Turn right here and follow an unmarked path over the old Fanes Bridge and continue uphill. At the end of a flat area a path branches off to the right. Follow this path, past a scree gully, until the climbers' path to the face leads off uphill to the right (cairn!). The rocky (and grassy!) ledges at the foot of the wall are gained from the right.

Start right at the bottom of the obvious corner leading up to a roof.

Climb the corner to the roof. Move left. Continue up and left (passing a little tree) to a prominent niche. Leave the niche and climb up to grassy ledges leading to the finish.

Follow the grassy ledge round to the left and climb down to a bent cembra-pine on the edge of the cliff (abseil slings); about 10 minutes. Four abseils (20m, 30m, 35m, 25m) to the ledges at the start of the route. Caution: the last abseil point on a thin little tree was (is?) a bit macabre!

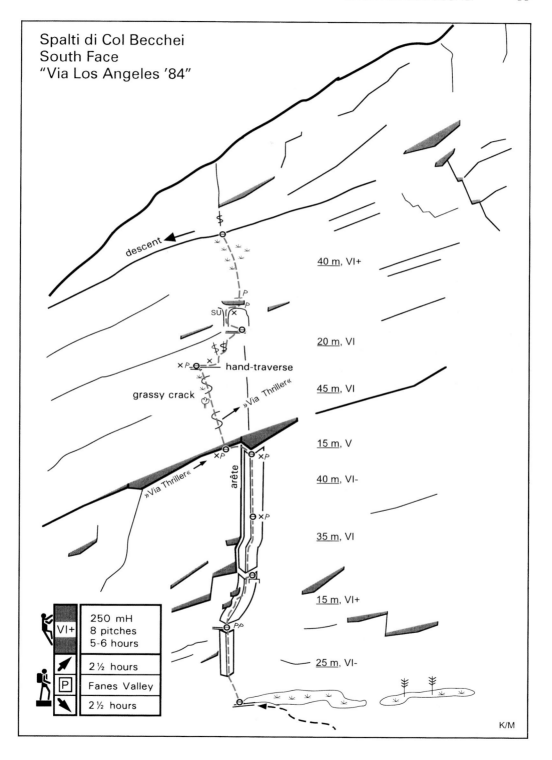

Spalti di Col Becchei
South Face
"Via Los Angeles '84"

descent

40 m, VI+

P
P
SÜ X

20 m, VI

$ $
P P
×P ─ ─ ×   hand-traverse

grassy crack   »Via Thriller«   45 m, VI

15 m, V

×P   ×P

»Via Thriller«   arête   40 m, VI-

×P

35 m, VI

15 m, VI+

P P

25 m, VI-

250 mH
VI+   8 pitches
5-6 hours

2 ½ hours

P   Fanes Valley

2 ½ hours

K/M

34 CIMA DEL LAGO   2632m

South-West Corner (Consiglio/dall'Oglio/Micarelli) IV+

The prominent mass of the Torre del Lago, bounding the Seescharte like a huge goalpost, is connected to the less distinct summit of the Cima del Lago by a huge, obvious corner. If ever the term 'open book corner' were to be applied to a route, then surely here. The route actually gains the corner only at a ledge a good third of the way up after first making a detour around a band of overhangs on the lower wall. The climbing on the lower section is a bit chossy but as soon as the corner is reached things improve quickly. There follows pitch after pitch of perfect corner climbing on great rock and at a fairly consistent level of difficulty.

Paolo Consiglio, Marino dall'Oglio, G. Micarelli. 2 August 1954.

Infrequent pegs on the lower pitches. Sufficient thereafter.

Rifugio Scotoni (1985m). Above St. Cassian on the Valparola Pass road a small road branches off to Capanna Alpina at a dried-up river bed. Follow the road for 45 minutes to the hut.

From Rifugio Scotoni take waymarked paths to the Lagazuoi Lake and continue towards Forcella del Lago. On reaching the foot of the Torre del Lago cliffs walk left and follow the climbers' path beneath the wall to below the big corner.

Start about 40m left of the highest point of the scree fan.

The lower section stays well to the left of the corner. Breach the obvious band of roofs on the left, at its weakest point. A good third of the way up the wall is a ledge – visible from below – which leads into the big corner. Climb the corner all the way.

From the summit, follow a vague path to the north-east to reach an abseil point. Make two abseils (10m, 20m). Continue down the path to Forcella del Lago; cairns. Pass through Forcella del Lago, following a path to the south and back to the Lagazuoi Lake (45 minutes).

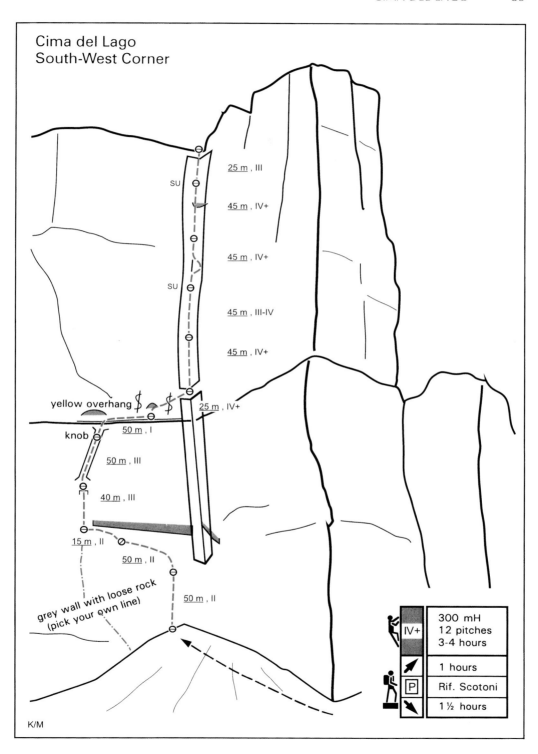

Cima del Lago
South-West Corner

25 m , III

SU

45 m , IV+

45 m , IV+

SU

45 m , III-IV

45 m , IV+

yellow overhang

25 m , IV+

knob

50 m , I

50 m , III

40 m , III

15 m , II

50 m , II

grey wall with loose rock
(pick your own line)

50 m , II

IV+	300 mH 12 pitches 3-4 hours
	1 hours
P	Rif. Scotoni
	1 ½ hours

K/M

35 CIMA SCOTONI   2874m

S.W. Face, "Lacedelli" (Lacedelli/Ghedina/Lorenzi) VI+/A1

Cima Scotoni's South-West Face enjoys a good reputation amongst the bigger faces of the Dolomites – there was even a time when it was considered to be the most difficult. Difficulty is, however, a relative thing and that will become apparent on this route right from the start. If there are sufficient pegs in place the modest grade VI aspirant will be able to manage with a few sections of A1. If there are none you will have to appoint someone of steely nerve as leader. The hard work on the initial pitches is well worthwhile. After the first ledge (where horizontal progress, i.e. ungainly crawling, is the order of the day) there are several very varied ropelengths, one after the other. The steep, golden-yellow rock is – unexpectedly – compact, sound and full of nice surprises. It is a pleasure to haul upwards on the solid edges and flakes. Beyond the second ledge the rock increasingly tends towards the 'building block' variety, so it is advisable to shun the summit experience and leave the face at this point by the left-hand exit.

Lino Lacedelli, Luigi Ghedina, Guido Lorenzi. 10–12 June 1952.

Normal pegs, variable in quality and number.

Rifugio Scotoni (1985m), see p.84

From Rifugio Scotoni, follow a well-used path to the Lagazuoi Lake, finally leaving the path to scramble up over rubble to the foot of the wide expanse of the South-West Face.

The wall is split by two terraces. The first of these ends roughly in the centre of the face at a roof which marks the top of a corner system. Start on easier angled ground at the foot of the wall and pick a way up in a direct line with this prominent corner. A short, yellow crack/groove provides the crux of the route if tackled free (and even with a little aid).

Follow the corner to the first terrace. Traverse about 70m to the left and continue up, keeping slightly right, to gain the second terrace. The difficulties end here.

Traverse left off the face along the second terrace and descend the climbers' path to the debris fields on the north side, to reach the notch between Cima Scotoni and Torre del Lago. Follow a waymarked path (Dolomite High Route No. 1) back to the Lagazuoi Lake and the hut.

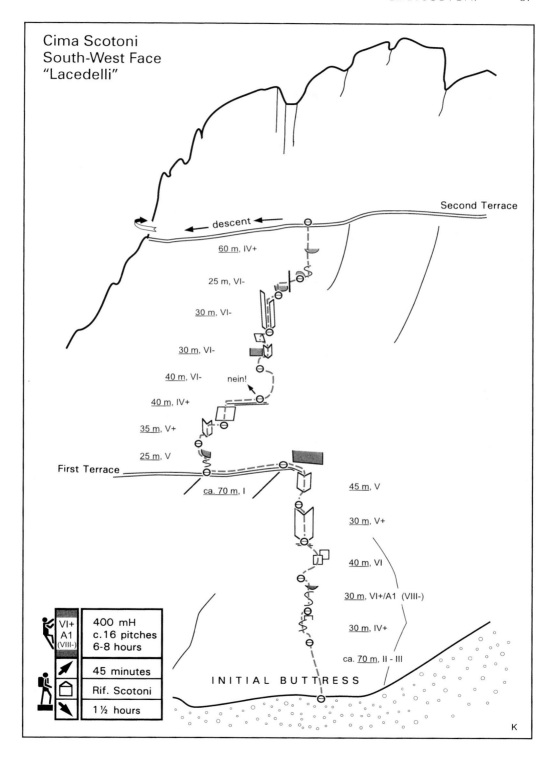

Cima Scotoni
South-West Face
"Lacedelli"

Second Terrace

descent

60 m, IV+

25 m, VI-

30 m, VI-

30 m, VI-

40 m, VI-   nein!

40 m, IV+

35 m, V+

25 m, V

First Terrace

ca. 70 m, I

45 m, V

30 m, V+

40 m, VI

30 m, VI+/A1 (VIII-)

30 m, IV+

ca. 70 m, II - III

INITIAL BUTTRESS

| VI+ A1 (VIII-) | 400 mH c.16 pitches 6-8 hours |
| 45 minutes |
| Rif. Scotoni |
| 1½ hours |

K

36 **LAGAZUIO NORD** 2804m

West Face, "Via del Drago" (Barbier/Giambisi/Platter) VI−

In the late 1960s, several young and talented climbers turned their minds quite independently to the idea of free-climbing, calling into question the validity of the old 'nail ups' and the entrenched ideas of the previous generation. In the Dolomites, the major protagonist was Reinhold Messner, who castigated climbing by artificial means (particularly where bolts were involved) as 'the murder of the impossible' and mourned 'the death of the dragon' in adventure climbing. The Belgian Claudio Barbier, one of the best Dolomite climbers of all time, contributed to this 'movement' with his own "Route of the Dragon". His audacious climb takes the steepest part of this yellow and black face, with a fine sense of what is just possible, searching out the most logical free-climbable line. The lower section of the face is taken on the right to the prominent band of overhangs, where an impressive traverse leads left to the obvious corner system. The rock hereabouts is black from the constant trickle of water, steep, rough and very solid – ideal for high level fun and games!

Claudio Barbier, Almo Giambisi, Carlo Platter.   26 September 1969.

Normal pitons in-situ; carry nuts and slings.

Falzarego Pass; park at the valley station of the lift.

Either take the funicular up and walk down to the Lagazuoi notch and the hut or take the path up all the way to the hut (1 hour, 450m of ascent). Follow a faint path below the West Face of the Lagazuoi South and traverse the slope across to the West Face of the Lagazuoi North.

Start in the chimney formed by the tower leaning against the main wall.

A short, steep, yellow wall leads to an airy traverse left under overhangs to reach the prominent corner system in the middle of the wall. This provides the line of the rest of the route.

From the top of the route, traverse right across ledges to the SW ridge (occasional cairns). Descend the SW ridge. Where the ridge steepens abruptly a ledge leads round leftwards to join a short scree gully. Scramble down the gully to the foot of the SW ridge (notch). Continue down the gully to the foot of the face and reverse the approach route to the Falzarego Pass.

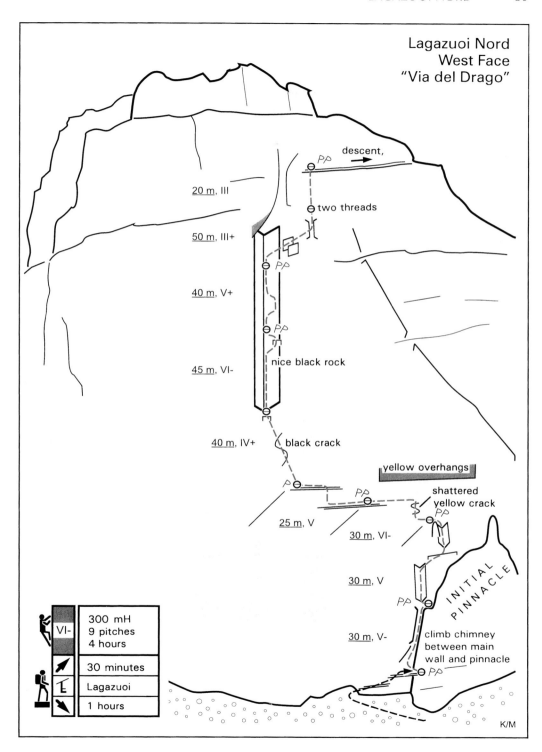

Lagazuoi Nord
West Face
"Via del Drago"

descent,

PP

two threads

20 m, III

50 m, III+

PP

40 m, V+

PP

45 m, VI-   nice black rock

40 m, IV+   black crack

yellow overhangs

shattered
yellow crack
PP

PP

25 m, V

30 m, VI-

30 m, V

INITIAL PINNACLE

PP

30 m, V-   climb chimney
between main
wall and pinnacle

PP

VI-	300 mH 9 pitches 4 hours
	30 minutes
	Lagazuoi
	1 hours

K/M

37 PICCOLO LAGAZUOI   2778m

W. Face, "Via M. Speziale" (Doglioni/Signoretti/Zannini/Barbiero) VI–

The majority of routes on the Piccolo Lagazuoi are characterised by their short, easy approaches, sunny aspects and often excellent rock quality. The heart of the "Via M. Speziale" is the big, black water streak on the West Face, leading to a broad, rubble-strewn ledge. It offers three dream pitches on steep, water-worn rock superbly protectable by countless thread runners. Thereafter, the route does tend to lose its way a little in the scrappy ledges and terraces which cut across the upper part of the face. The slabs of the penultimate pitch require a little trickery to overcome, while the overhanging crack on the final pitch is a pretty strenuous affair. It would be nicer if the black streak were that bit longer . . .

M. Doglioni, G. Signoretti, Andrea Zannini, M. Barbiero.   14 October 1986.

Some pegs in place but protection often from threads. Carry medium and large Friends or Hexentrics for the exit crack.

Park at the top of the Valparola Pass, diagonally opposite the ruined barracks.

A narrow path starts from the little parking place on the right-hand side of the road (coming from the Falzarego Pass) and leads up and along beneath the West Face of the Piccolo Lagazuoi. Scramble up scree to the foot of the wall.

Start directly below the black water streak, just to the left of a tower-like pillar of rock which forms an obvious corner with the main face.

Gain the big, black water streak by climbing in from the right and follow it to a ledge. Follow a vague line up easy ground to the second ledge and trend leftwards to the exit terrace.

Traverse right (east) along the exit terrace for about 300m to a little tower on the ridge. Scramble down a gully (II) to scree. Watch out for cairns and do not descend too early! Descend, keeping to the right, to the foot of the face.

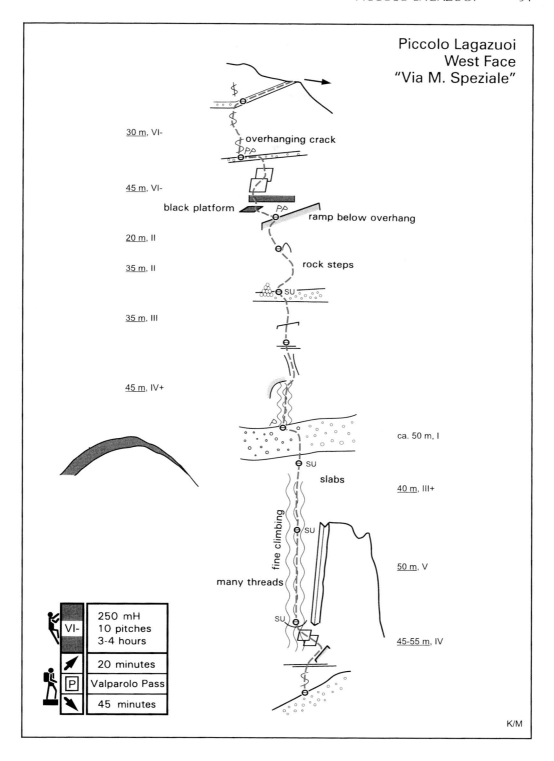

Piccolo Lagazuoi
West Face
"Via M. Speziale"

30 m, VI-

overhanging crack

45 m, VI-

black platform

ramp below overhang

20 m, II

35 m, II

rock steps

35 m, III

45 m, IV+

ca. 50 m, I

slabs

40 m, III+

fine climbing

many threads

50 m, V

45-55 m, IV

	250 mH
VI-	10 pitches
	3-4 hours
↗	20 minutes
P	Valparolo Pass
↘	45 minutes

K/M

38 PICCOLO LAGAZUOI   2778m

South-West Face, "Via del Buco" IV

The rather insignificant crags which lie directly on and in the Falzarego Pass are in fact one great big bolt-protected klettergarten – close to the road, with a short approach, a sunny aspect and generally excellent rock. One of the most enjoyable routes here is the "Via del Buco", which traces a line up the hold-covered limestone to the left of the obvious chimney. After five splendid pitches the slabby ramp ends abruptly and the route splits into a difficult and an easy variant. This has more in common with the rest of the climb but it does detract slightly from the beauty of the climbing, since the variation pitches seek the line of least resistance amidst the easy-angled ramps and the rock quality is no longer as awesomely good as on the lower section of the route. The more difficult original finish takes a corner system, the logical continuation of the chimney line below.

⊠   Unknown.

⚲   Abundant protection on the lower section: bolt belays etc. Normal pegs only on the easier variation finish [raising the question of whether the original route was piton-protected?].

🅿   Parking at the Falzarego Pass (valley station of the lift).

↗   Follow an indistinct path from the funicular station at the top of the pass before striking off directly to the foot of the face.

🄴   Start at the base of a corner in a little scree gully.

🅁   To the left of the cable car, the wall is split by a chimney system; left again is an area of slabs ending at the same height as the top of the chimney. The route follows the left hand side of the slabby ramp to a ledge. The easier variation takes a left-to-right dogleg to gain a muddy ramp which leads without further difficulty to the shoulder of the ridge.

↘   Traverse off to the west and descend a gully to a ledge which leads rightwards into a larger gully. Abseil from a point roughly mid-way along this ledge (abseil peg in-situ) and descend into the gully. Follow the gully down and left to reach the foot of the wall.

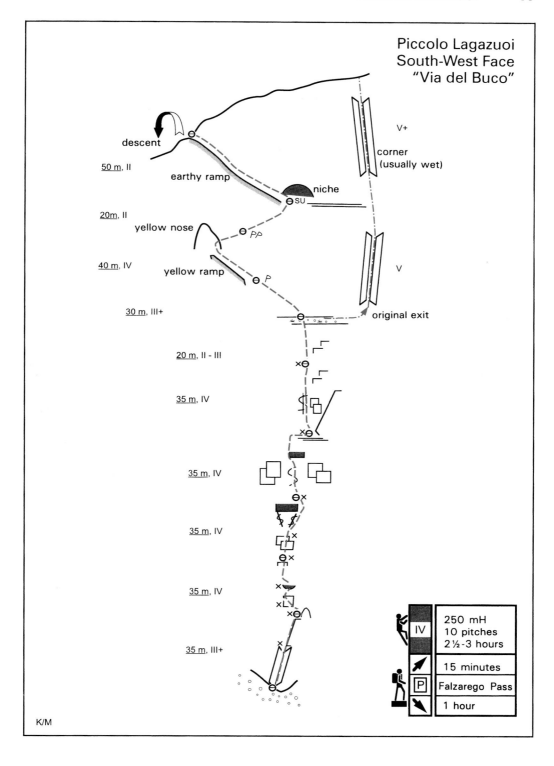

Piccolo Lagazuoi
South-West Face
"Via del Buco"

V+

corner
(usually wet)

descent

50 m, II

earthy ramp

niche

20m, II

SU

yellow nose

PP

40 m, IV

yellow ramp

V

P

30 m, III+

original exit

20 m, II - III

35 m, IV

35 m, IV

35 m, IV

35 m, IV

35 m, III+

IV	250 mH
	10 pitches
	2½-3 hours
	15 minutes
P	Falzarego Pass
	1 hour

K/M

39 HEXENSTEIN
SASS DI STRIA
2477m

South Rib (Cobertaldo/Pezzotti) IV+

The South Rib of the Hexenstein has been equipped with safe belay bolts and now offers those climbers looking for a relaxing route in grand surroundings a nice half-day's outing. The short approach and descent are devoid of potential dangers, while the south-facing aspect of the cliff and the solid – if well-handled – rock both add to the pleasure. This is an ideal route for those new to alpine climbing, as it contains everything from face climbing to chimneys and cracks in its short length. The escape through a slot from the South-West onto the South East Face is an interesting diversion. Those who avoid the nice grey crack on the last pitch by slinking off right miss (almost) the best bit of the route.

A. Cobertaldo, Lorenzo Pezzotti. 1 August 1939.

Bolt belays and sufficient pegs for protection in-situ.

Park at the valley station of the cable car in the Falzarego Pass.

From the top of the Pass, walk 1km along the road in the direction of the Valparola Pass (St. Kassian). On the left hand side of the road is a large boulder and a possible parking place. This marks the start of the path which leads beneath the South-East Face of the Hexenstein. Follow the path up (less distinct towards the end) to the foot of the South Rib.

E   Start at the left edge of a gully, bounded on its left by the South Rib and on its right by the arête forming the side of a little pinnacle. Climb up and left to join the rib.

R   Follow the right-hand side of the rib. Pass an obvious grassy ledge to reach a terrace leading round leftwards onto the South-West Face. Do not follow the terrace but go through a slot to a ledge on the South-East Face and climb this to the summit.

Descent is no problem. Scramble down the Normal Route (safety ropes and markers) to the north west and descend into the Valparola Pass.

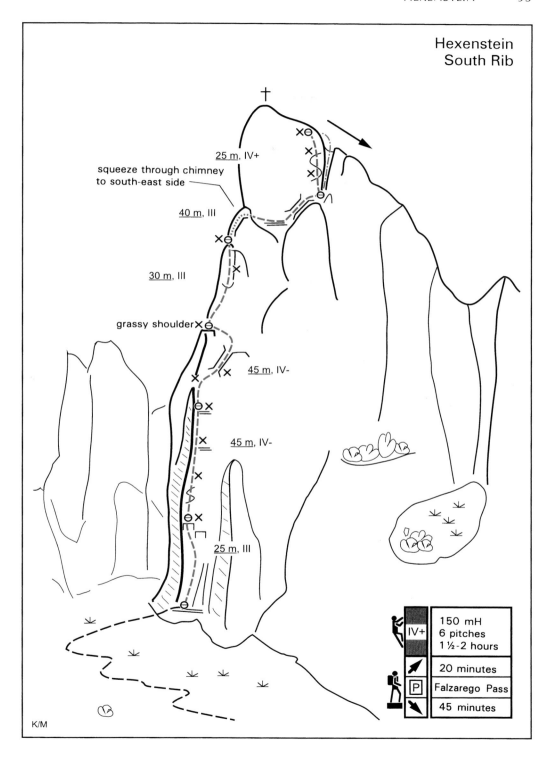

Hexenstein
South Rib

25 m, IV+

squeeze through chimney
to south-east side

40 m, III

30 m, III

grassy shoulder

45 m, IV-

45 m, IV-

25 m, III

IV+	150 mH 6 pitches 1 ½-2 hours
	20 minutes
P	Falzarego Pass
	45 minutes

K/M

40 TORRE DI FALZAREGO c.2500m

Falzarego Towers

The South Arête of Torre Piccola di Falzarego is a very popular climbers' objective; so much so that on fine holiday weekends it may be necessary to pre-book a place in the queue. After all, there are not that many routes of this grade that offer consistent difficulties, a south-facing aspect and a fine, airy line right up the edge of an outstandingly solid arête. Add a brace of cemented-in belay bolts and an approach march that takes a mere half an hour from the road and the reasons for the route's popularity should become clear. Be clever and climb against the flow of traffic and the whole thing is pure pleasure with no regrets. Alternatively, pick a day early in the year (the route comes into condition early) or start out in the afternoon. The descent from the Little Falzarego Tower dumps you automatically at the start of the West Face of Torre Grande di Falzarego, allowing you to prolong the fun a little.

TORRE PICCOLA DI FALZAREGO

South Arête (Comici/del Torso/Varale) IV+

- Emilio Comici, Sandro del Torso and Mary Varale. 10 August 1934.
- Protection is very good: cemented belay bolts and, in places, cemented protection pegs.
- Park about 1km east of the top of the Falzarego Pass road (valley station of the lift).

- Follow a footpath up towards the Falzarego Tower as far as an old army barracks. The route starts above this building.
- The usual start is located 10m to the right of an obvious chimney crack – directly below an old stone-pine tree and a painted number '10' – which formed the original start. The first (relatively hard but really nice) first pitch can be avoided by a right-to-left zig-zag detour across ledges.

(*previous page*) "The Valbonkante" (Rt. 22) towers above the Grassleiten Hut in the Rosengarten (Catinaccio) group. *Photo: F. Hauleitner*

(*left*) The Sella Towers (Routes 5 –10) provide a convenient introduction to the Dolomites for many climbers. *Photo: W. Neumayer.*

(*left*) The 600-metre East Face of the Rosengartenspitze (Cima Catinaccio), its obvious central line taken by the classic "Steger" route (Rt. 25, VI–) first climbed in 1929 by Hans Steger, Paula Wiesinger, Fred Masè Dari and Siegfried Lechner.

(*right*) On the South-East Face of Punta Emma (Rt. 27) – the grade V traverse across the slabby wall on the third pitch. This fine six-pitch route was another discovery of the Steger/Wiesinger team, climbed shortly before their Cima Catinaccio ascent.

(above) On the first pitch (VI–) of the long traverse of the classic "Big Micheluzzi" (Rt. 12) of Piz Ciavazes, with N. W. Face of Piz Pordoi on the right. *Photo: Tom Prentice*

(far left) In 1969 Reinhold Messner, climbing solo, added a fine direct finish to the classic "Vinazter/ Castiglione" route on Marmolada di Rocca's South Face (Rt 30). The climber is tackling the pocketed wall (VI– the first crux), one of the climb's best pitches *Photo H.Andergassen*

(near left) On the steep, pocketed wall (V+) of "Don Quixote" (Rt. 31), one of the most amenable rock climbs on Marmolada's mighty South Wall. The massif, the highest in the Dolomites (3343m), has glacier descents to the north or a cable-car from near the eastern top (M. D'Ombretta).

(above) The delectable, waterworn, limestone slab of the South Face of Sasso Nove (Nuenerspitze) offers a superb 250-metre climb (Rt. 32). This was pioneered in 1965 by the brothers Reinhold and Günther Messner with Hermine Lottesberger.

(below) Tofana di Rozes rises majestically above the main road on the western approach to Cortina

(right) The main line on Tofana's 800-metre South Face (Rt. 42) was first climbed in 1901 by a party led by Antonio Dimai and including the two Hungarian sisters Ilona and Rolanda Eötvös – one of the biggest events in world rock-climbing at that date. Here Anette Köhler is seen leading the 40m-traverse (IV) above the Little Amphitheatre high on the route.

The North-West Face of Piz Pordoi (2952m) towers above the Val Gardena / Cortina road. Its black, water-washed face holds the classic (IV+) "Fedele" (Rt. 15) which joins the Dibona Route (*inset*) for a fabulous summit climb from the Upper Terrace. *Photo: Tom Prentice*

Torre Grande di Falzarego West Face

Torre Piccola di Falzarego South Arête

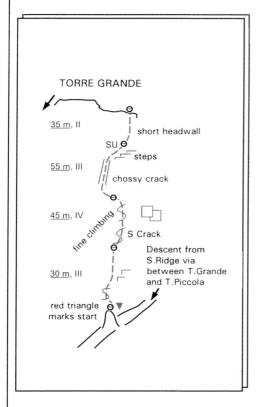

TORRE GRANDE

35 m, II

short headwall

SU

steps

55 m, III

chossy crack

45 m, IV

fine climbing

S Crack

Descent from
S.Ridge via
between T.Grande
and T.Piccola

30 m, III

red triangle
marks start

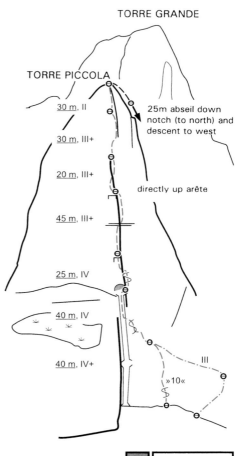

TORRE GRANDE

TORRE PICCOLA

30 m, II

25m abseil down
notch (to north) and
descent to west

30 m, III+

20 m, III+

directly up arête

45 m, III+

25 m, IV

40 m, IV

»10«

III

40 m, IV+

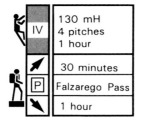

IV	130 mH 4 pitches 1 hour
	30 minutes
P	Falzarego Pass
	1 hour

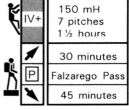

IV+	150 mH 7 pitches 1 ½ hours
	30 minutes
P	Falzarego Pass
	45 minutes

R The route takes a generally direct line up the South Arête of the tower. The signs of the passage of thousands of climbers and the odd red paint marks make it obvious.

↘ From the top of the tower, descend 15m to the north on the climbers' path to reach an abseil station. Abseil 25m into the gap between Torre Piccolo and Torre Grande. Scramble down the gully to the west. A path leads back to the start of the route (45 minutes). If time and inclination permit it is possible to link in an ascent of Torre Grande di Falzarego.

TORRE GRANDE DI FALZAREGO
West Face (Lassato Route) IV

Small, but perfectly formed, and with really nice, varied climbing for the grade, all on solid rock. Fairly short and therefore only really worthwhile if combined with the South Arête of Torre Piccolo di Falzarego.

⚔ S. Lussato. 13 August 1957.

🪝 Mainly cemented-in belay bolts and protection pegs.

P Park about 1 km east of the top of the Pass, on the Falzarego Pass road (lift).

↗ Either a 45 minute walk from the parking place along a narrow footpath to Torre Piccola and then along the climbers' path on its west side and up into the gully between the big and small towers. Or descend from Torre Piccola (see above) to the start of the route.

E Start at a little pinnacle just above the bottom of the gully separating the two towers. The start of the route is marked with a red triangle.

R Both the start and the route itself are marked with red paint. You can't miss either!

↘ From the summit, descend to the north down a short, chossy gully to a notch. From here, follow a less distinct path leading beneath the West Face to the start of the route with no further difficulties.

41 COL DEI BOS   2450m

South Arête, "Alverà" (Alverà/Menardi) V+

The Col dei Bos is a close neighbour of Tofana di Rozes and this explains why its compelling South Face enjoys relatively little attention. The great Tofana simply steals the show. That said, the rock hereabouts is of similarly good quality to its bigger neighbour, the approach and descent are short and the face catches the sun. The "Alverà Arête", which avoids the arête by climbing the wall to the left, offers nice, varied climbing on sound rock and at a consistent level of difficulty. It may be confidently recommended both to those parties operating in the upper levels of grade V and to those who can still find enjoyment on grade III, since the easier pitches straight after the crux offer climbing of a nature seldom found on grade III routes. The focal point of the climb is the prominent corner at about half height. This is also where the V+ crux is to be found – and you have to climb it clean. Things get a touch more serious again on the exit pitches, too, and if you choose the 'through route' through the cave you get to enter your name in the hidden summit book!

⚒	Silvio Alverà, Luigi (Igi) Menardi. 13 July 1947.
⚲	Relatively few belay and protection pegs in place. Definitely carry slings and a rack of nuts.
P	Park on the Cortina/Falzarego Pass road at the 'Da Ra Nona' bar near the 108.5km marker.
↗	Follow Path 412 for about 15 minutes to reach a gravel path at a debris filled gully. Scramble up the gully to the base of the wall.
E	The start of the route is up and to the right of the point where the gully meets the face.
R	The route first gains the prominent corner at about half height, before moving out right to the arête, only to move back left again to the exit pitches (topo p.100).
↘	From the top of the route, walk right to join an old military footpath. Follow this 'warpath' in a north-westerly direction down to Forcella dei Bois. Now walk down to the south, descending to reach a gravel path. Follow this to the right (west; short tunnel) to the bed of the stream and join the approach route. Reverse the approach route to the starting point.

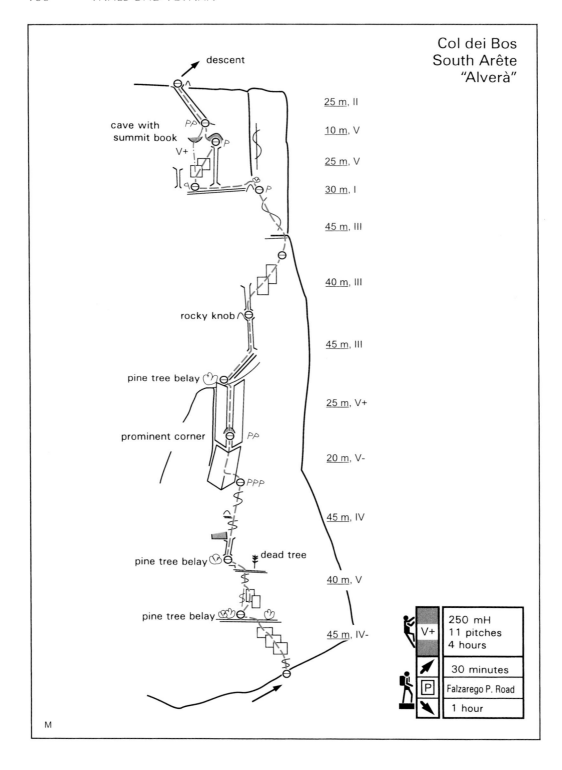

descent

Col dei Bos
South Arête
"Alverà"

cave with
summit book

V+

25 m, II

10 m, V

25 m, V

30 m, I

45 m, III

40 m, III

rocky knob

45 m, III

pine tree belay

25 m, V+

prominent corner

20 m, V-

45 m, IV

pine tree belay   dead tree

40 m, V

pine tree belay

45 m, IV-

	250 mH
V+	11 pitches
	4 hours
	30 minutes
P	Falzarego P. Road
	1 hour

M

42 TOFANA DI ROZES 3225m

South Face "Dimai/Eötvös" (Dimai/Eötvös/Siorpaës/Verzi) IV+

The massive castellations of Tofana di Rozes, with its proud array of South Face pillars, stands on its plinth like a great stone fortress offering a selection of worthwhile routes, each with the advantage of a short approach, a sunny, south-facing aspect, a grand panoramic view and splendid rock. The classic route is the South Face, climbed way back in 1901 by the adventurous young Hungarian Baronesses Ilona and Rolanda Eötvös, led by the Ampezzo mountain guide Antonio Dimai – an impressive performance even by today's standards! The route climbs the most imposing part of the face to gain the large amphitheatre and then goes left to a second, smaller amphitheatre and the summit. This long, impressive route requires stamina to succeed and should not be judged by pure climbing difficulty alone, for there are long sections where easy climbing predominates. It is the 'mountain experience' that takes pride of place here. The rock is very good throughout, you will find piles of loose stones scattered around on the flat sections. Be aware of the stonefall danger on the traverse of the big amphitheatre – move fast here! The more technically demanding upper section involves corner and chimney pitches and an unusually fine, exposed traverse.

Antonio Dimai, Ilona and Rolanda Eötvös, Giovanni Siorpaës, Angelo Verzi.   August 1901.

Few pegs on the lower two-thirds of the route but most necessary belay and protection pegs in-situ on the more difficult pitches. In general, placing protection requires initiative. Take a range of nuts, and slings for threads!

Rifugio Dibona (2000m). At the kilometer 113.8 marker on the Falzarego Pass road, a metalled road branches off to the right to Malga Federola. This is drivable (the last section is unmetalled) and leads right up to the hut and car-park.

From Rifugio Dibona take the wide path up to Rifugio Cantore/Rifugio Giussani, branching off right after a short distance on the path leading directly up to beneath the South Face of the Tofana. Traverse below the face to a prominent gully in a fall line from the large amphitheatre (and the summit).

Start at the right hand edge of this gully and scramble up smooth, slabby rocks to a ledge.

The lower part of the climb takes the rock to the right of the obvious gully leading into the large amphitheatre. Traverse the amphitheatre and make a further rising traverse to duck round the rib into the smaller amphitheatre. A corner and chimney system at the left-hand edge of this amphitheatre forms the logical way out. Climb it to a constriction in the chimney where things become very steep and make a superb, exposed, 40m leftwards traverse. Continue to a shoulder after which a final difficult chimney gains easier ground. Follow the loose arête to the summit.

From the summit, descend the Normal Route to Rifugio Guissani – taking the ridge to the north until erosion marks lead off to the right. Scramble down a series of flat rock steps and boulders (well marked) to reach the hut and a path which leads back to Rifugio Dibona.

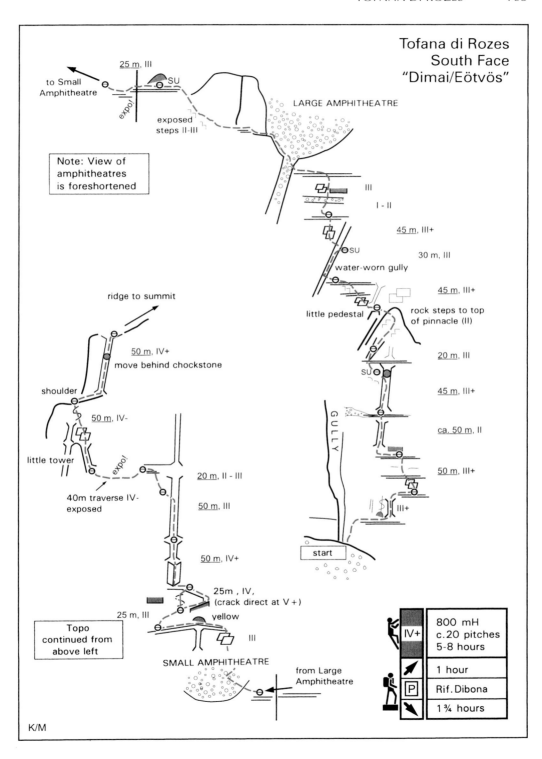

Tofana di Rozes
South Face
"Dimai/Eötvös"

to Small
Amphitheatre

25 m, III

SU

expo!

exposed
steps II-III

LARGE AMPHITHEATRE

Note: View of
amphitheatres
is foreshortened

III

I - II

45 m, III+

30 m, III

SU

water-worn gully

ridge to summit

45 m, III+

little pedestal

rock steps to top
of pinnacle (II)

50 m, IV+
move behind chockstone

shoulder

20 m, III

SU

45 m, III+

50 m, IV-

little tower

expo!

ca. 50 m, II

40m traverse IV-
exposed

20 m, II - III

50 m, III+

50 m, III

GULLY

III+

50 m, IV+

start

25m , IV,
(crack direct at V +)

25 m, III

yellow

Topo
continued from
above left

III

SMALL AMPHITHEATRE

from Large
Amphitheatre

IV+	800 mH c.20 pitches 5-8 hours
↗	1 hour
P	Rif. Dibona
↘	1¾ hours

K/M

43 TOFANA DI ROZES   2650m

South Face Buttress 1, "South Arête" (Pompanin/Alverà) V

In terms of height and mass, the far right buttress of the wide expanse of the Tofana's South Face is both the smallest and the most elegant. It has an almost perfect line, a slender, sharply delineated arête slicing steeply skywards and ending on the broad East Flank of the Tofana. Along the crest of this 'little' Tofana buttress runs the line of the route – worthwhile and enjoyable climbing on sound rock and, on the sections of the route which hug the arête itself, a 'free as a bird' sense of exposure to relish. This is an ideal training climb for the greater challenges of the neighbouring Tofana routes.

Ugo Pompanin, Albino Alverà.   August 1946.

Sufficient pegs in-situ on the more difficult pitches but nuts and slings are needed elsewhere for protection.

Rifugio Dibona (2000m). At the kilometre 113.8 marker on the Falzarego Pass road, a metalled road branches off to the right to Malga Federola. This is drivable (last section unmetalled) and leads up to the hut and a large car-park.

From Rifugio Dibona take the wide track up towards Rifugio Giussani, branching off left to below the South Face of the First Buttress.

Start to the left of the edge of the arête, at the foot of an obvious corner to the right of the gully dividing the smaller and larger of the Tofana Buttresses.

Climb the arête direct, with occasional logical diversions to the left and right; see photo p.101.

From the top of the route follow an erosion marked climbers' path horizontally to the north. Where the ground shelves away, descend to the waymarked hikers' path leading right, past the old Rifugio Cantone and back to Rifugio Dibona.

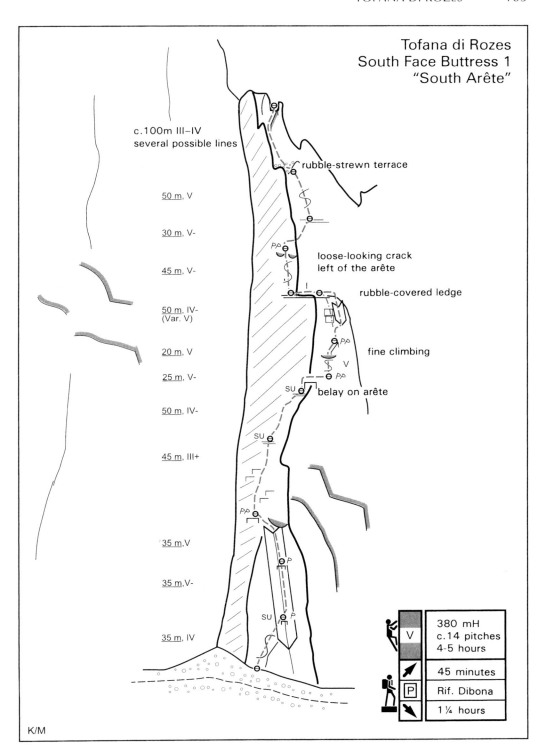

Tofana di Rozes
South Face Buttress 1
"South Arête"

c.100m III–IV
several possible lines

rubble-strewn terrace

50 m, V

30 m, V-

45 m, V-
loose-looking crack
left of the arête

rubble-covered ledge

50 m, IV-
(Var. V)

fine climbing

20 m, V

25 m, V-

V

belay on arête

50 m, IV-

45 m, III+

35 m,V

35 m,V-

35 m, IV

V
380 mH
c.14 pitches
4-5 hours

45 minutes

P   Rif. Dibona

1 ¼ hours

K/M

44 TOFANA DI ROZES   2820m

South Face Buttress 2, "Pillar Rib" (Costantini/Ghedina) VI–

The most famous route on the right-hand sector of the Tofana's South Face is the "Pilastro" or "Tofana Pillar" (VII+). Left of this is the elegant line of the wonderful "Pillar Rib", now a classic lower grade VI free climb. This very varied and interesting route has a few exposed sections, particularly on the crux pitch, the big traverse below the yellow roof. Excellent quality plate limestone predominates; the only dubious rock is the shattered yellow stuff found in a few places under the roof. After the big traverse the route follows the rib itself and here the route finding sometimes becomes less than obvious but without the climbing losing any of its appeal. The consistent level of difficulty, the excellent rock and the splendid positions make this a route of class!

🗡 Ettore Costantini, Luigi Ghedina. September 1946

🖼 All necessary pegs in-situ; carry slings for threads.

🅿 Rifugio Dibona (2000m). At the kilometre 113.8 marker on the Falzarego Pass road, a metalled road branches off to the right to Malga Federola. This road leads up to the hut (car-park).

↗ From the Rif. Dibona take the wide track up towards Rif. Cantore/Giussani. Branch off left and traverse below the South Face of the Tofana to reach the broad mass of the South Face Buttress.

🅴 Start to the right of the big gully on the left of the buttress. Scramble up to a narrow ledge which leads across to the rib. (A finger-shaped little pinnacle on the ledge marks the start of the "Pilastro", the next route). Traverse the ledge to the foot of a shallow crack right of the rib.

🆁 Climb right of the rib, heading for the obvious yellow roof. Traverse left below the second roof and go round the arête of the buttress. Follow the edge of the rib to the top (topo p.108).

↘ From the top of the route follow a path north and ascend a few metres to the notch which is the key to the path to Rif. Guissani. From there, follow the path leading back to Rifugio Dibona.

45 TOFANA DI ROZES   2820m

South Face Buttress 2, "Pilastro" (Costantini/Apollonio) VII+

The classic hard route of the South Face of the Tofana is the "Pilastro", which goes straight up the middle of the proudest of the three South Face Buttresses. It offers continuously difficult and varied climbing calling for stamina and commitment until two-thirds height, where it peters out into easier terrain. The first view of the compact, grey armour of the lower slabs of the buttress holds the promise of great things to come and, sure enough, the rock turns out to be wonderfully sound and well-endowed with holds. After the first terrace, things start getting exposed as the route breaches the steep yellow wall. The 'official' crux sections are at the two roofs and here it is a matter of athleticism versus gravity. The crux done, both the redpoint aspirant and the fifi-hook specialist can perch, raven-like, in a little niche and collect themselves for an encore – the 'unofficial' (and real) crux of the climb: an impending, out-of-balance, and usually damp chimney crack.

⚔ Ettore Costantini, Romano Apollonio.   14 July 1944.

⚲ Sufficient belay and protection pegs in-situ; carry slings and nuts.

P Rifugio Dibona (2000m). For approach, see p.106.

↗ Take the Rif. Cantore path and branch off left to reach the second of the South Face Buttresses.

E The route begins to the right of the big gully which bounds the buttress on the left. Scramble up to a narrow ledge which leads across to the rib. Start in a corner to the right of a finger-shaped little pinnacle.

R The route at first follows an obvious crack slanting upwards to the right through the zone of grey slabs, breaching the twin band of yellow roofs about halfway up the face. Thereafter, a chimney system provides the continuation line. Where this ends, trend up and left to the arête and climb easy ground on the other side of this to the top; topo p.108.

↘ From the top of the route follow a path north and ascend a few metres to the notch which is the key to the path to Rif. Guissani. From there, follow the path leading back to Rifugio Dibona.

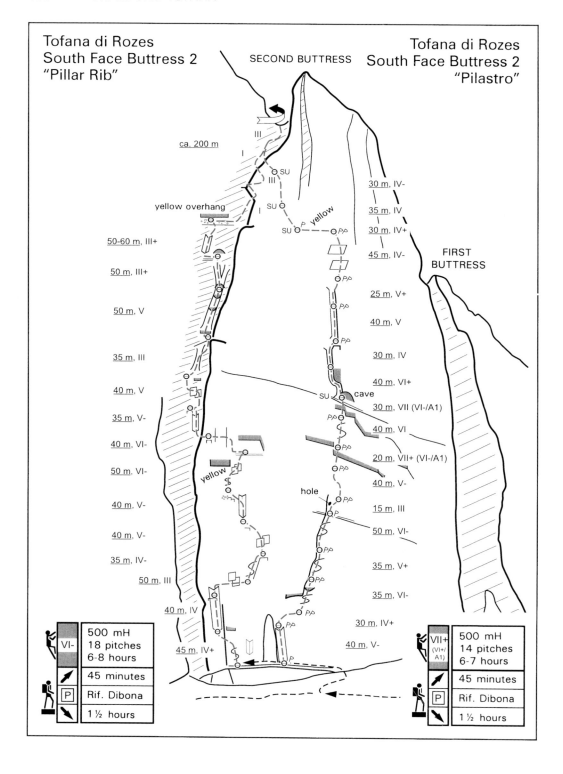

Tofana di Rozes
South Face Buttress 2
"Pillar Rib"

Tofana di Rozes
South Face Buttress 2
"Pilastro"

SECOND BUTTRESS

ca. 200 m

III

I

III   SU

yellow overhang

SU

I   SU

SU   P   yellow   PP

50-60 m, III+

50 m, III+

PP

50 m, V

35 m, III

40 m, V

SU   cave

35 m, V-

PP

40 m, VI-

50 m, VI-

yellow

40 m, V-

PP

hole   PP

40 m, V-   P

35 m, IV-

50 m, III

PP

40 m, IV

PP

45 m, IV+

P   P

30 m, IV-

35 m, IV

30 m, IV+

45 m, IV-

FIRST
BUTTRESS

PP

25 m, V+

PP

40 m, V

PP

30 m, IV

40 m, VI+

30 m, VII (VI-/A1)

40 m, VI

20 m, VII+ (VI-/A1)

40 m, V-

15 m, III

50 m, VI-

35 m, V+

35 m, VI-

30 m, IV+

40 m, V-

	VI-	500 mH
		18 pitches
		6-8 hours
		45 minutes
	P	Rif. Dibona
		1½ hours

	VII+ (VI+/A1)	500 mH
		14 pitches
		6-7 hours
		45 minutes
	P	Rif. Dibona
		1½ hours

CRODA DA LAGO, NUVOLAU

Enthroned atop the high ground of the Nuvolau plateau, the Cinque Torri are the traditional local crags and the forcing ground of the Ampezzo mountain guides. Here, the famous "Scoiattoli" have trained and tested out new ideas for many years. Small wonder, since even the 'old guard' used to appreciate short approach walks and solid rock! Although there are also many routes in the modern idiom to be discovered up there,

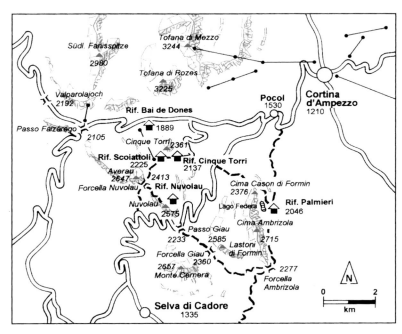

including several harder one-pitch climbs, the routes described here are the trio of classic multi-pitch climbs and Torre Barancio offers a nice little beginners' summit.

The Cinque Torri are easily reached from the Falzarego Pass road. Rifugio Scoiattoli, located within easy striking distance of the towers, can be approached either on foot from the "Bai de Dones" parking space or by taking the chair-lift. The Averau also occupies the high ground of the Nuvolau and its short but very worthwhile South Face can be reached equally easily from either Rifugio Scoiattoli or Passo Giau.

To the south-east of the Nuvolau high plains and Passo Giau stretches the elongated spur of Croda da Lago where are to be found the two selected climbs that start this chapter. The approach from Passo Giau is fast, yet few climbers find their way up here and as a result the atmosphere is one of tranquility and remoteness, far away from the cares of the world. The two routes are the good-natured North-West Corner of Cima Cason di Formin and the fine, demanding North-West Buttress of Lastoni di Formin. Both can be done in a day from Passo Giau. The recommended valley base for the whole area is Cortina d'Ampezzo.

46 CIMA CASON DI FORMIN 2376m

North-West Corner, "Dallago" (Costantini/Delago) V

Anyone who has ever been to Cortina d'Ampezzo is probably familiar with the strikingly obvious long ridge of Croda da Lago but most know it only as a view from afar, since, surprisingly, relatively few people ever find their way up there to climb. The fact that the textbook corner line on Cima Cason di Formin was first climbed as late as 1970 illustrates the fine qualities of the area well. Even today the backwater feel persists. Yet this obvious classic line has no cause to hide its face. If one avoids the first two pitches – and pretty poky they are, too – one is left with a joyous haul up seven pitches of sustained grade IV climbing. No scrambling, no choss and rubble – unusual for these parts and on its own a good enough reason for the few extra steps on the approach walk. There is also the splendid peace and quiet mostly found on this mountain.

D. Costantini, Franz Dallago.   23 September 1970.

Few pegs in place. Do not forget the slings (threads) and the nuts.

The Rio Curto bridge (parking) on the Pocol/Passo Giau road, 6½ km from the top of the pass.

Follow Path 437 for about 30 minutes towards Rifugio Palmieri (Croda da Lago Hut) to a point where two paths cross. Take Path 435 to the right and into the Formin Valley. Finally, strike off directly towards the North-West Corner (visible from the path).

Start at the foot of a grey crack (V) or climb rock steps to the left (III–IV).

The North-West Face of Cima Cason di Formin characterised by two obvious corner systems forming a huge V-shape. The route follows the right hand of these two corners, finishing on a rocky shoulder.

From the shoulder, scramble up over choss and go right to a gully which narrows towards the top. Either squeeze through a narrow cleft (III) or avoid this by climbing the grey wall on the left (V). Pass underneath a large chockstone to gain the south side. Descend a scree gully for a little way towards Rifugio Palmier and then traverse left to the notch which bounds Cason di Formin. Scramble down the gully to the start of the route (approx. 45 minutes); marked by the occasional cairn.

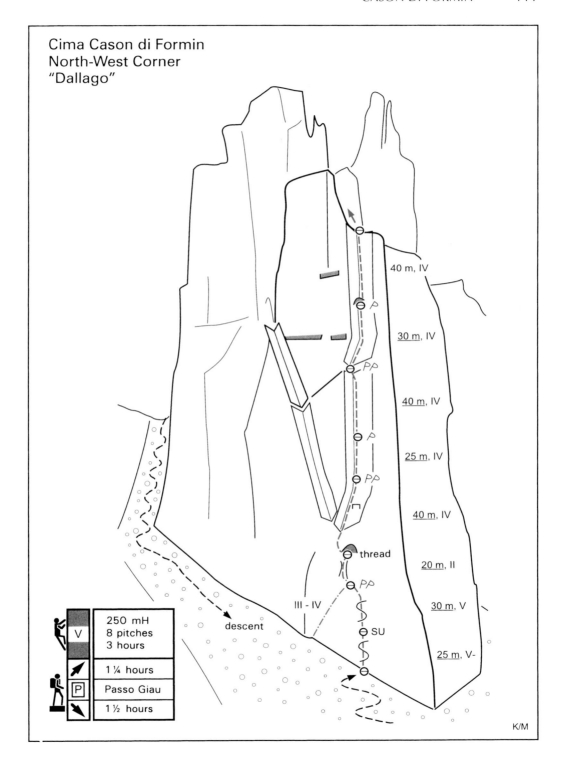

Cima Cason di Formin
North-West Corner
"Dallago"

40 m, IV

P

30 m, IV

PP

40 m, IV

P

PP

40 m, IV

thread

20 m, II

PP

III - IV

30 m, V

descent

SU

25 m, V-

V

250 mH
8 pitches
3 hours

1 ¼ hours

P   Passo Giau

1 ½ hours

K/M

47 LASTONI DI FORMIN   2585m

North-West Buttress (Buzzi/Calzi/Priolo/Zeper) VI+

The Lastoni di Formin stand in front of the ridge of Croda da Lago; the even proportions of the twin buttresses, standing exactly parallel to each other, draw the eye upwards from the viewpoint on the road to Passo Giau. The left-hand of the two pillars contains the challenging route described here. Despite its many fine sections, it has a rather austere and serious character. The route-finding is not always totally obvious and the technically interesting though often physically demanding climbing gets harder and harder towards the top. The rock is generally very good and still relatively free of polish. Crack and corner climbing predominate – fun on the lower pitches, imposingly steep and strenuous on the crux. The exposed traverse at two-thirds height gives the whole thing that little extra pinch of spice.

⚔ G. Buzzi, G. Calzi, R. Priolo, N. Zeper.   14 September 1974.

⚒ All necessary belay pegs in-situ; protection pegs on the difficult pitches only. Hammer and small selection of pegs recommended.

🅿 Path 436 to Forcella Giau branches off left at the 7.5 km marker post on the Cortina /Passo Giau road; park here.

↗ Follow the path for a while before leaving it to head directly up through the meadows and across scree to the Buttress.

🄴 Start to the right of the rib of the buttress on a small tower whose base protrudes furthest down into the scree slope.

🆁 Follow cracks and corners to the right of the rib of the buttress. At about two-thirds height, traverse around the rib on an exposed little rail. Climb the rib to the summit.

↘ Cross the flat summit plateau to the south-east (no path) to reach the Rossa del Formin notch at the southernmost end of the Croda da Lago ridge. Descend to the south, then to the west and traverse below the South Faces of the Lastoni to reach Forcella Giau and the starting point.

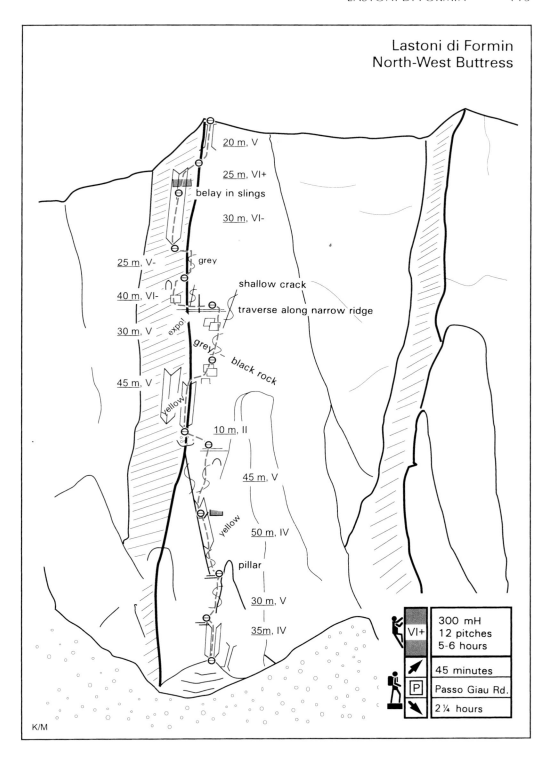

Lastoni di Formin
North-West Buttress

20 m, V

25 m, VI+

belay in slings

30 m, VI-

25 m, V-   grey

shallow crack

40 m, VI-

traverse along narrow ridge

30 m, V   expol

grey   black rock

45 m, V   yellow

10 m, II

45 m, V

yellow

50 m, IV

pillar

30 m, V

35m, IV

VI+	300 mH 12 pitches 5-6 hours
	45 minutes
P	Passo Giau Rd.
	2¼ hours

K/M

48 MOUNT AVERAU   2647m

South West Face, "Alverà" (Alverà/Pompanin/Illing/Apollinio) IV+

It is not particularly big. It is not particularly impressive. But the Averau, perched on a rise between the Falzarego Pass and Passo Giau, will tempt you onto its sunny South-West Face with an utterly worth-while route where the grade IV climber is king for the day! When it catches the sunlight, the golden-yellow face fulfils many a Dolomite cliché, while the fairly steep (for the grade), hold-covered rock will not dis-appoint even on closer scru-tiny. The central feature of the climb is an exposed traverse along a vague seam at about half height, positioned exactly where you would least expect to find such a thing. The traverse turns out to be much juggier and far less complicated than it at first appears and the same goes for the very steep pitch out of the niche which follows. A small route, but perfectly formed – and guaranteed to hold your attention!

🍴 Albino Alverà, Ugo Pompanin, Ugo Illing, Armando Apollonio. 29 June 1945.

⚲ Many of the belays are equipped with bolts. Sufficient protection pegs in-situ.

🅿 Passo Giau (2233m).

↗ Take the Path 452 to the Averau Hut. From the hut, follow the waymarked path in the direction of the Falzarego Pass (to the west) for about 200m and head uphill towards an obvious wide chimney running down left of the South Arête. Scramble up the chimney – or the rocks to the right (II–III) – and quit it on the left to climb up diagonally leftwards to a boulder-strewn ledge and the start of the route.

🅴 Start on the rubble-strewn ledge at a chimney, just left of an ill-defined arête.

🆁 Climb a chimney system to about halfway up the Face, then traverse right in an exposed position and continue stright up to the top.

↘ From the summit, follow a well-trodden path to the north down into the 'Amphitheatre'. From the right-hand (lower) edge of the amphitheatre (large cairn), a via-ferrata leads back down to the Averau Hut. From there, take Path 452 back to Passo Giau.

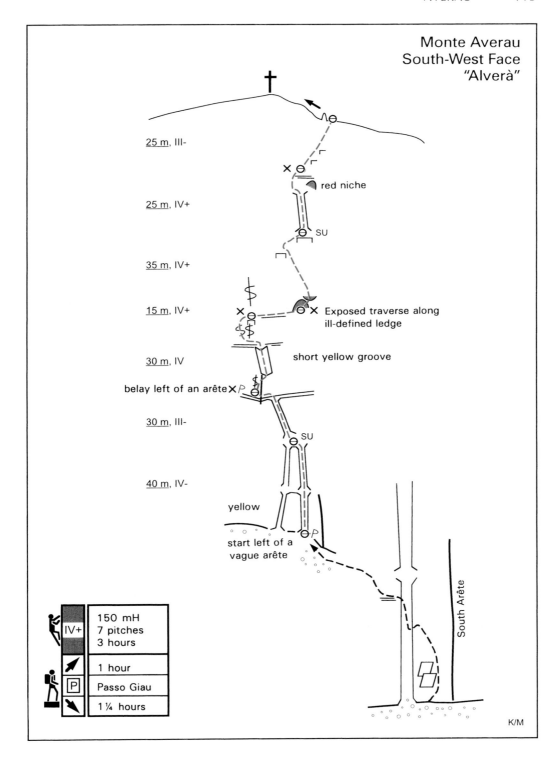

Monte Averau
South-West Face
"Alverà"

25 m, III-

× ⊖ 🔴 red niche

25 m, IV+

⊖ SU

35 m, IV+

15 m, IV+   × ⊖ × Exposed traverse along
ill-defined ledge

short yellow groove

30 m, IV

belay left of an arête × P ⊖

30 m, III-

⊖ SU

40 m, IV-

yellow

⊖ P

start left of a
vague arête

South Arête

IV+	150 mH 7 pitches 3 hours
🡥	1 hour
P	Passo Giau
🡦	1¼ hours

K/M

49 CINQUE TORRI

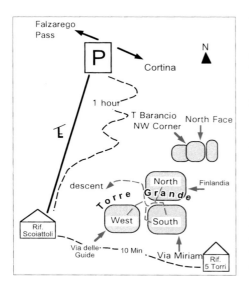

The Cinque Torri stand proud atop the high plateau of the Novolau, a huge mass of rock split as if by the devil's hand. Viewed from a distance, they appear almost mystic, like the great holy place of some ancient cult. Yet up there on the green grassy spur they resemble more a picture book idyll, a vast children's playground with massive building blocks of stone scattered there simply to amuse. And seen from here, the neighbouring Tofana di Rozes shows itself off from its best side, which makes for a wonderful and grandiose ambience. At the weekends, lots of big kids come here to play. Small wonder, for after all the area has much to discover at every level of difficulty: classic, multi-pitch routes; hard, one-pitch test-pieces; and several beautiful easier routes that are ideal training climbs.

P Park at "Bai de Dones" parking spot on the Cortina d'Ampezzo/Falzarego Pass road – valley station of the chairlift to Rifugio Scoiattoli (2225m). The path to Monte Averau and Nuvolau also starts here. When the lift is not running it is possible to drive up the little track to Rifugio Cinque Torri; the track branches off the Falzarego Pass road at the km 112.2 marker post.

One hour on foot (5 mins by lift) to Rifugio Scoiattoli and from there five minutes more on a wide path to the Cinque Torri or the eponymous hut below the South Faces. The hut is a fine base for those wishing to spend longer up here.

TORRE GRANDE, WEST SUMMIT   2350m
South-West Face, "Via delle Guide" (Dallamono/Ghirardini) IV

The "Via delle Guide" to the West Summit of Torre Grande is the most amenable multi-pitch route on the Cinque Torri and, by tradition, the classic beginners' climb. With the exception of the first pitch, the difficulties are few. The rock is sound and does not yet attain a worrying degree of steepness. The protection is as close to perfect as matters. All in all, an ideal route to get a feel for the area and a great warm-up climb.

 Pietro Dallamano, Renato Ghirardini. 15 July 1930.

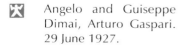 Cemented-in belay and protection pegs.

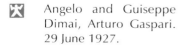 Start just right of the South-West Arête at the highest point of the scree fan. Above the start is a little belt of roofs; this is breached on the right, at its weakest point.

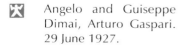 Climb up, in a fairly direct line, to the summit. The exact line is obvious – just follow the signs of many ascents (about 100m, 90 minutes; topo p.118).

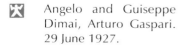 Abseil 25m from the northern summit slabs (cemented peg) down the north side to a ledge which is followed east to where a further abseil (20m) gains the gully between the West and North Summits. Head north down the gully (optional abseil from an iron stake) and follow a vague path, keeping left, around the West Summit and back to the start (20 minutes).

TORRE GRANDE, SOUTH SUMMIT   2361m

South Face, "Via Miriam" (Dimai/Gasperi) V+

This climb outwits the spectacular roof on Torre Grande's South Face. It was first climbed by the Cortina guides Arturo Gasperi and the two Dimais, and repeated eight days later (as the

guides had planned) by the Americans Miriam O'Brien and Margaret Hellburn with Angelo Dimai, his father Antonio and Angelo Dibona.* Nowadays, this is the classic route on the Cinque Torri. Its popularity has resulted in a few unpleasantly polished sections, particularly on the entry pitch.

* See p44 of *Give Me the Hills* by Miriam Underhill (O'Brien), Methuen, London, 1956, which gives a full account of this.

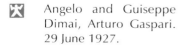 Angelo and Guiseppe Dimai, Arturo Gaspari. 29 June 1927.

Cinque Torri

(A) Torre Grande, North Summit, "Via Finlandia", VII–
(B) Torre Grande, South Summit, "Via Miriam", V+
(C) Torre Grande, West Summit, "Via delle Guide", IV
(D) Torre Barancio, North Face, IV
(E) Torre Barrancio, North-West Corner, IV

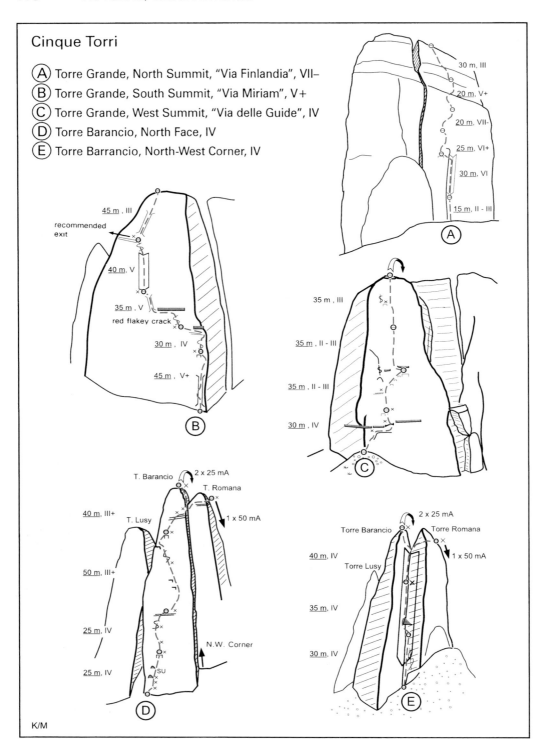

K/M

Cemented-in belay and protection pegs. A few additional nuts advisable.

Start at the lowest point of the South Face, just left of the South-East Arête.

Climb the chimney crack just to the left of the South-East Arête. Continue up going left of the arête, and traverse left beneath the obvious large roof to where it peters out (impressive, but not too difficult!). Climb the corner which follows to its end and continue easily to the top (about 150m, 2 hours).

There are two possible descents:

a) Abseil 20m from a spike into the chimney which splits the summit to gain a ledge (big chockstones in the gully between the South and North Summits). Abseil 20m down and left from a thread to a chockstone. Traverse out of the gully (west) between the summits; protected by via-ferrata cables.

b) Down climb the last pitch of the route to the stance. Follow the ledge around (west) to a terrace. Go north to a saddle. Now descend a gully, heading north (possible abseil from an iron spike) and continue, keeping left, around the West Summit and back to the start of the route (30 minutes).

TORRE GRANDE, NORTH SUMMIT 2350m

East Face, "Via Finlandia" (Gstrein/Jokinen) VII–

A gift to the climbing community of the Cinque Torri from Finnish guests visiting the Dolomites, the "Via Finlandia" combines difficult, demanding and varied climbing to give one of the finest multi-pitch routes in the lower grade VII level of difficulty. The line of the entry pitch is determined by a prominent groove, after which the climb snakes its way skilfully between the overhangs on this steep rocky bastion. A pleasurable experience for those who have already had a taste of the Seventh Grade.

W. Gstrein, M. Jokinen. 27 July 1959.

Bolt belays and normal pitons for protection.

On the left section of the East Face of the North Summit of Torre Grande is the obvious roof-capped groove which provides the entry pitch.

Climb up to the groove, then the groove itself. Quit it on the left and continue in a zig-zag fashion to easier ground and the summit (100 m, 2 hours).

Down-climb to the south-west (II) and abseil (anchor in-situ) down the deep gully between the South and North Summits to the middle terrace. Gain the opposite side of the gully with the aid of a fixed rope and finally descend the North Gully (20 minutes).

TORRE BARANCIO   2308m
North-West Corner (Dibona/Apollonio/Stefani) IV

If you are drawn to classic lines, enjoy elegant bridging and fancy a bit of practice placing nuts, the textbook corner between Torre Romana and Torre Barancio can be highly recommended. It can also be easily combined, according to whim, with the lovely North Face of Torre Barancio, to give a grade IV climb almost without equal anywhere in the area.

Ignazio Dibona, Pietro Apollonio, Dino Stefani. September 1934.

Just a few well-spaced pegs and a single solitary bolt! Well-protected with nuts.

Start at the foot of the obvious corner between the two towers.

The Barancio and Romana towers are linked by a classic open-book corner; this provides the line of the route. Follow it all the way, moving left right at the top o exit onto the summit of Torre Barancio; 100 m, 1 hour; topo p. 118.

 Two possible descents: (a) From the top of Torre Barancio, make two steep 25m abseils to the south; cemented-in abseil rings (15 minutes). (b) On the South-East Arête of Torre Romana is a big, cemented-in abseil peg. Abseil 50m to the south.

TORRE BARANCIO   2308m
North Face, "Dibona" (Dibona/Apollonio/Stefani) IV

The shadowy North Face of the Torre Barancio is one of the best easy routes in the whole of the extensive Cinque Torre area. It gives well-protected, steep climbing on ideal rock and is technically quite demanding for the grade. A word of encouragement to all those who find the first pitch hard: the compact, slabby rock gets a more liberal sprinkling of holds the higher you get!

Ignazio Dibona, Pietro Apollonio, Dino Stefani.   September 1934.

Despite the good protection it is recommended you carry a few slings for threads.

The route starts at the left hand end of the North Face, below a niche in the rock.

Climb the wall. Exit at the top onto either Torre Barancio or Torre Romana (100m, 1 hour; topo p.118).

See above.

POMAGAGNON, CRISTALLO, CADINSPITZEN

The Pomagagnon group completes the circle of mountains to the north of Cortina. The most westerly summit of this chain, Punta Fiames, with the "Fiames Arête" and the "Via Comune", the showpiece climbs of Cortina. And rightly so, for these two routes are certainly amongst the very best of their grade in the whole of the Dolomites. They are situated on the sunny side of the mountain and this and the relatively low altitude means they can be climbed quite early (or late) in the year. This factor, when combined with the quality and historical interest of the climbs, makes them particularly valuable to climbers on a tight schedule.

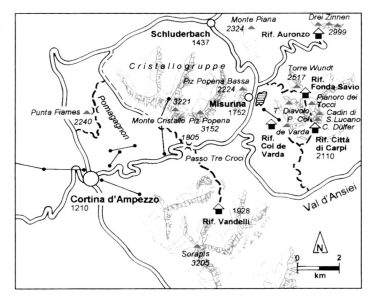

Situated directly above the Misurina Lake, Piz Popena Basso (or Monte Popena) is attributed geographically to the Cristallo Group which joins the Pomagagnon ridge at its eastern end. It forms part of a relatively low-altitude rock ridge barring the way to the high summits of the Cristallo. With its relatively short and often very well-protected easterly-facing towers and the simple approach and descent it has the atmosphere of a *klettergarten* yet with a grandiose backdrop, surrounded by the Cristallo, Sorapis, Tre Cime and Cadinspitzen. Here, too, one can enjoy unstressed climbing early or late in the year.

Directly opposite the Piz Popena Basso lie the Cadinspitzen. As a climbing area, it remains relatively unknown outside Dolomite circles although the peaks do house several exceptionally fine and, from a historical point of view, very interesting routes. Of particular value is the area around the cosy and very welcoming Rifugio Fonda Savio at the Passo dei Tocci which has several worthwhile and enjoyable short climbs which have recently been equipped with belay bolts. What has been created here is a kind of alpine *klettergarten* with short, well-protected, south-facing routes on very good rock. The most important valley base for the whole area is Cortina d'Ampezzo.

50 PUNTA FIAMES 2240m

South Face, "Via Comune" (Heath/Dimai/Verzi) IV+

Without doubt, the "Via Comune" offers one of the most worthwhile grade IV climbs in the Dolomites – 15 lovely pitches, at a very consistent III and IV level. One should, however, have an absolute mastery of climbing at this grade, since the rock is not only very solid but also very compact and this means there are relatively few natural protection placements to be found. The stances are equipped with bolts and on the crux chimney pitch and the wonderful headwall there are also a few protection pegs, but only a few! The most difficult passages are concentrated in and around the chimney at roughly half-height. It is reached by an exposed traverse and a short but very steep and smooth bit of wall. The chimney itself ends beneath a roof and looks more fierce than it actually is. If dripping wet, it can be avoided on the left (V+). As a final farewell gift, the route's penultimate pitch has a splendidly juggy piece of face climbing.

 J. L. Heath, Antonio Dimai, Angelo Verzi. 7 July 1901.

 All belays equipped with bolts. Hardly any protection pegs.

 Park at the hospital (Istituto Elioterapeutico) on the road out of Cortina to the north.

Follow a path behind the clinic buildings through meadows, bearing right after 500m to enter the forest and join up with a wide forestry track. As soon as this track leaves the forest, turn sharp right and follow a less well defined path across a bare slope to a traversing path leading up and across to Punta Fiames. Where this path drops down, turn off to the right and scramble up a dirty gully, emerging onto a ledge. Climb a series of chimneys (II–III) and go up and left to a terrace covered in pine trees. Go up and left again to the foot of a chimney.

E Start at the foot of a chimney which rises up to the left.

R The lower part follows a prominent corner to a ledge about ⅓ of the way up the face. Go along the ledge to the left, to pine bushes left of the arête. From here, the line is not obvious. Gain the chimneys which lead to the West Ridge. Bear right, following the *via ferrata* to the summit.

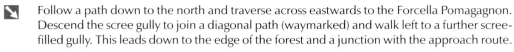 Follow a path down to the north and traverse across eastwards to the Forcella Pomagagnon. Descend the scree gully to join a diagonal path (waymarked) and walk left to a further scree-filled gully. This leads down to the edge of the forest and a junction with the approach route.

53 PIZ POPENA BASSO   2224m

East Face, "Mazzorana/Adler" IV+

On this little mountain, with the grandiose backdrop of the Sorapis, Candinspitzen and Tre Cime, the climber's life may be enjoyed to the full – a spot of climbing, followed by a lie down in the sun and a bit of daydreaming at the top of the route and if you haven't fallen asleep an easy trot back down for some more climbing! The "Mazzorana/ Adler" is the recommended warm-up route. The lower part is a little grassy and vegetated but the route gets better and better towards the top.

🗙 Piero Mazzorana, Mulli Adler.   17 August 1936.

🕭 Cemented-in belay and protection pegs.

P Park at the Misurina Hotel complex at the lake of the same name (1752m).

↗ To the north, behind the Hotel Misurina, is the start of a nice little unmarked path, which leads through the pinewoods directly to the foot of the East Face.

E Start at the top of a scree gully, behind a small pinnacle. The start is marked with a red arrow and a triangle. The first cemented-in peg is located just to the right of the corner.

R Remember to leave the initial corner at about half-height!

↘ From the top of the route, follow a path to the north through pine trees to a small wooded hollow. From here, a path marked by cairns leads back down to the foot of the crag (15 minutes).

54 TORRE WUNDT   2517m

South Face, "Mazzorana" (Mazzorana/del Torso) IV–

The most worthwhile climbs in the imme-diate vicinity of the Rifugio Fonda Savio, a beautifully situated hut in the Passo dei Tocci, have recently been completely re-equipped with sturdy belay bolts. Of these routes, the South Face of the Torre Wundt is reckoned to be one of the very best easy climbs around. As befits its status, it is also one of the most frequently climbed routes in the area. When rush hour threatens it can be a great help to relax a while at the nearby hut and wait your turn over apfelstrudel and cappuccino; after all, you can always bag this nice little peak at a more unorthodox time and avoid the crowds completely. The climbing itself is an equally pleasant diversion and apart from a few sections of lower grade IV rarely exceeds III. You should, however, be confident of your ability to lead IV, since between the good bolt belays protection pegs are rare. For this reason this is not a suitable climb for novices as, apart from the aforementioned challenge, the descent also calls for competent abseiling and navigation skills over pathless terrain.

⚔	Piero Mazzorana, Sandro del Torso. 7 September 1938.
🔑	Most stances have bolt belays, as do all of the abseils.
🏠	Rifugio Fonda Savio (2359m). A signposted track leads off right from the Misurina – Tre Cime road (limited parking spaces). Follow it to the valley station of the funicular (no public service, goods only) and take a waymarked path up to the hut. Luggage transported by prior arrangement.
↗	Follow the path from Rifugio Fonda Savio down to a point below the false summit of Torre Wundt. An indistinct path leads over scree and boulders to the foot of the South Face.
E	Start at the bottom of a corner.
R	Climb the rightward slanting corner system and the continuation chimneys. Finally, follow a ramp up and left to the summit.
↘	Walk to the west to a notch between the North and South summits and climb down about 5m to a drilled abseil ring. Make four diagonal leftwards abseils (30m, 25m, 25m, 25m) to easier-angled terrain. Bear left to a notch. Now go west around the mountain. Cross two further notches and descend to a gully. Descend to the south to the corrie.

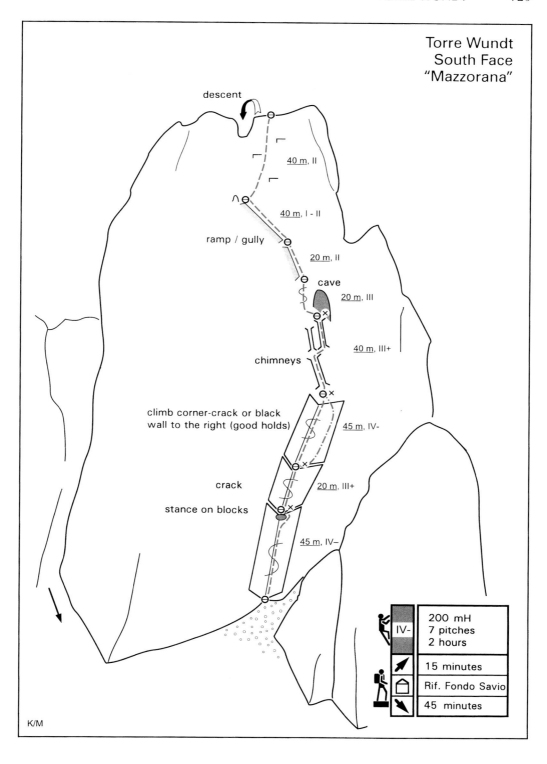

Torre Wundt
South Face
"Mazzorana"

descent

40 m, II

40 m, I - II

ramp / gully

20 m, II

cave   20 m, III

40 m, III+

chimneys

climb corner-crack or black
wall to the right (good holds)   45 m, IV-

crack   20 m, III+

stance on blocks

45 m, IV–

IV-	200 mH 7 pitches 2 hours
	15 minutes
	Rif. Fondo Savio
	45 minutes

K/M

55 PIANORO DEI TOCCI   2675m

East Face, "Quinz Corner" (Quinz/Vecellio) VI

Within easy striking distance of the hut, the East Face of Pianoro dei Tocci has a huge and impressive corner line which glows golden in the sun and is visible from a some distance. This is the line of a short but very stiff route. The stances are equipped with solid ring bolts but in between high levels of adrenaline are guaranteed. The route gives steep and at times bold and athletic crack and corner climbing of the finest quality on predominantly sound rock. The airy crux on the third pitch requires the leader to place the protection himself. The easiest way off is to abseil from the last belay. Obsessive peak-baggers will doubtless be tempted by a little additional easy climbing and a solitary summit experience. The drawback here is that the poorly protected final scramble has then to be down-climbed.

Valerio Quinz, A. Vecellio.   10 September 1951.

Bolt belays but between them … nothing! Take medium to large nuts and two 45m ropes for the abseil.

Rifugio Fonda Savio (2359m). See p.128.

Path 116 towards Forcella del Nevajo to the signpost and then climb up to the foot of the face.

E Scramble up easy slabs to below and left of the corner.

R Climb the yellow corner crack.

Abseil back down the route from the last bolt belay. 45m ropes necessary!

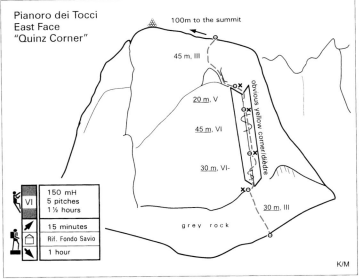

Pianoro dei Tocci
East Face
"Quinz Corner"

100m to the summit

45 m, III

20 m, V

45 m, VI

obvious yellow corner/diédre

30 m, VI-

30 m, III

grey rock

VI	150 mH	
	5 pitches	
	1 ½ hours	
	15 minutes	
	Rif. Fondo Savio	
	1 hour	

K/M

56 IL GOBBO   2560m

North Face, "Fanton/Vecellio"   III+

Positively the ideal beginners' route in the area around the cosy little Fonda Savio Hut is the North Face of the Gobbo, the smallest of the trio of towers that also includes Torre Leo and Torre del Diavolo. It was from this impudent little summit that the Baronesses of Eötvös many years ago launched their assault on the Devil himself; in fact, they reached the top of the Gobbo by a very similar route to the one described here. Nowadays, this nice little climb is perfectly protected by bolts [!!] and offers more in its four pitches than many a longer route – juggy face climbing, airy chimneys and, to round things off, a short but exposed ridge leading to the summit. [A 1910 route retrobolted to make it safe for beginners, the ultimate 'dumbing down'.]

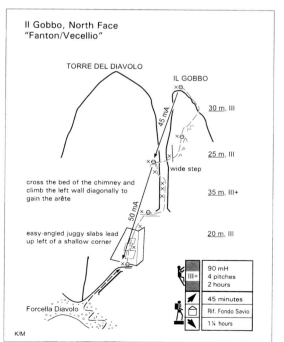

Il Gobbo, North Face
"Fanton/Vecellio"

TORRE DEL DIAVOLO

IL GOBBO

30 m, III

45 mA

25 m, III

wide step

cross the bed of the chimney and climb the left wall diagonally to gain the arête

35 m, III+

50 mA

easy-angled juggy slabs lead up left of a shallow corner

20 m, III

Forcella Diavolo

K/M

III+	90 mH
	4 pitches
	2 hours
	45 minutes
	Rif. Fondo Savio
	1¼ hours

Umberto Fanton, E. Vecellio. 2 Oct. 1910.

The route is equipped with ring bolts.

Rifugio Fonda Savio (2359m). For approach see p.128.

From the hut, follow path 117 up to the Forcella Diavolo.

E Just before the notch a short gully slants up to the right. The start of the route is at a bolt at the foot of the leaning slabs of Torre Diavolo's North Face.

R Climb the slabs up and right to gain the chimney between Torre del Diavolo and Il Gobbo. Climb the chimney and exit right onto the Gobbo's North Face. Follow the ridge to the airy summit.

Abseil back down the route or as shown on the topo (50m ropes).

57 TORRE DEL DIAVOLO   2598m

E. Face (Torre Leo) & S. Face (Dülfer/von Bernuth/Dibona/Stösser) VI–

Though not a high summit, for a time Torre del Diavolo dismissed with satanic scorn every normal attempt to climb it. After many a suitor had been rebuffed, it was eventually the Baronesses Ilona and Rolanda von Eötvös who, in 1903 in the company of their guides Antonio Dimai, Giovanni Siorpaës and Angelo Verzi, were the first to gain the devil's head. Their method was to snare the summit with a rope thrown across from Il Gobbo, thereby making a 'tyrolean traverse' with which to make the crossing. It was left to Hans Dülfer to make the first proper ascent ten years later. With a devilishly wide bridging manoeuvre he managed to get across from Torre Leo and get established on the South Face, which he then climbed to the summit. Nowadays, the usual route is actually a combination of three different climbs: up the "Dibona" to the gap between Torre Leo and the Diavolo, then the "Stösser/Schutt" to gain the summit of Torre Leo. From here we follow Dülfer and his wild bridging move.

Those who are a little short have been driven to despair and even retreat at this point and even those climbers with the stature of a guardsman often require several attempts before they dare commit themselves to the jump. An impressive and rather curious route which, for all its brevity, should not be underestimated. Something for those with a taste for the unusual.

🍴	Hans Dülfer, Werner von Bernuth. 15 Aug. 1913. Angelo Dibona, Walter Stösser, Fred Schutt.
⚲	The protection arrangements consist of everything from 'nothing to speak of' to bolt belays. Nuts and some slings are essential. 50m ropes for the abseils.
🏠	Rifugio Fonda Savio (2359m). For approach see p.128.
↗	From the hut, follow path 117 up to Forcella Diavolo.
E	Start in a little corner on the south side of the gap. Make a short traverse out left to the prominent chimney separating Torre del Diavolo from Torre Leo.
R	Climb the chimney to a chockstone. Make a rising traverse out onto the N.E. side of Torre Leo. From its summit move down into the chimney between the two towers and make a long step across onto the South Face of Torre del Diavolo. Follow the obvious crack to the top.
↘	Down-climb (II) 20m to the north (back towards Il Gobbo) to an abseil point. Abseil 50m to a ledge above the chimney separating Torre del Diavolo from Il Gobbo (peg). Abseil a further 50m to the north-east. Head east back down to Forcella Diavolo (approx. 50m, I).

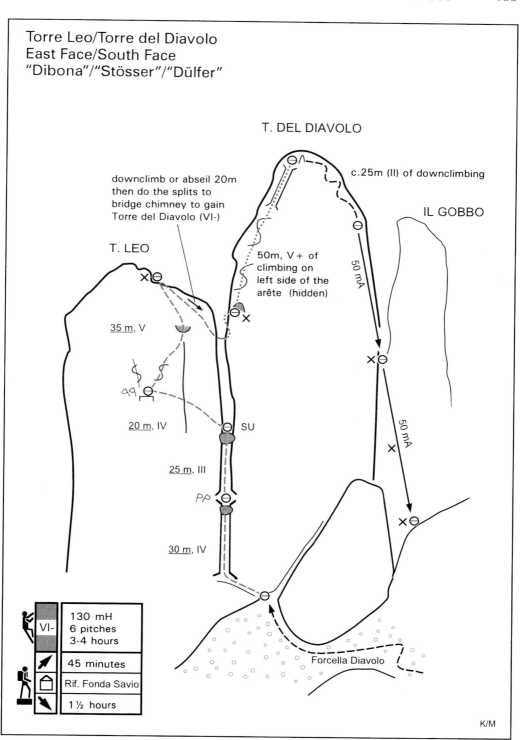

Torre Leo/Torre del Diavolo
East Face/South Face
"Dibona"/"Stösser"/"Dülfer"

T. DEL DIAVOLO

c.25m (II) of downclimbing

IL GOBBO

downclimb or abseil 20m
then do the splits to
bridge chimney to gain
Torre del Diavolo (VI-)

T. LEO

50m, V+ of
climbing on
left side of the
arête (hidden)

50 mA

35 m, V

20 m, IV

25 m, III

30 m, IV

SU

PP

50 mA

130 mH
6 pitches
3-4 hours

45 minutes

Rif. Fonda Savio

1 ½ hours

Forcella Diavolo

VI-

K/M

58 PUNTA COL DE VARDA   2504m

North-West Corner, "Comici" (Comici/del Torso) IV

Viewed from the valley one is hard pressed to make out this lovely peak, located directly in front of the central Candinspitzen. The chairlift up to Col de Varda does however provide the climber with a great seat in the gods from which to study the route and the straightforward approach. The climb takes the prominent cracks and chimneys in the corner system. Here the middle-grade climber just out for a bit of fun really does profit from Emilio Comici's legendary eye for an elegant line. Although the left-hand exit to avoid the headwall does not follow exactly the super-direct original line of the master ('let a drop of water fall – and that is the line I will follow') it does make the route more consistent. The result is a climb whose difficulties hover around a fairly tame III to IV level. The rock is rich in coralline fossils but one should not go hunting for them in the depths of this amenable chimney system. The best way to keep your boots dry after rain and to avoid 'offwidth rash' is to refrain from crawling into the back and climb it by elegant bridging. In the hedonist's version described here, the route is a nice 'half day Comici' which has yet to achieve the level of high gloss and polish of its great cousin, despite the easy chairlift access and its increasing popularity.

☒ Emilio Comici, Sandro del Torso. 1 September 1934.

⚲ Some pitons in-situ. Good natural protection available.

🅿 Park at the station of the Col de Varda chairlift, on the southern shore of Lake Misurina (1752m).

↗ From the top station at Col de Varda (2115m – a walk of one hour from Lake Misurna), follow the Sentiero Bonacossa northwards until a faint climbers' path leads up and right over scree to the foot of the face.

🄴 Start to the left of the bottom of the chimney splitting the North-West Face in a direct line with the summit.

🅁 The lower, overhanging section of the chimney is avoided by climbing in from the left. Once gained, the chimney is followed to beneath the impending headwall which is avoided by a rising leftwards traverse out onto ledges on the North Face.

↘ From the summit, climb down (II) into the gap between Punta Col de Varda and the main massif and then descend scree and rubble (south) to the foot of the wall. The gap can be easily reached by following the cairns eastwards from where the real climbing ends, below the summit.

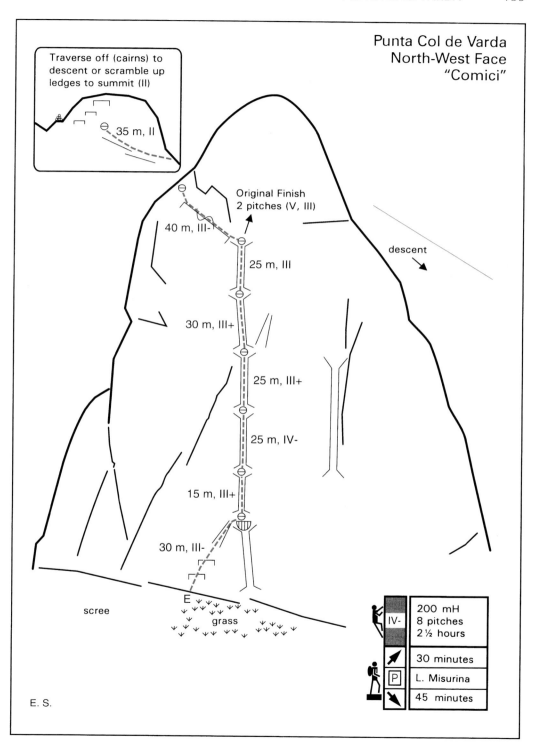

Traverse off (cairns) to descent or scramble up ledges to summit (II)

35 m, II

Punta Col de Varda
North-West Face
"Comici"

Original Finish
2 pitches (V, III)

descent

40 m, III-

25 m, III

30 m, III+

25 m, III+

25 m, IV-

15 m, III+

30 m, III-

E

scree

grass

IV-	200 mH 8 pitches 2 ½ hours
	30 minutes
P	L. Misurina
	45 minutes

E. S.

59 CAMPANILE DÜLFER 2706m

East Rib, "Dülfer" (Dülfer/von Bernuth) V–

The Campanile Dülfer stands directly in front of Cima Eötvös. At first glance it is not discernible as an independent tower as the notch which divides the two peaks is very narrow. The Campanile achieved fame through its first ascentionist Hans Dülfer but owes its notoriety to the sensational descent – the abseil from the summit into the narrow notch being exceedingly thrilling. It provided Walter Pause with good material for a tale in his alpine chamber of horrors, wherein a potential climbing horror story actually ends without serious mishap. Reliable abseil anchors, modern sit harnesses and the nowadays-ubiquitous 50m double ropes have consigned the horror stories to the annals of history. These days one can concentrate on the climbing itself, for this is the real reason for the Campanile's fame. The rock is wonderfully solid and juggy and the very few signs of passage mean that every ascent feels like the first.

Hans Dülfer, Werner von Bernuth. 25 August 1913.

Relatively few pitons in-situ but plentiful natural protection: slings on spikes, threads and nuts.

Rifugio Citta di Carpi (2110m). This beautifully situated hut is reached in 90 minutes by a waymarked path from the south end of Lake Misurina (valley station of the lift, 1752m) via Col de Varda (chairlift up to this point). The route is also accessible from Rifugio Fonda Savio (2359m); see p.128 for details.

From Rifugio Citta di Carpi, walk up the Sentiero Durissimi (path) which passes below Campanile Dülfer. At the base of the tower go right, over scree, to the start of the route. The alternative approach from Rifugio Fonda Savio (2359m) takes 2 hours and follows a waymarked path from the hut via Forcella del Nevajo and Forcella Verzi. On the far side of the col, a painstaking descent of the Sentiero Durissimi leads across rubble and scree down to Campanile Dülfer.

E Start right of the rib at a short crack leading to an easier ramp. This slants up to the right beneath a capping roof.

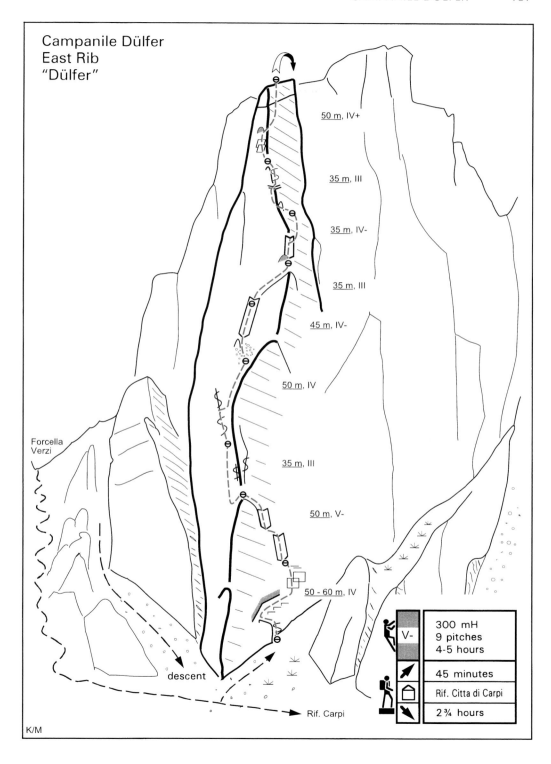

Campanile Dülfer
East Rib
"Dülfer"

50 m, IV+

35 m, III

35 m, IV-

35 m, III

45 m, IV-

50 m, IV

Forcella
Verzi

35 m, III

50 m, V-

50 - 60 m, IV

descent

Rif. Carpi

K/M

V-	300 mH 9 pitches 4-5 hours
↗	45 minutes
⌂	Rif. Citta di Carpi
↘	2 ¾ hours

R Gain the first ledge on the rib by a wide right-to-left zigzag then follow splendidly juggy cracks and corners to the left of the rib. The upper third of the route takes the rib direct to the summit.

Climb down 10m on the north-east side of the tower to an abseil point. Abseil 45m (airy) into the narrow gap between Campanile Dülfer and Cima Eötvös. If 45m ropes are used, the bad stance 10m below the first abseil station can be ignored. Make two abseils west out of the gap (40m, 40m) and leave the gully by a chossy ledge leading round to the right. Cross numerous little gullies to the main gully running down from Forcella Verzi (see sketch). Either cross the gully and descend to Rifugio Fonda Savio or scramble down the gully to the foot of the face and continue to Rifugio Citta di Carpi.

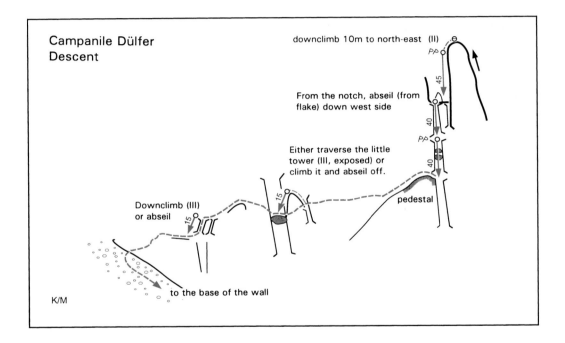

Campanile Dülfer
Descent

downclimb 10m to north-east (II)

From the notch, abseil (from flake) down west side

Either traverse the little tower (III, exposed) or climb it and abseil off.

pedestal

Downclimb (III) or abseil

to the base of the wall

K/M

DREI ZINNEN
TRE CIME DI LAVAREDO

The world-famous Drei Zinnen group is only a very tiny part of the huge mountain wilderness of the Sexten (Sesto) range yet they have become the emblem which epitomises the Dolomites. During the summer months hordes of tourists pass along the wide track from the Auronzo Hut to the Paternsattel in order to view the Tre Cime from the north. And the "North Face Show" on offer is indeed very impressive. Small wonder that these faces were long considered unclimbable and that – as always, when the word 'impossible' is bandied about – generations of climbers, drawn like moths to a lamp, have wrestled their way up their routes on uncompromisingly steep walls. The Drei Zinnen routes described here are all classics, every one of them, climbs with great history. Even the names of the first ascentionists read like a 'Who's Who' of climbing history: Grohmann, Preuss, Dülfer, Comici, Cassin …
Situated on the far side of the Paternsattel, the Paternkofel offers a nice grade III route on its North-North West Arête with the reward of fabulous views across to the three great peaks. Yet the strategic position of this mountain is inextricably linked with a darker chapter of history. During the Great War it was a bitterly contested military position with commensurate loss of life. The most central base for the routes described in this area is Rifugio Auronzo but thanks to the toll road to the hut from Misurina, all these routes can be done as single-day climbs. If one is planning to do several routes it is certainly worth using Rifugio Auronzo or the nearby Rifugio Lavaredo, since the convenience of the toll road does come at a price.

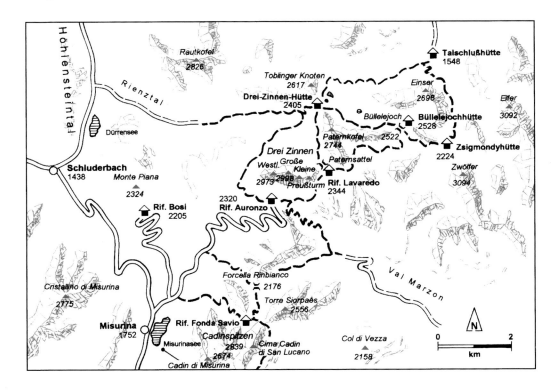

60 GROSSE ZINNE
CIMA GRANDE DI LAVAREDO
2998m

South Face, "Normal Route" (Grohmann/Innerkofler/Salcher) III

For some people this historic climb is simply a tedious necessity – the descent after completing one of the climbs on the steeper faces. For others it is often the only possible way of climbing the mountain. Here, unlike some other Dolomite peaks, the Normal Route is actually a very worthwhile climb – long and quite difficult, it should neither be denigrated nor underestimated. The rock has been polished to a nice shine so that the route-finding is straightforward. The scenery is magnificent but from midday onwards, the traffic on the climb detracts from quiet contemplation and can be rather irksome.

Paul Grohmann, Franz Innerkofler, Peter Salcher.   21 August 1869.

The difficult sections of the route have belay/abseil pitons. Natural protection is plentiful.

Rifugio Auronzo (2330m) and car-park, reached from Misurina along the signposted toll road.

Head at first along the road in the direction of Rifugio Lavaredo. Leave the road at the chapel and follow a less well-defined trail uphill over scree and into the gully between Cima Grande and Cima Piccola.

About 80m below the skyline notch an obvious ramplike gully branches off to the left. This is the start of the route and is impossible to miss (follow your nose!).

The leftwards-slanting gully leads up to a narrow gap between a pinnacle and the main mass of the face. Climb up, crossing two further notches, to the lower terrace of the South Face. Continue up the right hand part of the South Face to the upper terrace ("Ringband"). Follow this round to the left to reach a gully system which splits the headwall and leads to the top.

Descend the route. Allow at least two hours to the foot of the face.

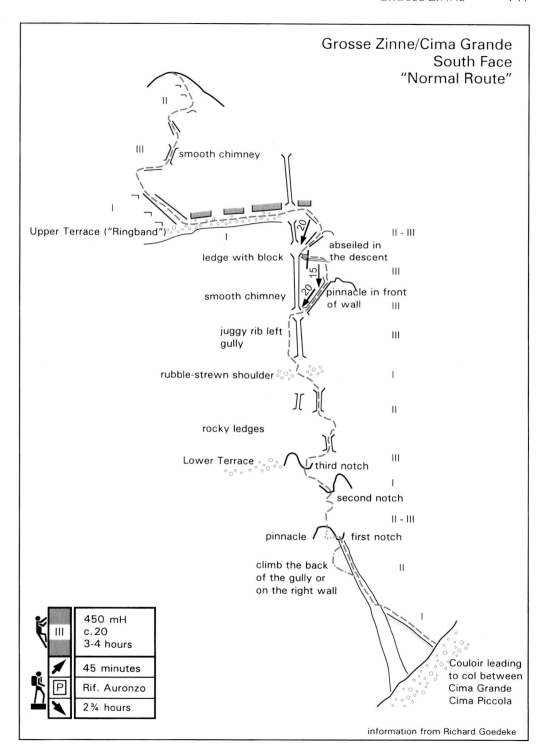

Grosse Zinne/Cima Grande
South Face
"Normal Route"

II

III   smooth chimney

I

Upper Terrace ("Ringband")

I

20

ledge with block   abseiled in   II - III
                    the descent

III

20 15

smooth chimney   pinnacle in front
                  of wall   III

juggy rib left   III
gully

rubble-strewn shoulder   I

II

rocky ledges

III

Lower Terrace   third notch

second notch   I

II - III

pinnacle   first notch

climb the back   II
of the gully or
on the right wall

I

450 mH
III   c.20
      3-4 hours

45 minutes

P   Rif. Auronzo

2¾ hours

Couloir leading
to col between
Cima Grande
Cima Piccola

information from Richard Goedeke

61 GROSSE ZINNE
CIMA GRANDE DI LAVAREDO

2998m

West Face, "Dülfer" (Dülfer/von Bernuth) V+

The Grosse Zinne has, for most visitors only two sides, the famous north side and the anonymous south side. But hidden away in a gully to the west, is the towering West Face, almost as beautifully sculpted as the North Face yet more elegant and compact in its dimensions. The best thing about this wall is the corner line splitting it, straight as a die, steep, exposed and wonderfully solid. 1913 saw the great German pioneer Hans Dülfer (partnered by Werner von Bernuth) capture this line and add it to his collection of gems in what was probably his most successful year in the mountains.

Hans Dülfer, Werner von Bernuth.   August 1913.

Sufficient belay and protection pegs in-situ. Placing nuts on this route is pure pleasure; medium to large sizes recommended.

P Rifugio Auronzo (2330m) and car-park, reached from Misurina along the signposted toll road.

Head along the road towards the Rifugio Lavaredo. Branch off and follow a less well-defined trail into the gully between Cima Ovest and Cima Grande. Climb out of the east side of the gully across ledges to gain a little tower on the West Face.

E Start at a little tower on the wall.

R The big corner in the face tucked in left of the South-West Arête gives the line of the route. The bottom of the corner is gained from the left. The capping overhang is turned on the right to reach a chimney which looks horrible but turns out to be wonderfully amenable, even when wet.

The route ends on the "Ringband", which is followed round to the south to a gully dropping down to the south; cairn. Climb/abseil down the Normal Route (route 60, see topo p.141); two hours to the foot of the face.

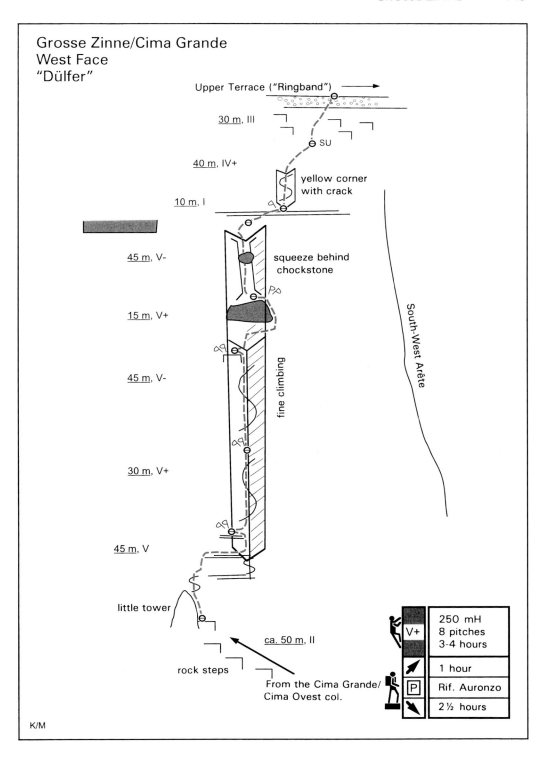

Grosse Zinne/Cima Grande
West Face
"Dülfer"

Upper Terrace ("Ringband")

30 m, III

SU

40 m, IV+

yellow corner
with crack

10 m, I

45 m, V–

squeeze behind
chockstone

15 m, V+

45 m, V–

fine climbing

30 m, V+

South-West Arête

45 m, V

little tower

ca. 50 m, II

rock steps

From the Cima Grande/
Cima Ovest col.

V+

250 mH
8 pitches
3–4 hours

1 hour

P   Rif. Auronzo

2 ½ hours

K/M

62 GROSSE ZINNE
CIMA GRANDE DI LAVAREDO
2998m

North Face, "Comici" (Comici/Dimai) VII–

This is one of the great alpine North Faces and one with a great deal of prestige attached. The verticality of the wall is so unique, the word 'impossible' was applied to it for so long and the actual first ascent was so spectacular that it could not be otherwise. There are only a very few routes on which the climber is at the mercy of such vertiginous steepness over such a long stretch as this one. The face really is a Big Wall. This is a feeling one has to first get used to and what for some is grounds for euphoria will simply terrify others. The climbing itself is very strenuous for eight pitches, consistently steep and difficult. Thereafter things get easier but the terrain remains far from undemanding. On the hard pitches the rock has been polished clean; further up one does come across throwaway holds. Those aspiring to the redpoint should bear in mind that one of the most difficult bits comes right at the start, before you are really firing on all four cylinders.

🗡	Emilio Comici, Giuseppe and Angelo Dimai. 12/14 August 1933.
🔧	On the lower, more difficult sections, the route is strewn with countless pitons of varying degrees of quality. An additional rack of nuts is essential!
🅿	Rifugio Auronzo (2330m) and car-park, reached from Misurina along the signposted toll road.
↗	Follow the waymarked track to Rifugio Lavaredo and continue to the col of the Paternsattel. Cross the col and traverse the scree slopes on the other side until beneath the North Face.
🄴	Start at a stepped leaning pillar on the right hand sector of the North Face. Climb a gully on the left of the pillar to reach the highest point of the pillar and a little terrace.
🆁	The route climbs the right hand side of the North Face in a more or less direct line leading up to the water streaks and the big corner dropping down from the "Ringband" terrace.
↘	Follow the "Ringband" round to the right (looking up) and traverse onto the south side. The descent of the Normal Route starts at a south-facing gully (cairn); sections of III, several abseils. See topo p.141.

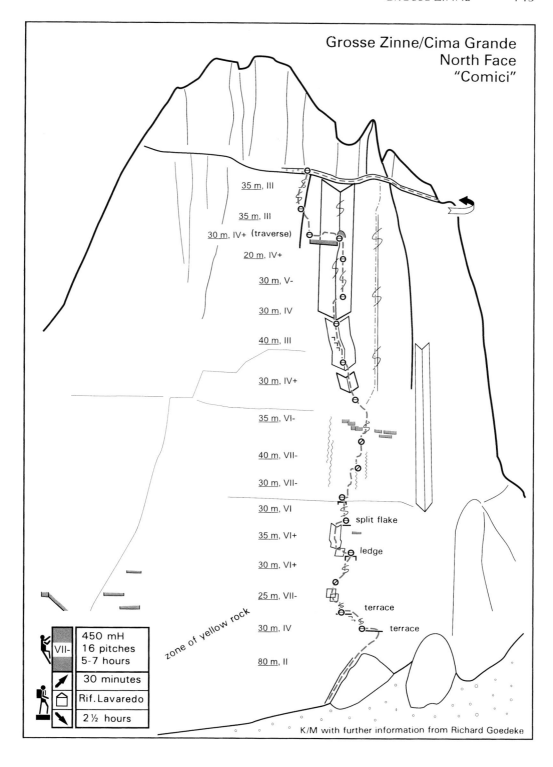

Grosse Zinne/Cima Grande
North Face
"Comici"

35 m, III

35 m, III

30 m, IV+ (traverse)

20 m, IV+

30 m, V-

30 m, IV

40 m, III

30 m, IV+

35 m, VI-

40 m, VII-

30 m, VII-

30 m, VI

35 m, VI+ — split flake

30 m, VI+ — ledge

25 m, VII-

30 m, IV — terrace

80 m, II — terrace

zone of yellow rock

VII-
450 mH
16 pitches
5-7 hours

30 minutes

Rif. Lavaredo

2 ½ hours

K/M with further information from Richard Goedeke

63 KLEINE ZINNE
CIMA PICCOLA
2857m

South Arête, "The Yellow Edge" (Comici/Zanutti/Varale) VI

It was with glowing words that Emilio Comici described the first ascent of the famed Yellow Edge (a.k.a. Spigolo Giallo or Gelbekante) as 'the most exposed climb one can imagine ... Two days of raging battle we experienced on this route, clinging astride it to microscopic holds, while she defended herself with torrents of falling stones.' The 'torrents of falling stones' have long since been committed to the valley floor; the 'microscopic holds' are no longer as small but are polished by the sweat of fear, especially on the lower part; nor will you find yourself clinging to an arête – it is far more likely that you will be buried deep inside strenuous cracks and chimneys. What remains is the breathtaking exposure and the fantastic feeling that comes with climbing a 'golden' line.

- Emilio Comici, Renato Zanutti, Mary Varale. 8 September 1933.
- All belay and protection pegs in-situ. Nuts are useful on the chimney pitches.

- Rifugio Auronzo (2330m) and car-park, approached via the toll road from Misurina.
- Follow the toll road to Rifugio Lavaredo until below the Yellow Edge. At this point climb screes directly to its foot. 45 minutes from the Rif. Auronzo.
- Start just left of the arête at a prominent polished corner.
- After the initial corner pitch, the route moves right of the arête to gain easier ground on the South-East Face. Only at half height does it return to the arête, reaching the first summit via corners and chimneys to the right of the arête.

- Descend the Normal Route (solid abseil pitons): traverse from the first summit to the top of the summit headwall and make two 20m abseils down a gully to the west. Further left, make four 20m abseils down the wall to a terrace. Descend to the south to a pinnacle and go over this to the gully between Cima Grande and Cima Piccola. Descend to the south.

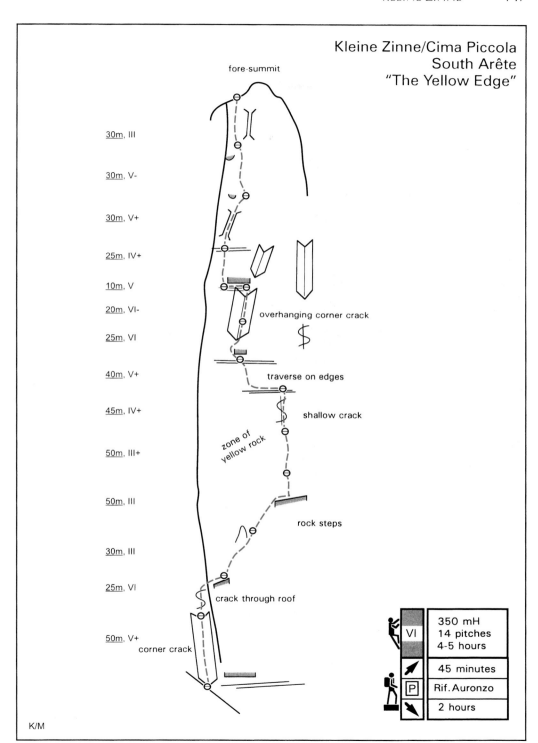

Kleine Zinne/Cima Piccola
South Arête
"The Yellow Edge"

fore-summit

30m, III

30m, V-

30m, V+

25m, IV+

10m, V

20m, VI-

25m, VI

overhanging corner crack

40m, V+

traverse on edges

45m, IV+

shallow crack

zone of
yellow rock

50m, III+

50m, III

rock steps

30m, III

25m, VI

crack through roof

50m, V+
corner crack

VI   350 mH
      14 pitches
      4-5 hours

      45 minutes

P   Rif. Auronzo

      2 hours

K/M

64 KLEINSTE ZINNE 2700m
CIMA PICCOLISSIMA (PREUSSTURM)

North-East Face, "Preussriss" or "Preuss Crack" (Preuss/Relly) V

The "Preussriss" (mostly a chimney) slices in a direct line through the entire North-East Face of the smallest of the "Cime", the only one named [by German speakers at least] after its first ascentionist. It is something of a 'must do route' in matters of free-climbing history, and well worth doing for its quality as well. Those who clip the pitons on the "Preuss Wall" with a sense of relief might recall that on the first ascent in 1911 not a single piton was used. To abide by his own strict rule of only climbing up things he could comfortably reverse Preuss, the uncompromising and hugely talented 'Pope of Free Climbing', first down-climbed the critical wall before addressing the steep and very airy chimney/crack which followed. Nowadays one finds several pitons (notably on that crux wall), which are welcome for those who are not made of the same stuff as Preuss. [How sad that Preuss's ideas were not more influential during the following years of technical alpinism].

☒ Paul Preuss, Paul Relly. 6 September 1911.

⚲ Belay and protection pegs in-situ. Belays can often be backed up with threads.

P Rifugio Auronzo (2330m) and car-park, approached from Misurina along the toll road.

↗ Follow the road past Rif. Lavaredo and up to the Paternsattel; on the far side of the col, go left to the foot of the pinnacle at the base of the tower. Traverse onto the north side and up rock steps to a ledge which leads round to the left onto the east side of the pinnacle.

E Start on the ledge of the pinnacle to the left of the North-East Arête, at the foot of a corner; peg belays. The pinnacle can also be avoided by climbing up first right then left to gain the stance below the "Preuss Wall".

R Climb the corner to a ledge leading back right and gain the notch between the lower pinnacle and Cima Piccolissima. Leave the notch by a difficult bit of face climbing to reach a ledge which leads rightwards to the belay below the "Preuss Wall". Climb the wall to a left-leading ramp. The route finding now becomes obvious. Follow the prominent crack/chimney splitting the North Face right to the top.

↘ Gain the Cima Piccolissima/Punta Frida col. The steep "Dülfer Couloir" to the south is descended by a series of long abseils (cemented-in ring bolts). Note: Take care to avoid triggering stonefalls in the couloir.

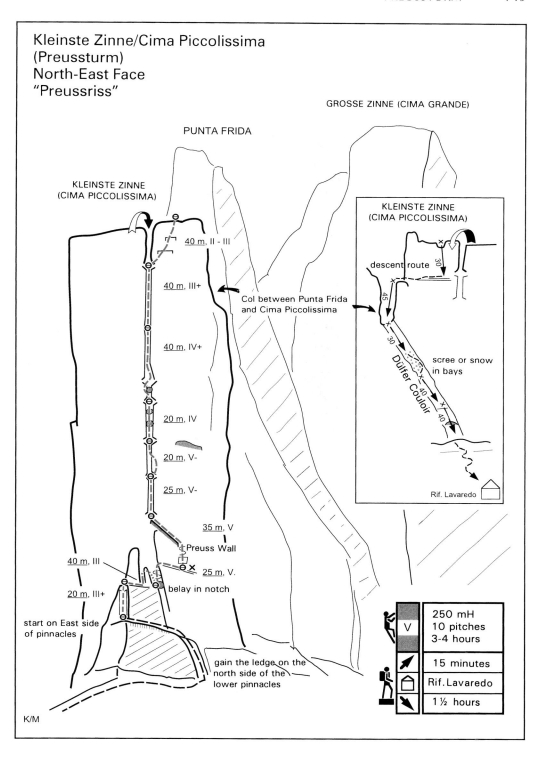

Kleinste Zinne/Cima Piccolissima
(Preussturm)
North-East Face
"Preussriss"

GROSSE ZINNE (CIMA GRANDE)

PUNTA FRIDA

KLEINSTE ZINNE
(CIMA PICCOLISSIMA)

40 m, II - III

40 m, III+

Col between Punta Frida
and Cima Piccolissima

40 m, IV+

20 m, IV

20 m, V-

25 m, V-

35 m, V

Preuss Wall

40 m, III

25 m, V.

20 m, III+

belay in notch

start on East side
of pinnacles

gain the ledge on the
north side of the
lower pinnacles

KLEINSTE ZINNE
(CIMA PICCOLISSIMA)

descent route

30

45

30

Dülfer Couloir

scree or snow
in bays

40

40

Rif. Lavaredo

	250 mH
V	10 pitches
	3-4 hours
	15 minutes
	Rif. Lavaredo
	1½ hours

K/M

65 KLEINSTE ZINNE   2700m
CIMA PICCOLISSIMA (PREUSSTURM)

South Face, "Cassin" (Cassin/Vitali/Pozzi) VII–

Although Cima Piccolissima is the smallest of all the Cime, the vertical sweep of its walls easily measures up to the others. On the southern side in particular where the other peaks offer looser facets the Picolissima boasts a fierce cliff. A full four years before making his most famous climb, the Walker Spur, Riccardo Cassin and his companions had fought their way up this impressive face using some pitons for aid. Today, the route is a popular free climb with one pitch in the lower seventh grade and plentiful sections of VI and V. The little flakes and edges on this steep bastion are mostly solid, even if at first glance they do not necessarily appear so. Only on the last two pitches before the summit are there any really friable bits and these can be confidently avoided by heading straight for the descent route.

✠ Riccardo Cassin, Gigi Vitali, Luigi Pozzi. August 1934.

⚲ All belay pegs and many protection pegs in-situ. Double ropes needed for the abseils

P Rifugio Auronzo (2330m) and car-park, approached from Misurina along the toll road.

↗ From the Rif. Auronzo take the track to Rifugio Lavaredo and continue to the Paternsattel. Traverse beneath the South Face to the Dülfer Couloir, the deep gully between Cima Piccolissima and Punta Frida.

E Climb a little way out of the gully to a ledge at the foot of the initial corner.

R Follow cracks and shallow corners up the centre of the face to a traverse line giving access to a corner. This leads to the top of a pillar two-thirds of the way up the face. Continue just left of the South-West Arête to a terrace. One can traverse off to the descent route from here. The continuation pitches to the summit are loose in parts.

↘ Descend the Dülfer Couloir, the breathtakingly narrow, wild and often wet gully between Cima Piccolissima and Punta Frida. A series of long abseils from cemented-in ring bolts lead back to the start of the climb. Stonefall danger to and from other parties in the couloir.

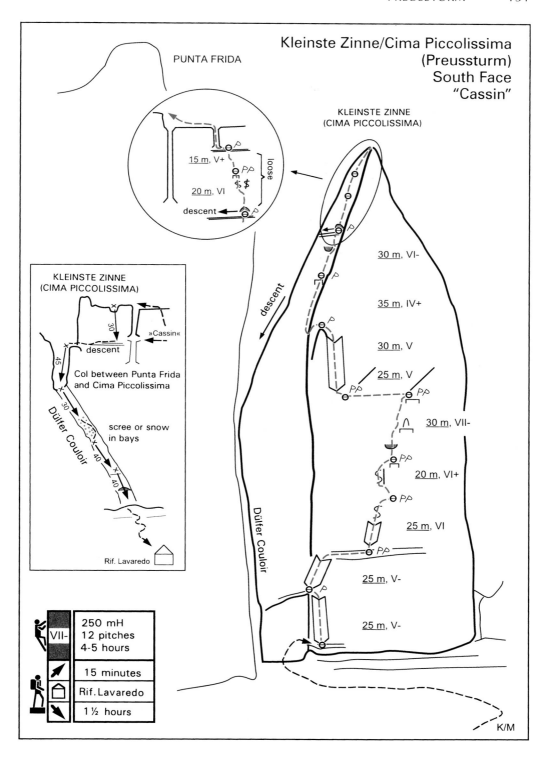

Kleinste Zinne/Cima Piccolissima
(Preussturm)
South Face
"Cassin"

PUNTA FRIDA

KLEINSTE ZINNE
(CIMA PICCOLISSIMA)

15 m, V+

loose

20 m, VI

descent

KLEINSTE ZINNE
(CIMA PICCOLISSIMA)

30 m, VI-

35 m, IV+

30 m, V

25 m, V

30 m, VII-

20 m, VI+

25 m, VI

25 m, V-

25 m, V-

»Cassin«

descent

Col between Punta Frida
and Cima Piccolissima

scree or snow
in bays

Dülfer Couloir

Rif. Lavaredo

Dülfer Couloir

VII-

250 mH
12 pitches
4-5 hours

15 minutes

Rif. Lavaredo

1½ hours

K/M

66 PATERNKOFEL   2744m
PATERNO

North-North-West Ridge (Innerkofler/Biendl) III+

An ideal first route for beginners or those new to the area is the combination of the Innerkofler via ferrata and the North-North-West Ridge of Paterno, although the loose initial gully may cause the sceptic to raise doubts about the continuation of the undertaking. The following seven rope-lengths then remain at a perfectly accept-able level on the 'rickety scale' and give some very airy and diverting face and arête climbing for the grade, all on solid rock. Included in the arrangements are the beautifully shaped pilgrims' summit of the members of the 'iron road fellow-ship' the grandiose views of all the big routes in the Tre Cime group, and a poten-tial lump on the head from the approach (use a helmet and torch in the tunnel)! The end result of the expedition, despite the damp and constricting war-time caving trip, will likely turn out to be more lighthearted than dark and obscure.

Sepp and Christian Innerkofler, E. Biendl. 1 September 1886.

Only a few in-situ pitons but well-protected by nuts and threads. Torches for the tunnel.

From Misurina take the toll road to Rifugio Auronzo (2330m) and car-park. Continue along the track past Rifugio Lavaredo, cross the Paternsattel, and thence around the head of the cwm to Rifugio Locatelli (2405m).

Approach via the Sepp Innerkofler *Via Ferrata* ("Gallerie del Paterno") to beyond the tunnel.

At the first left bend of the via ferrata after the tunnel exit, bear right to the apron of a scree fan below a loose gully.

The gully leads to an overhang which is avoided on the left. Go up left, then right to the gap behind the uppermost tower on the ridge. Climb up trending left (belay) then back right to join the arête. Climb the arête, moving right eventually to join the summit ridge.

Descend by the waymarked Normal Route to the "Gamsscharte" (Chamois Notch). From here, either follow the "Gallerie del Paterno" back to Rifugio Locatelli or the old military path back to the Paternsattel and the approach track.

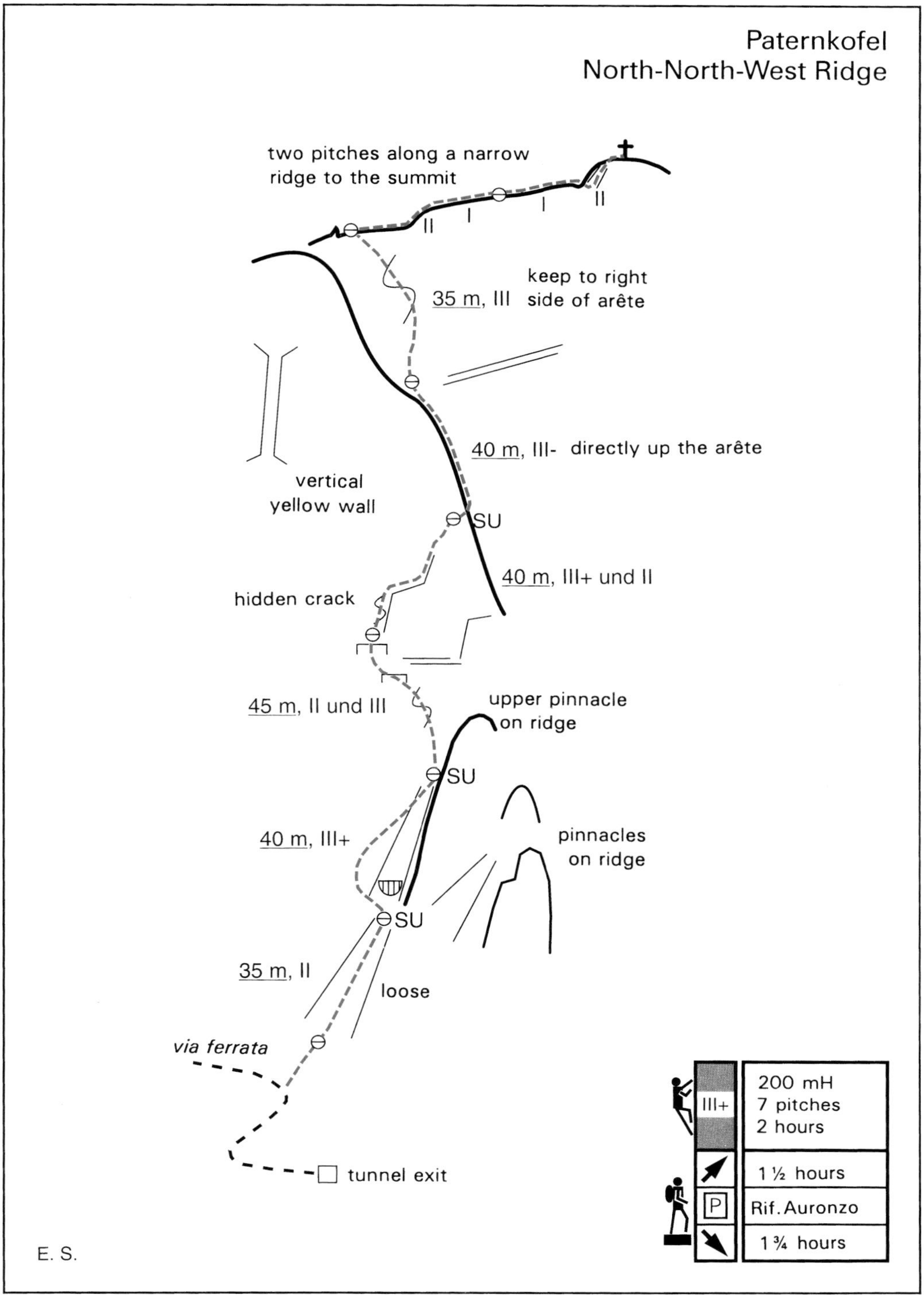

Paternkofel
North-North-West Ridge

two pitches along a narrow
ridge to the summit

II I   I   II

keep to right
35 m, III side of arête

40 m, III- directly up the arête

vertical
yellow wall

SU

40 m, III+ und II

hidden crack

45 m, II und III

upper pinnacle
on ridge

SU

pinnacles
on ridge

40 m, III+

SU

35 m, II

loose

via ferrata

tunnel exit

III+	200 mH
	7 pitches
	2 hours
	1 ½ hours
P	Rif. Auronzo
	1 ¾ hours

E. S.

BOSCONERO AND MEZZODI

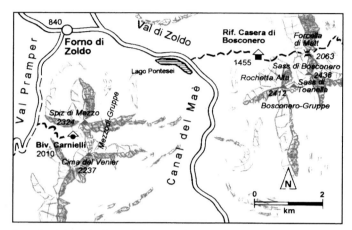

The Bosconero and Mezzodi Groups are two of the secret venues hidden deep in the Zoldo Dolomites in the eastern part of the range. Although, in clear conditions, the Bosconero group can be seen clearly from Cortina d'Ampezzo, rising as sharply-defined, chalk-white teeth of rock, they only attracted the attentions of the climbers relatively recently. The main thrust of development was in the 1960s and 1970s and this despite the fact that the big faces like Rocchetta Alta attain Tre Cime proportions. But though they have the scale, they do not have the fame so that during weekdays one is left to enjoy them in a paradise of peace and quiet, before the weekend climbers from Belluno arrive to play.

The point of departure for the routes in this area is also a little piece of paradise as Rifugio Casera di Bosconero (1455m) is beautifully situated in a clearing below the West Face of Rocchetta Alta. The hut sleeps 40 and during the summer months offers a kindly and simple hospitality. To watch Fillipo the sumpter-mule and the dwarf goat Theresa (employed as a lawnmower) playing their hilarious games together with the hut dog completes the picture of this backcountry idyll.

The hut is reached from Forno di Zoldo (840m) in the Mae Valley north-west of Longarone (campsite, and the best valley base for the whole region). The picturesque and varied approach path starts at Lago di Pontesi (signpost) kilometres down the valley from Forno.

The walls of the Bosconero offer few easier climbs and even these are quite demanding, requiring competence on often loose and vegetated alpine terrain.

From the wonderful wild country of the Mezzodi Group we have selected only one route: the "Schleierkante of the Zoldo Dolomites", the North-West Arête of Spiz di Mezzo. The point of departure for this climb is Bivacco Carnielli (2010m), which perches like an eagle's nest, wild and remote, atop a pine-clad shoulder below the West Face of Spiz di Mezzo. This is an area that will appeal to those with a romantic streak.

67 SASS DI BOSCONERO   2436m

North-West Arête, "Antispigolo" (Pretto/De Pellegrini) IV+

Although the "Antispigolo" is one of the easier routes in the Bosconero Group it is still a long and arduous climb and should not be underestimated. It climbs the arête of a series of three stacked pillars running up the North-West Face of Sass di Bosconero. This airy itinerary is mainly on very solid rock and the less steep sections are relatively free of wear and tear. The best rock is always to be found right on the edge of the steep arête where the climbing is often thrillingly exposed. Those who seek to avoid the issue by climbing the rather average face away from the arête will be robbing themselves of this pleasurable experience.

⚒   L. Pretto, Bruno De Pellegrini.   11 July 1964.

🔎   Odd belay and protection pegs on the harder pitches. Nuts and slings essential. 600m.

🏠   Rifugio Casera di Bosconero (1455m). From the car-park at Lago Pontesei, follow the way-marked path to the hut. 90 minutes.

↗   Follow the path to Forcella dell Matt to the start of the gully leading up into the notch. Bear right over broken ground to reach the grassy plinth below and in front of the "Antispigolo".

E   Start at the highest point of the plinth.

R   The West Face of Sass di Bosconero is arranged into three obvious pillars with prominent arêtes. The route starts up the edge of the right-hand and smallest pillar. Where the arête peters out go left a few metres along a ledge and climb 50m to a system of narrow ledges. Traverse 90m left along the ledges to gain the arête of the middle pillar. Climb straight up the edge of this pillar for 5 pitches to reach a rubble-covered ledge. Go left 80m to reach the next arête. Climb it on its left hand side to the summit (2 pitches) (topo p. 156).

↘   Follow the climbers' path down into Forcella de la Toanella. Scramble down the Toanella Gully (signposted) and back to the hut.

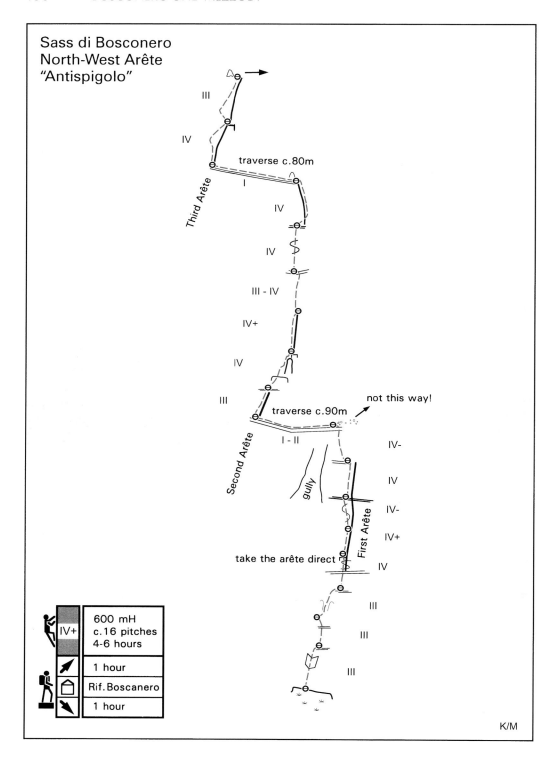

Sass di Bosconero
North-West Arête
"Antispigolo"

III

IV

traverse c.80m

Third Arête

I

IV

IV

III - IV

IV+

IV

III

traverse c.90m

not this way!

I - II

IV-

Second Arête

gully

IV

IV-

First Arête

IV+

take the arête direct

IV

III

III

III

600 mH c.16 pitches 4-6 hours
1 hour
Rif. Boscanero
1 hour

IV+

K/M

68 ROCCHETTA ALTA   2412m

N.W. Arête, "Spigolo Strobel" (Menardi/Lorenzi/Da Pozzo/Zardini) VII–

The "Spigolo Strobel", first climbed by members of the Ampezzo "Scoiattoli" group and named after Albino "Strobel" Michielli, is certainly among the most beautiful of the harder arêtes in the Dolomites. Twelve pitches long, and every one of them cast from the same mould: few of them easier than grade VI, all on very compact, solid rock and, with the exception of the entry pitches, no chossy interludes to spoil the flow. Such wonderful consistency in a route is not found very often! Here is crack and corner climbing in every conceivable variation, while the overhang on the crux pitch requires both skill and strength to surmount. The fact that 500 metres of grade VI climbing is no easy stroll soon makes itself felt and the route provides a stern test of stamina. For those at home with hard grade VI climbing, this is the route for you!

☒ Bruno Menardi, Lorenzo & S. Lorenzi, Luciano Da Pozzo, Giusto Zardini. 14–15 June 1964.

🗝 Belay and protection pegs in-situ. Nuts required. Take at least 15 quick-draws. 600m.

⌂ Rifugio Casera di Bosconero (1455m). Reached in 90 minutes using the path from Lago Pontesei (parking).

↗ Follow the Forcella Toanella path to below Rocchetta Alta. Scramble up rightwards to gain a niche in the gully between the North-West Arête and the West Buttress.

E The climb starts in the deep gash at the foot of a chimney leading up to a ledge (c. 120m, II–III). The real difficulties begin at the ledge.

R Follow a line just right of the obvious North-West Arête (topo p.158).

↘ From the top of the last pitch, scramble up the right-hand gully (or its left edge) for about 100m to a notch. Either continue up and right to the summit (it is a long way!) or traverse east along terraces towards Sasso Toanello. As soon as Sasso Toanello comes into view, start traversing down towards the lowest stand of pines. Descend through these and down-climb approx. 50m to a larger terrace. This terrace leads into the gully between Rocchetta Alta and Sasso Toanello. Descend the gully and return to the hut.

Rocchetta Alta
North-West Arête
"Spigalo Strobel"

c.200m to North Summit

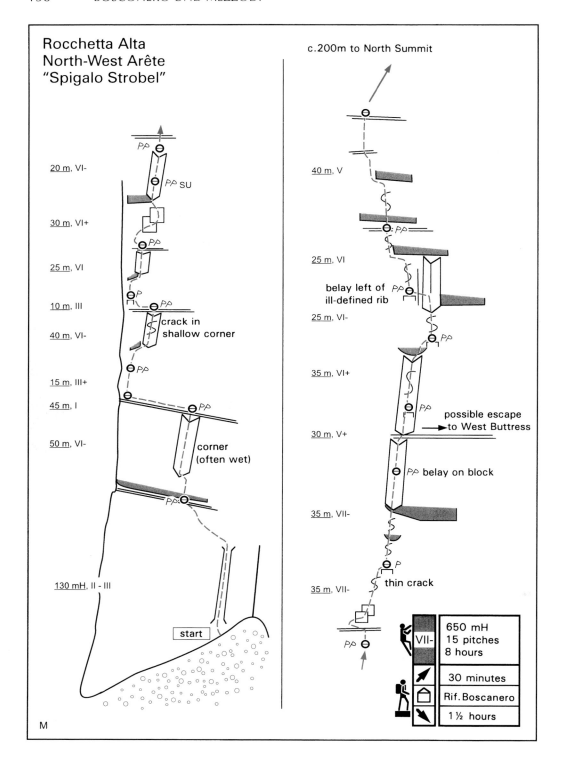

20 m, VI-

30 m, VI+

25 m, VI

10 m, III

40 m, VI-   crack in
                 shallow corner

15 m, III+

45 m, I

50 m, VI-   corner
                 (often wet)

130 mH, II - III

start

M

40 m, V

25 m, VI

belay left of
ill-defined rib

25 m, VI-

35 m, VI+

possible escape
to West Buttress

30 m, V+

belay on block

35 m, VII-

thin crack

35 m, VII-

| 650 mH |
| 15 pitches |
| 8 hours |
| 30 minutes |
| Rif. Boscanero |
| 1½ hours |

VII-

69 SPIZ DI MEZZO   2324m

North-West Arête (Gianeselli/Somavilla/Viel) V+

The North-West Arête of the Spiz di Mezzo is an uncompromisingly steep climb which, from the point of view of aesthetics and unity of line, bears favourable comparison with the "Schleierkante" of Cima della Madonna. The quality of the climbing is also frequently compared to that paradigm of Dolomite rock-climbing but the comparison does seem a mite too euphoric, since the climbing on Spiz di Mezzo is technically much more difficult and the whole atmosphere far wilder, more remote and serious than the oft-climbed Schleierkante. The rock is steep, compact and highly featured and only shows its rather unpleasant side on the entry pitches. Varied and at times very steep crack and corner climbing predominates, combining on the central section to give several outstandingly beautiful pitches.

Gianni Gianeselli, Piero Somavilla, G. Viel. 13 August 1967.

Some belay and protection pegs in-situ. Nuts obligatory, plus a small selection of pitons.

Bivacco Carnielli (2010m). From Forno di Zoldo, follow the road into Val Pramper as far as the barrier. From here, take the narrow path up and right to the hut – 2 hours.

From Bivacco Carnielli, walk below the West Face of Spiz di Mezzo to a kind of rocky pulpit directly below the North-West Arête.

Start at twin parallel cracks to the right of the arête. Climb rock steps via the left-hand, more prominent crack. Several possible lines at the start.

Stay on the right hand side of the arête all the way (topo p.160).

From the summit, descend the South Arête towards a hollow between Spiz di Mezzo and Spiz Sud. Abseil 20m into the gap. Go across a few metres to a cairn and make two 25m abseils down a chimney to the west. Down-climb (or abseil 20m) and cross a rock spur between two gullies. Climb down the right-hand gully and bear left to gain the terrace and the bivouac.

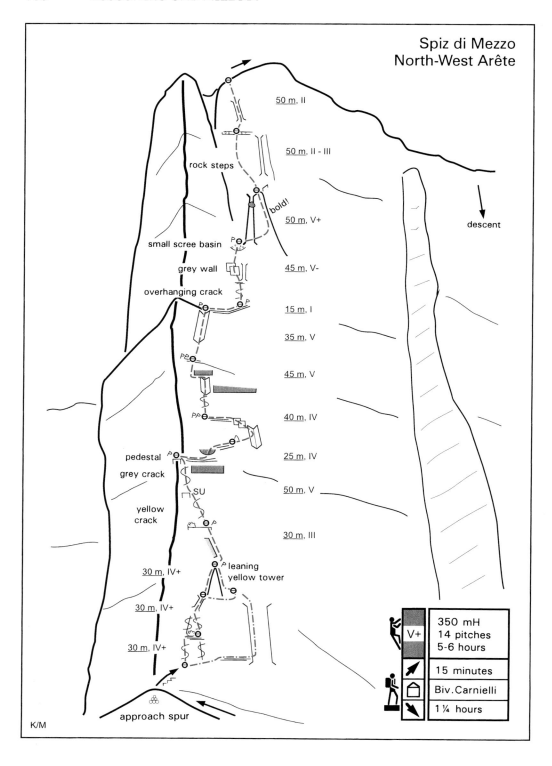

Spiz di Mezzo
North-West Arête

50 m, II

50 m, II - III

rock steps

bold!

50 m, V+

descent

small scree basin

grey wall   45 m, V-

overhanging crack

15 m, I

35 m, V

45 m, V

40 m, IV

pedestal   25 m, IV

grey crack

SU   50 m, V

yellow
crack

30 m, III

leaning
yellow tower

30 m, IV+

30 m, IV+

30 m, IV+

approach spur

V+	350 mH
	14 pitches
	5-6 hours
	15 minutes
	Biv.Carnielli
	1¼ hours

K/M

(previous page) The fifth pitch (V–) of "Pillar Rib" on Tofana's South Face Buttress 2 (Rt. 44). This fine and sustained grade VI– climb was first pioneered in 1946 by Ettore Costantini and Luigi Ghedina. It provides a very worthwhile alternative to the adjoining, more celebrated, "Pilastro".

(right) The West Face of Piccola Lagazuoi, close to the Valparola Pass, offers the 250-metre "Via M. Speziale" (Rt. 37). Its three initial pitches on water-washed rock are particularly fine, notably the grade V second pitch seen here.

(above) The steep chimney/crack pitch (V–) leading to the upper crest of the "Fiames Arête". This is Cortina's local classic climb (Rt. 51), a very bold ascent when first done (1909) by Francesco Jori and Käthe Bröske. *Photo: Rudi Lindner*

(right) The Pomagagnon cliffs north of Cortina. The "Fiames Arête", sharply etched by the evening sun, is on the left

The South Face (right side) of Marmolada D'Ombretta (3347m) with "Don Quixote" (Rt. 31) finishing up the spur right of the obvious long gully right of the summit peaks: Numbers of harder routes are to the right and off picture to the left including the celebrated "Fisch" (VII, 1981) that finishes near the summit (cable-car station, see p76). *Photo: Tom Prentice*

(above) The long, "Antispigolo" of Sass di Boscanero (Rt. 67) provides over 500m of consistent grade IV arête climbing. Here, Anette Köhler climbs the first arête pitch above the initial terrace.

(left) The South-East Faces of Cima Ovest, Cima Grande and Cima Piccola (Rts. 60 and 63). The "Yellow Edge" is the line of light and shade on the right.

(right) The critical 40m-traverse on the South Face of Torre Venezia in the Monte Civetta massif (Rt.74). Attilio Tissi (with Giovanni Andrich and Attilio Bortoli) led this grade VI pitch which proved the key to a great climb. *Photo: Rollo Steffens*

(left) The "Grey Piller" of Monte Mulaz (Rt. 76) is a tough, ten-pitch free climb in the Pala group. Hard cracks on this second pitch (VI–)give access to a descending leftward traverse to the crux corner (VI).

(right) On the "Guides Route" of Crozzon di Brenta (Rt. 59) approaching the overhanging crack where the difficulties begin to accumulate.

(overleaf) The view from the "Guides Route" on the Crozzon di Brenta. Rifugio Brentei is seen below, set strategically in the centre of a magnificently scupted cirque amidst the great Brenta peaks.

MOIAZZA AND CIVETTA

The Civetta and Moiazza regions are independent yet closely related mountain groups. The Moiazza is really the southern part of the Civetta, since the two are separated only by a gap on the ridge. Their characters, however, could hardly be more contrasting. The face that Monte Civetta presents to the world is its broad, 1000m high North-West Face, rising in an unbroken sweep of wall above the village of Alleghe.

The Moiazza has a less sharply defined profile; here, the view is dominated more by broad, relatively randomly assembled sweeps of rock. Perhaps this is one reason why it has

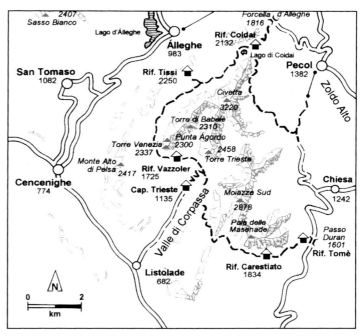

remained relatively unknown as a climbing area to other than local climbers. Yet in Pala delle Masenade we have an objective which measures up in every respect to the demands of the modern climber. Here, the focus is firmly on the climbing and not the summit. Approaches and descents are short and unproblematic and the sunny walls offer solid, hold-covered rock. The routes described can be done as one-day undertakings from Passo Duran.

On the southern side of the Civetta Group group the picture is dominated by such imposing peaks as Torre Trieste and Torre Venezia. On the routes of Monte Civetta's North-West Face what counts is sheer size and seriousness, rather than unfettered climbing enjoyment.* Things are quite different on the south side, however. Torre Venezia is a dream mountain with routes to match, while the elegant climbing on the South Arête of Torre di Babele is almost without equal. Indeed the whole area around Rifugio Vazzoler (1725m) – the usual point of departure for all the routes described here – is one of the most idyllic spots in the entire Dolomites with a marvellous garden of alpine flowers right next to the hut.

---

* English-speaking climbers may be surprised that the great routes on Monte Civetta's North Face receive no attention in this guide – such classics as the Phillip/Flamm, the Andrich/Fae, the Aste/Sussati and the Solleder/Lettenbauer will be on the agenda of any serious big wall enthusiast, as indeed would be the Cassin/Ratti routes on Torre Trieste and Cima Ovest (Tre Cime group). Memmel and Köhler are adamant in leaving such climbs out of their selection for the reasons given above – their stress is towards climbing quality and sporting enjoyment rather than challenge – a clear indicator of the change of attitudes that has evolved in recent years.

70 PALA DELLE MASENADE   2413m

S. Face, "Colatoio Nero" (Decima/Brustolon/Della Santa/Todeso) V+

Pala delle Masenade is a wide, massive wall of rock rising up opposite the Cariestiato Hut. On its south-western arête the water has carved out the flute of "Colatoio Nero", accomplishing much painstaking and detailed work on behalf of the climbers. Here is to be found nice little *goutes d'eau* finger pockets, rough, juggy flakes and solid threads. The route, thus naturally 'doctored' is, in dry conditions, one of the most worthwhile in the Dolomites. There is rock as solid as one could possibly dream of, the line logical and positioned to catch the sun. The difficulties are homogeneous, the approach short, the descent unproblematic and the climbing offers many splendid and varied pitches, often in wonderfully airy positions.

L. Decima, P. C. Brustolon, Sonia Della Santa and F. Todesco. 8 October 1976.

Some belay and protection pegs in-situ. Take nuts and slings for the threads!

Rifugio Carestiato (1834m), reached in 45 minutes by a path from the top of Passo Duran (Rifugio Tome).

Follow the path in the direction of Rifugio Vazzoler. The path traverses beneath the face. Leave it just before the two tower-like pillars in front of the main mass of the wall and head straight up (no path) to the start of the route.

Start on the slabby rock to the right of the initial corner.

The South-West Face of Pala delle Masenade has two parallel towers at its base. Above these towers is an area of the face with big yellow overhangs. To their right, a water-worn scoop runs down the ill-defined arête. This "couloir" is reached by climbing the initial corner pitch.

The route ends at a small water-worn basin with a grassy terrace leading out left (west). This terrace is followed until a vague path leads down to the south.

Pala delle Masenade
South Face
"Colatoio Nero"

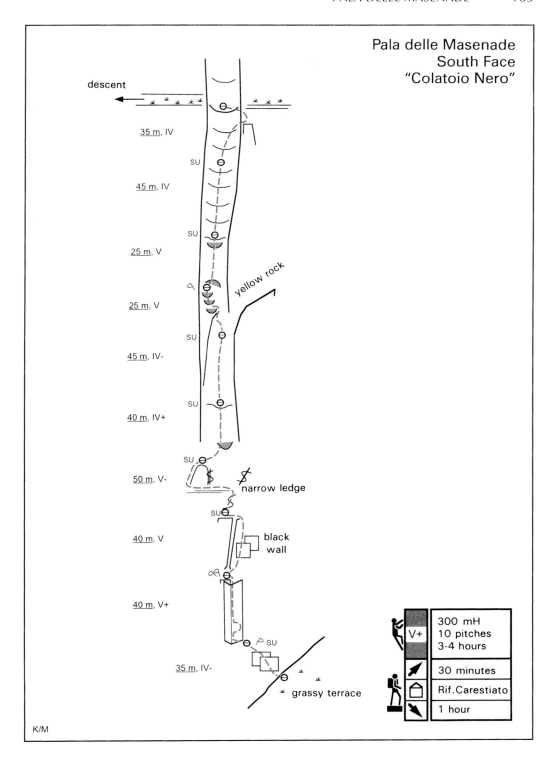

descent

35 m, IV

SU

45 m, IV

SU

25 m, V

25 m, V

yellow rock

SU

45 m, IV-

SU

40 m, IV+

SU

50 m, V-

narrow ledge

SU

40 m, V

black
wall

40 m, V+

SU

35 m, IV-

grassy terrace

V+	300 mH
10 pitches
3-4 hours
	30 minutes
⌂	Rif. Carestiato
	1 hour

K/M

71 PALA DELLE MASENADE 2413m

South-East Face, "Soldà" (Soldà/Kraus) VI

Viewed from Rifugio Carestiato, the broad South-East Face of Pala delle Masenade looks very steep and compact, so much so that it appears at first glance unimaginable that a classic grade VI route could find a way up this wall. Indeed, the "Solda" is certainly no give-away. Almost consistent grade VI difficulties require a considerable degree of climbing ability and a cool leader's head, e.g. on the steep pitches up through the water-streaks or the following rope length where after the traverse an overhang has to be free-climbed in a very airy and exposed position. The pitches comprising the middle section of the route are particularly fine – powerful technical climbing on good quality rock. The pitch immediately below the second terrace forms the heart and soul of the route – what a pity the climb does not continue in the same style; instead the rock deteriorates slightly towards the top.

Gino Soldà, Hans Kraus.   20 August 1959.

All necessary belay and protection pegs in situ.

Rifugio Carestiato (1834m), reached in 45 minutes along a waymarked path from the top of the Passo Duran (Rifugio Tome).

Follow the path in the direction of Rifugio Vazzoler for about 10 minutes. Leave the path and head to the right up a scree gully containing some big boulders.

Start at the apex of the scree gully, where it meets the cliff, at a rightwards slanting, easy-angled corner ending directly below the big, black water-streaks.

To the right of the South-East Arête the face is marked by two water-streaks. The route follows the left hand of the two water-streaks and traverses left beneath a belt of roofs.

Do not climb right up to the summit but follow the wide top-out ledge down to join the "Via ferrata Constantini". Descend this.

Pala delle Masenade
South-East Face
"Soldà"

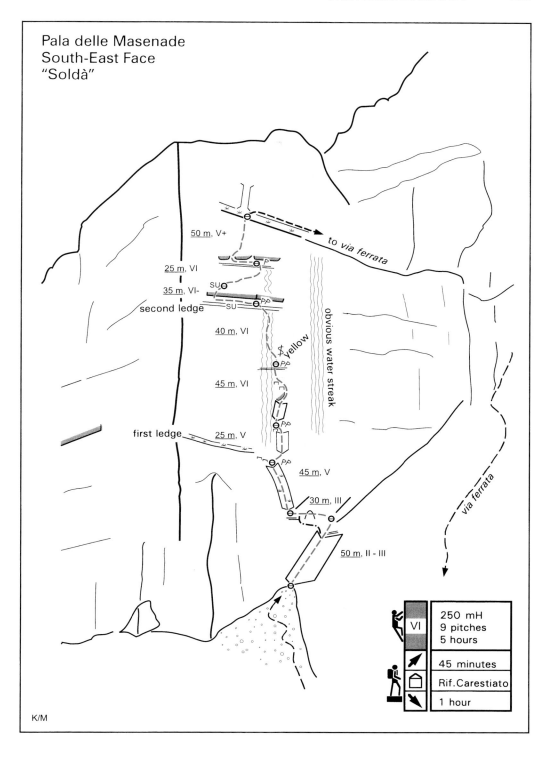

50 m, V+

to via ferrata

25 m, VI

35 m, VI-

second ledge

SU

P

SU

PP

40 m, VI

yellow

PP

obvious water streak

45 m, VI

PP

first ledge

25 m, V

PP

45 m, V

30 m, III

50 m, II - III

via ferrata

VI

250 mH
9 pitches
5 hours

45 minutes

Rif. Carestiato

1 hour

K/M

72 PUNTA AGORDO   2300m

W. Face, "Agordo Dièdre" (Da Roit/Zanvettor/Facciotto/Penasa) V

Punta Agordo is separated from the neighbouring Torre Venezia by a large gully but does not have the appearance of a prominent indepen-dent summit. An obvious point of reference is the rocky shoulder formed by the South-West Arête below the summit headwall. The prominent feature of the "Agordo Dièdre", the best-known and nicest route on the mountain, reaches this terrace direct. The actual corner climbing is relatively short-lived and the continuity of the route as a whole is rather spoiled by the rubble-strewn shoulder. But the rock in the corner is very compact and smoothed by the tireless action of the water and stonefall, which makes for interesting climbing and quite sparse protection.

Armando (Tama) Da Roit, Carlo Zanvettor, Mario Facciotto, Attilio Penasa. 1941.

Some belay and protection pegs in place. The crux pitch is poorly protected. Nuts and slings required.

Rifugio Vazzoler (1725m), approached from Listolade along a little road to the Capanna Trieste (possible parking). Follow the track to the hut. 90 minutes. See p.170.

From Rifugio Vazzoler, head towards Rifugio Tissi as far as a meadow strewn with large boulders. Follow the climbers' path up and right to the rock plinth at the base of the wall leading to the corner proper.

The real climbing starts at a crack to the right of the angle of the dièdre.

Climb the dièdre to the rubble-covered terrace. Zig zag up to the summit headwall and climb it by a double crack.

Go 10m north to a pine tree. Abseil 15m into the gap between Punta Agordo and the tower to the north. Climb the tower for a short way and traverse across ledges on the west flank to a tunnel leading to the east side. Descend a gully (II) to where a traverse can be made across towards Forcella di Pelsa. Beyond this notch is the junction with the normal descent route from Torre Venezia; see diagram p.172.

Punta Agordo
West Face
"Agordo Dièdre"

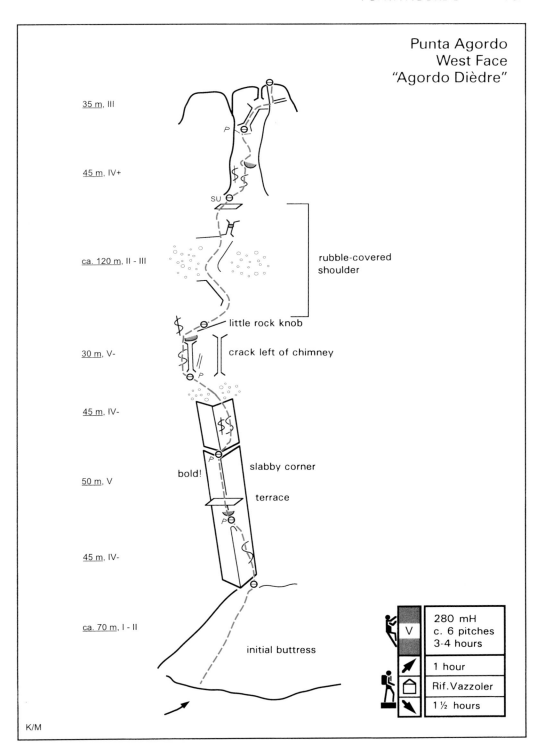

35 m, III

45 m, IV+

SU

ca. 120 m, II - III

rubble-covered
shoulder

little rock knob

30 m, V-

crack left of chimney

45 m, IV-

50 m, V

bold!

slabby corner

terrace

45 m, IV-

ca. 70 m, I - II

initial buttress

V	280 mH
	c. 6 pitches
	3-4 hours
	1 hour
	Rif. Vazzoler
	1 ½ hours

K/M

73 TORRE VENEZIA   2337m

South-West Arête, "Andrich/Fae" V+

Up beyond the rural idyll of the Vazzoler, Torre Venezia rises to an impressive height. Those climbers wishing to approach the South-West Arête from the Vazzoler Hut will first have to circumnavigate half of the mountain, a trip which provides a good opportunity for a detailed study of the grandiose South Face. The arête itself is not very long but here not one metre of climbing is wasted on banalities. The serious business starts right from the first belay; after all, you are already right in the middle of the face, thanks to the entry terrace. Those hoping to enjoy the exposed climbing with some measure of relaxation should be completely certain they are up to climbing at this level of difficulty. On the upper part of the route, a celebratory corner line on iron-hard rock awaits – enjoyable bridging guaranteed!

☗ Alvise Andrich, Ernani Fae.   17 August 1934.

⚲ Sufficient belay and protection pegs in-situ.

⌂ Rifugio Vazzoler (1725m), approached from Listolade along a little road to Capanna Trieste (possible parking). Follow the track to the hut. 90 minutes. See p. 170.

↗ Take the Rifugio Tissi path to a meadow beneath the West Faces of Punta Agordo and Torre Venezia. Scramble up the gully between the two to gain a narrow pine-covered ledge leading rightwards onto the West Face of Torre Venezia.

E Start at the foot of a crack at the end of the ledge.

R The lower part stays just right of the ill-defined arête. Further up, climb the prominent corner with the black water-streaks, leading to the "Circular Terrace" below the summit area.

↘ The descent (marked in red) is an abseil piste with ring pegs. Follow the Circular Terrace round to the left and onto the NNE Face. Descend 10m to the first anchor followed by six medium length abseils. Continue into the gully between Torre Venezia and Punta Agordo. Descend the gully (two 10m abseils). Go right across ledges to a tree-covered shoulder and down this to the hut. See diagram p.172.

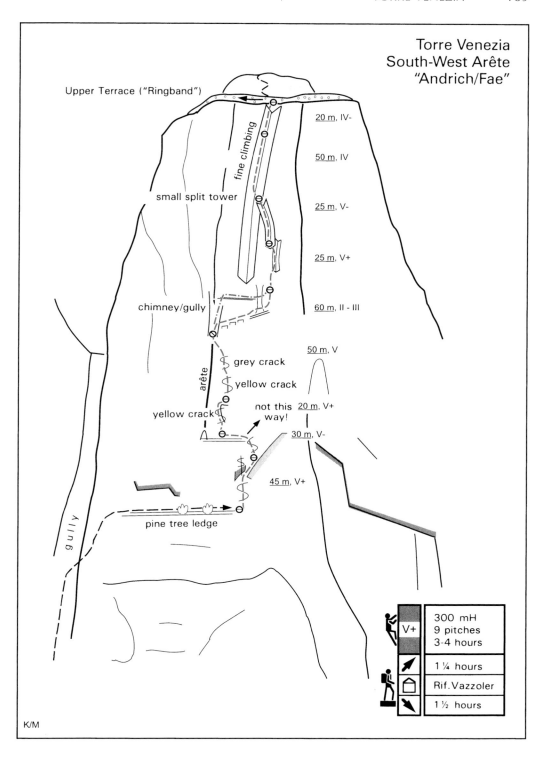

Torre Venezia
South-West Arête
"Andrich/Fae"

Upper Terrace ("Ringband")

fine climbing

20 m, IV-

50 m, IV

small split tower

25 m, V-

25 m, V+

chimney/gully

60 m, II - III

arête

grey crack

50 m, V

yellow crack

not this 20 m, V+
way!

yellow crack

30 m, V-

45 m, V+

pine tree ledge

gully

K/M

V+ | 300 mH
9 pitches
3-4 hours

1 ¼ hours

Rif. Vazzoler

1 ½ hours

74 TORRE VENEZIA   2337m

South Face, "Tissi" (Tissi/Andrich/Bortoli) VI–

The "Tissi" route on Torre Venezia was for many years rated as one of the classic Extremes in the Dolomites. It was helped to the reputation by the crux pitch, the "40 metre traverse" (actually only 30 metres). Traverses are always just the thing for justifying a route's reputation, particularly when they take such a steep and exposed bit of wall as this one. What at first glance looks hard, turns out to be merely airy gymnastics on splendidly positive and solid holds. You just have to take care not create too much rope drag. In addition to this celebrated traverse, interest is also to be found on the steep corner preceding it, to say nothing of the rest of the climb. Indeed the difficulties are pretty sustained right up to the last pitch, which deposits you, a little the worse for wear, on the "Circular Terrace". The rock quality is excellent, if a little grassy on the initial pitches.

☒ Attilio Tissi, Giovanni Andrich, Attilio Bortoli.   1933.

⚲ All necessary belay and protection pegs in-situ, the latter plentiful on the two crux pitches. Some thread belays – take some long slings!

⌂ Rifugio Vazzoler (1725m), approached from Listolade (682m). From the centre of the village a little metalled road branches off to the left into the Corpassa Valley (coming from Cecenighe this is signposted). This leads up to the Capanna Trieste (parking). Follow the track to the hut. 90 minutes.

↗ From the Vazzoler Hut, head for the Rifugio Tissi until below the South Face of the Torre Venezia. A climbers' path over scree leads to the foot of the Face.

🄴 Start just right of the arête bounding the prominent South Dièdre (which leads up directly into the zone of roofs).

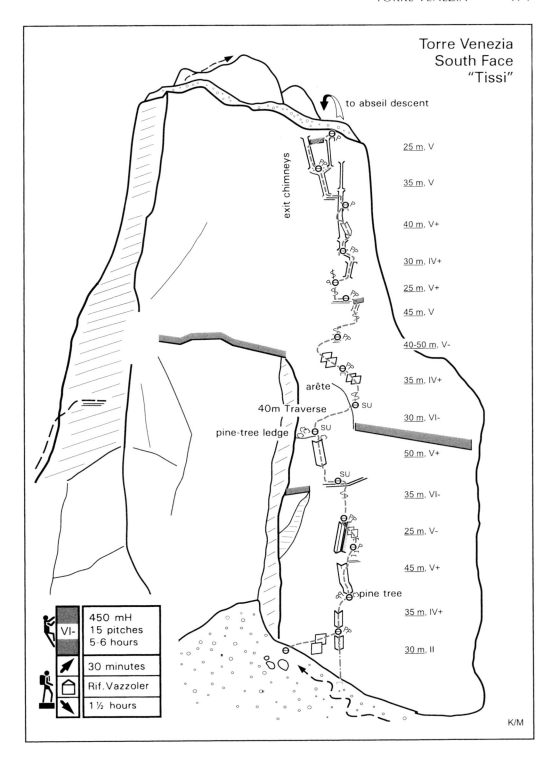

Torre Venezia
South Face
"Tissi"

to abseil descent

exit chimneys

25 m, V

35 m, V

40 m, V+

30 m, IV+

25 m, V+

45 m, V

40-50 m, V-

35 m, IV+

arête

40m Traverse

SU

30 m, VI-

pine-tree ledge   SU

50 m, V+

SU

35 m, VI-

25 m, V-

45 m, V+

pine tree

35 m, IV+

30 m, II

450 mH
15 pitches
5-6 hours

VI-

30 minutes

Rif. Vazzoler

1 ½ hours

K/M

R Climb the middle part of the South Face, right of the prominent South Dièdre leading to the belt of roofs at half height. The famous "40 metre traverse" arrives at this level. After the traverse the route works a way up to gain the obvious chimney system, leading to on the "Circular Terrace". Those wishing to carry on to the summit should follow the "Circular Terrace" round the North Side to gain and climb the South-West Arête (I).

Follow the "Circular Terrace" round to the right and onto the NNE Face. The descent via the Normal Route is marked in red and equipped with solid ring pegs; see p. 168.

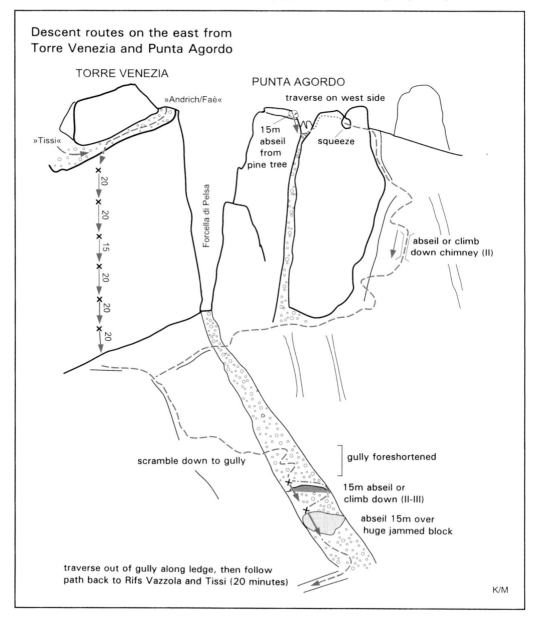

Descent routes on the east from
Torre Venezia and Punta Agordo

TORRE VENEZIA

PUNTA AGORDO

»Andrich/Faè«

traverse on west side

»Tissi«

15m abseil from pine tree

squeeze

Forcella di Pelsa

× 20
× 20
× 15
× 20
× 20
× 20

abseil or climb down chimney (II)

scramble down to gully

gully foreshortened

15m abseil or climb down (II-III)

abseil 15m over huge jammed block

traverse out of gully along ledge, then follow path back to Rifs Vazzola and Tissi (20 minutes)

K/M

75 TORRE DI BABELE   2310m

South Arête, "Soldà" VI–

The elegant line of the "Soldà" route on the Torre di Babele does not actually climb the lower section of the South Arête but takes the gully wall to its left. The arête proper is gained via an obvious ledge halfway up the face (there are several such ledges and, as a result, just as many opportunities to go off-route). If the climbing up to the ledge is pleasantly engaging, thereafter it is quite simply fantastic: varied, technically demanding, steep cracks, corners and face climbing on splendidly compact limestone. The difficulties should not, however, be underestimated, since the climbing is 'free' in the truest sense of the word – protection pitons are few and far between. On the descent, the mountain then shows its disintegrating side. It is a relatively unpleasant descent, with danger from stonefall in places, particularly when several parties are out and about.

- Gino and Italo Soldà.   1937.

- All necessary belay pegs in-situ. Pitons for protection something of a rarity, especially on the upper section! Take nuts.

- Rifugio Vazzoler (1725m), approached from Listolade along a little road to Capanna Trieste (possible parking). Follow a track to the hut (90 minutes, see p.170).

- From Rifugio Vazzoler, follow the Rifugio Tissi path briefly until an obvious little path heads off to the woods on the right leading to Val Cantoni and the gully between the Gnomo and Torre di Babele. Ascend the gully until a traverse line right leads out along a ledge to a large jammed block.

- Start just before, or right on top of, this jammed block.

- Climb up just left of the actual arête. At half height, go right along a ledge to gain a crack and corner system just right of the arête. Follow it to the South Shoulder (topo p. 174).

- Descend to the west from a little notch on the shoulder, keeping right (II) and abseil into the gully between the Gnomo and Cima dell'Elefante. Scramble down the gully into Val Cantoni and back to the base of the cliff.

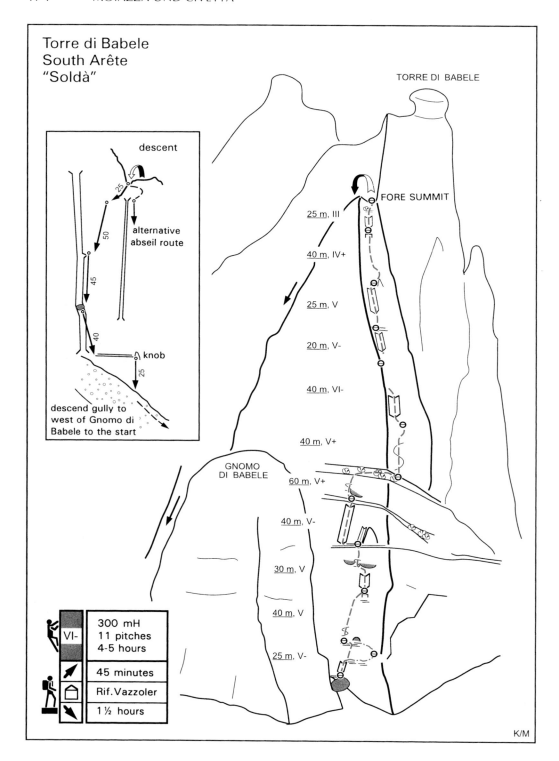

Torre di Babele
South Arête
"Soldà"

TORRE DI BABELE

descent

25

50

alternative
abseil route

45

40

knob

25

descend gully to
west of Gnomo di
Babele to the start

FORE SUMMIT

25 m, III

40 m, IV+

25 m, V

20 m, V-

40 m, VI-

40 m, V+

GNOMO
DI BABELE

60 m, V+

40 m, V-

30 m, V

40 m, V

25 m, V-

VI-	300 mH 11 pitches 4-5 hours	
	45 minutes	
	Rif. Vazzoler	
	1½ hours	

K/M

PALA

The Pala region is among the best areas in the Dolomites for the middle-grade climber.* Hardly anywhere else will you find so many 'big', worthwhile routes in the mid-range of difficulty. The price for this climbing enjoyment has to be paid in sweat and toil on the walk-in, however, as the mountains here are not close to the main roads. By way of compensation, the Pala rock is of unique quality. Mostly very sound and lavishly covered in holds, it has a light and airy feel to it, like a well-stirred cream pudding poured from its mould and left to harden, with countless air bubbles which have collapsed to form splendid finger pockets and threads. The structure of the crags is very uniform and there are few obvious features to aid orientation. This sometimes makes the climbing a little ill-defined but, as a rule, one simply has to choose

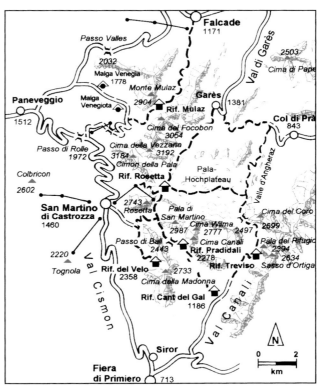

the nicest of several eminently climbable possibilities. One odd feature of the Pala region is the mist, which likes to rise from the Po river plateau to play hide and seek with the mountains and consequently make a complete fool of the climber. There are days when the mornings are so overcast one would swear that bad weather is on the way and then at midday the sun shines mockingly from clear blue skies. The alternative version exists, too, of course, and this can prove to be far more unpleasant, since most of the Pala peaks have long and, at times, complicated descents, another reason why this is no place for alpine novices. The routes described here are not really possible as one-day excursions, unless of course one counts oneself among that species of alpine athlete who derives pleasure from hard and fast walking.

The most important and most centrally located valley base is San Martino di Castrozza (campsite, Rosetta funicular). The tourist trap of Val Canali, in the southern Pala, is similarly endowed with a campsite, several guesthouses and cafes and is best approached from Fiera di Primiero. The vehicular track to Passo Cereda goes straight there. Rifugio Treviso, situated in Val Canali, is an ideal base for the routes in this area.

* Here the authors are referring to climbs of IV, V and VI–. Putting difficulties to one side, in terms of length, remoteness and seriousness the climbs should still be treated as major undertakings.

76 MONTE MULAZ   2904m

West Face, "Grey Pillar" (Mayr/Koch) VI

The compact, grey West Face of Monte Mulaz rises straight from the lush green meadows of Val Venegia and one suspects even from a distance that the rock up there must be good – a suspicion that is soon confirmed. Here is high quality limestone with lots of great pockets, comparable to the best rock of the Marmolada's South Face. But the walk-in is long and the actual pleasures rather short-lived. Also, the route is a little disjointed as the difficulties are confined to the first three pitches, although the crux pitch is, in fact, outstanding – a very steep and bold grade VI corner crack. If, after this, you are happy with grade IV territory then the route is to be most warmly recommended. Particularly so since from the summit has a magnificent view.

H. Mayr, M. Koch. 5 August 1956.

All necessary belay pegs and some protection pegs in-situ on the difficult part. On the crux pitch medium-sized nuts are useful for additional protection.

Turn off the Passo Rolle/Passo Valles road and park on the track to Malga Venegia.

From Malga Venegia, walk along the track (closed to vehicles), past Malga Venegiota, until a path leads left to Passo Di Valles. Follow this up to the steep meadows above the trees. Follow a little stream up across the meadows to the foot of the cliffs. Scramble rightwards up grassy rocks to the right of a gully to where it bends sharply to the right. At this point traverse left along a narrow ledge, then go straight up to the first belay.

Start below the huge basin-like depression to the right of the prominent pillar, at the left-hand edge of a deep niche in the wall.

The grey pillar is the logical line up the West Face. Start up a prominent crack system right of the edge of the pillar. After a short right-left dogleg the route joins the arête of the pillar for the upper section.

Descend to the east in the direction of Passo del Mulaz. Then follow the path from Rifugio Mulaz (Rifugio Volpi) back down into Val Venegia.

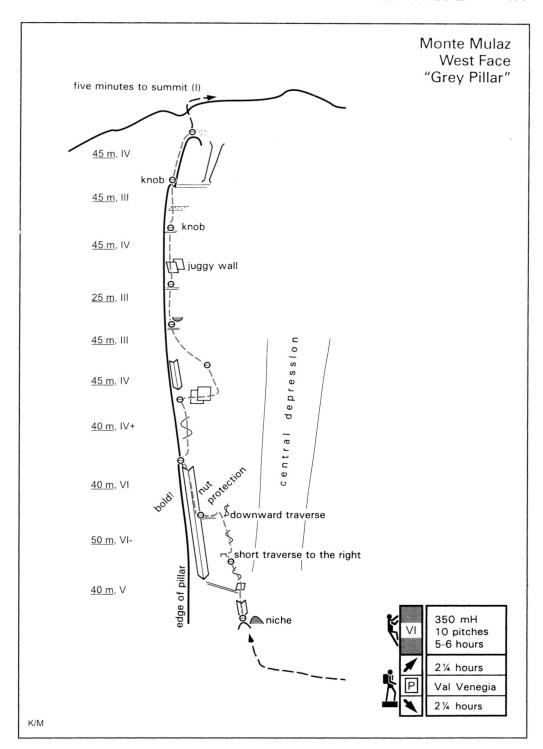

Monte Mulaz
West Face
"Grey Pillar"

five minutes to summit (I)

45 m, IV

knob

45 m, III

knob

45 m, IV

juggy wall

25 m, III

45 m, III

45 m, IV

40 m, IV+

central depression

40 m, VI

bold!   nut protection

downward traverse

50 m, VI-

short traverse to the right

40 m, V

edge of pillar

niche

VI	350 mH 10 pitches 5-6 hours
	2¼ hours
P	Val Venegia
	2¼ hours

K/M

77 CIMA DELLA MADONNA 2733m

North-West Arête, "Schleierkante" (Langes/Merlet) V+

The "Schleierkante" (Bridalveil Arête, also known as the "Scarf Arête" or "Spigolo del Vello") is considered the most beautiful rock climb in the Eastern Alps. An Alpine Mecca, whose rock has amazingly remained relatively unaffected by the passage of the faithful pilgrims. The cloud-piercing line of the route is sublime and the rock is indeed iron-solid and lavishly endowed with good holds, but does this climb in particular deserve such praise. The West Arête of the Ortiga and the "Gran Pilaster" are of comparable quality, yet few of our comrades seem to know that. There appears to be no explanation for this difference in popularity. Nevertheless this is a climb one simply has to have done, an obligation which will at the latest become apparent on viewing the route from the valley.

Günther Langes, Erwin Merlet. 19 July 1920.

All necessary belay and protection pegs in place. Lots of threads!

Rifugio del Velo (2358m). Turn left off the San Martino/Fiera di Primiero road and drive up the track to Rifugio Malga Civertaghe (parking). A path leads on to Rifugio Velo. 2 hours.

Traverse up and left from the hut to join the *via ferrata* leading back left into the gully. Follow it to the foot of the arête.

E Where the *via ferrata* trail goes left climb the buttress for 100m (II). At a shallow ledge turn right to where the wall steepens.

R Climb the crest of the arête. The arête of the first pillar can either be climbed direct or via a crack (the original way).

Descend by the Normal Route (waymarked and equipped with abseil rings). Follow the summit ridge to the "Winkler Chimney". Move down and left to a small rock pulpit with a cemented-in abseil ring. Make two 20m abseils. Climb down the gully, traverse right and go down again to a steep drop; abseil into a notch. Descend the gully on the right to a second gully branching off to the right which is descended to the last steep rock step. Abseil 20m then head back to the hut.

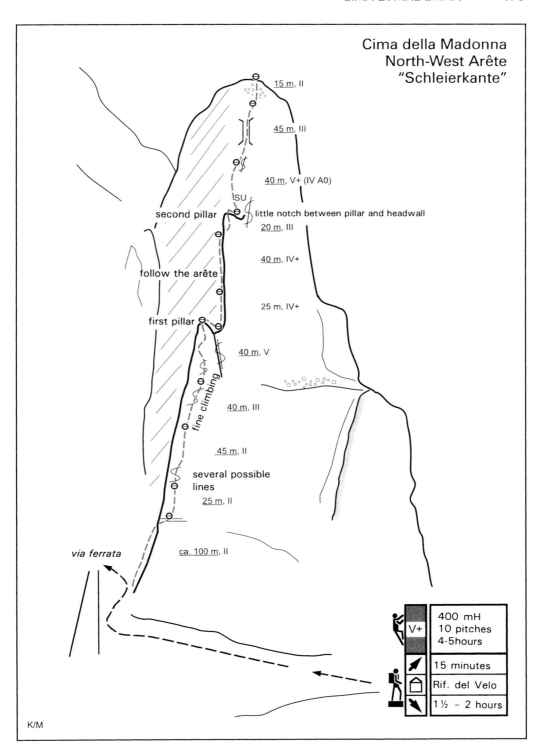

Cima della Madonna
North-West Arête
"Schleierkante"

15 m, II

45 m, III

40 m, V+ (IV A0)

SU

second pillar — little notch between pillar and headwall

20 m, III

40 m, IV+

follow the arête

25 m, IV+

first pillar

40 m, V

fine climbing

40 m, III

45 m, II

several possible
lines

25 m, II

via ferrata

ca. 100 m, II

	V+	400 mH 10 pitches 4-5hours
		15 minutes
		Rif. del Velo
		1 ½ – 2 hours

K/M

78 CIMA CANALI   2900m

West Face, "Buhlriss" (Buhl/Herweg) VI–

The central pillar of the mighty West Face of Cima Canali is split down its entire length by a crack, the "Buhlriss". The climbing is as complete as the line itself: straight as a die, uncompromising and, rather unusually for a crack of this width, elegant, too. With the exception of the crux pitch (an overhanging wall) the climbing is predominantly bridging (the crack soon widening to a chimney). Eleven long pitches, each one more beautiful and exposed than the last, and you stand on the top of the pillar. From here the long route back to the valley begins with the remaining 200m of easy climbing to the summit. The descent from this big mountain is wearisome and complicated. In mist, of the kind which loves to hang around the Pala, or during stormy weather the smiles rapidly disappear. For this reason alone it is well to tackle this magnificent route during settled weather.

Hermann Buhl, Hermann Herweg. 9 September 1950.

Belay and protection pegs in situ. Plenty of threads on the upper part (slings!).

Rifugio Pradidali (2278m). From the Fiera di Primiero/Passo Cereda road, branch off along a little road to the upper Val Canali. Park at the Restaurant Cant del Gal (1186m). Follow Path 709 for about 3 hours to the hut. Alternatively, approach from San Martino di Castrozza via the top station of the Rosetta funicular and the path over Passo di Ball (2 hours).

Up over choss and rubble (no path) between Cima Wilma and Cima Canali and traverse rightwards across ledges onto the West Face.

The start is marked with a cairn and located almost at the end of the ledge, below an overhang which is bounded on its right by a crack. Gain the crack.

Climb the crack/chimney line to the top of the pillar. From here, follow the red markers up easy rocks to the summit.

From the summit, first descend to the east, then follow the South Ridge down to Forcella Figlia della Canali. Down-climb to the left of the big gully of the West Face to the foot of the face (II–III, cairns and red markers) – one 20m abseil obligatory. Two further sections of down-climbing can be descended by 20m abseils, if preferred.

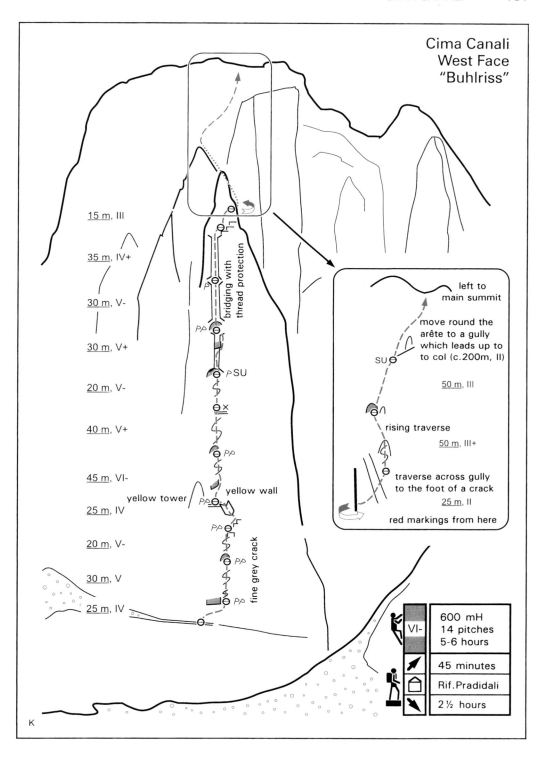

Cima Canali
West Face
"Buhlriss"

15 m, III

35 m, IV+

30 m, V-

30 m, V+

20 m, V-

40 m, V+

45 m, VI-

25 m, IV

20 m, V-

30 m, V

25 m, IV

bridging with
thread protection

ρ

PP

ρ SU

×

PP

yellow tower   yellow wall

PP

PP

PP

PP

fine grey crack

left to
main summit

move round the
arête to a gully
which leads up to
to col (c.200m, II)

SU

50 m, III

rising traverse

50 m, III+

traverse across gully
to the foot of a crack

25 m, II

red markings from here

K

VI-

600 mH
14 pitches
5-6 hours

45 minutes

Rif. Pradidali

2 ½ hours

79 CIMA WILMA   2777m

South-West Arête, "Castiglioni/Detassis" V

Cima Wilma, neighbour of the mighty Cima Canali, dispatches an envoy to the south-west in the shape of a prominent arête, on which Ettore Castiglioni and Bruno Detassis left their mark for all time. The route approaches the impressive overhangs on the arête, only to circumvent them in a most refined fashion and thus gain the big, black, couloir-like corner that drops down from a notch on the ridge between Punta Gretl and the main summit. Particularly delightful are the pitches which flirt with the overhangs on the arête: the juggy grey slabs and the steep cracks which form the link pitches to the "couloir". The climbing in the corner is also entertaining, but the last pitch before the terrace does provide a rather more difficult intermezzo. The ridge continuation tends to lose itself in 'pick your own line' territory where the rock quality also takes a turn for the worse.

⚔ Ettore Castiglioni, Bruno Detassis. 1934.

🛠 Belay and protection pegs generally in-situ. Carry a rack of nuts and some slings. 50m ropes recommended (for the abseils) and check the anchors (normal pitons/slings) before use.

🏠 Rifugio Pradidali (2278m). For approach, see p. 180.

↗ From Rifugio Pradidali, scramble up over debris (no path) between Cima Wilma and Cima Canali and bear left to the foot of the cliffs.

E The start is located right at the base of the South-West Arête, at a little, grey corner. To the left is the bottom of the prominent ramp of the Normal Route.

R Climb up, keeping right of the arête, and into the black couloir, avoiding all the overhangs on the arête on their right. Follow the line of the black couloir to a terrace. Climb easier gullies and grooves to the ridge and up this to the summit.

↘ From the main summit, follow cairns down to the north-west until a traverse right (north) gains the first abseil station. Make six abseils down the west-facing gully (20m, 20m, 40m, 20m, 30m, 20m). Traverse the gully (cairn) and continue with three more abseils down to the west (25m, 25m, 50m). Finally, descend the deep ramp back to the foot of the face (II–III).

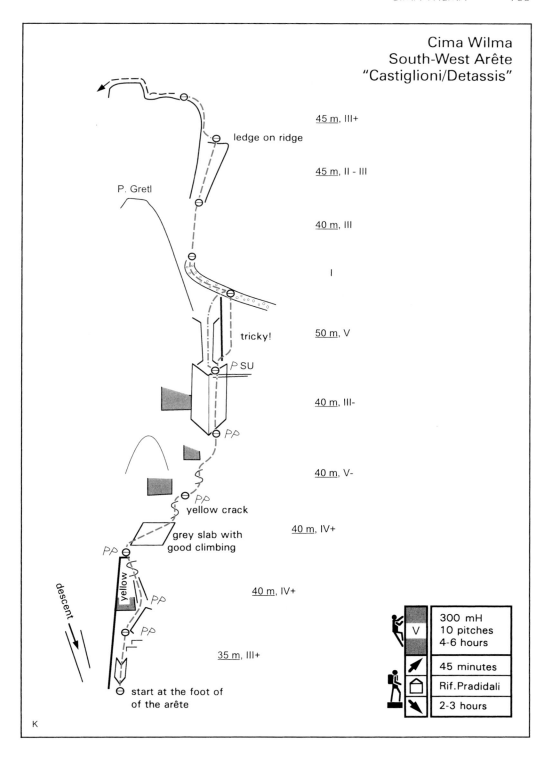

Cima Wilma
South-West Arête
"Castiglioni/Detassis"

45 m, III+

ledge on ridge

45 m, II - III

P. Gretl

40 m, III

I

tricky!   50 m, V

P SU

40 m, III-

PP

40 m, V-

PP
yellow crack

grey slab with   40 m, IV+
good climbing

PP

yellow

descent   40 m, IV+

PP

PP

35 m, III+

start at the foot of
of the arête

V	300 mH 10 pitches 4-6 hours
	45 minutes
	Rif. Pradidali
	2-3 hours

K

80 PALA DI SAN MARTINO   2987m

South-West Pillar, "Gran Pilaster" (Langes/Merlet) IV–

The uniform mass of the soaring South-West Pillar of Pala di San Martino immediately catches the eye when glimpsed from San Martino di Castrozza. The honour implicit in the sound of the name "Gran Pilaster" is thoroughly appropriate, both to the mountain and to the route. When one gazes up at this grandiose pillar of rock it is barely believable that such a feature might be tackled by the competent grade IV climber. It is certainly one of the most beautiful routes at this level of difficulty in the Dolomites. The difficulties are consistently around the lower grade IV or upper grade III level, the climbing is varied and on best quality, juggy Pala rock with plentiful natural protection possibilities, typical of this region. The climb initially takes a 200m chimney with much elegant bridging. The upper section then joins the airy arête of the pillar, a great line climbed on lovely pocketed slabs. The descent, however, is again quite demanding. Long, exposed in places and with complicated route-finding, despite the red marker paint, it requires care and concentration on the grade II terrain. If you are planning to do the route in a single day from the Rosetta lift station you need to be very sure of your abilities at this grade.

⚔ Günther Langes, Erwin Merlet. 24 July 1920.

🗝 Numerous belay and protection pegs in place. Take plenty of slings for threads and belays. Carry a few nuts.

🏠 Rifugio Rosetta (2578m). 5 minutes from the top station of the Rosetta funicular (valley station at San Martino di Castrozza).

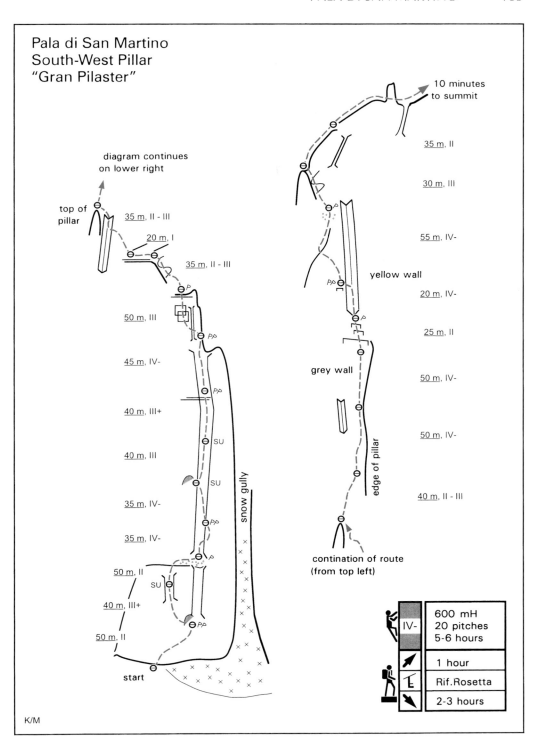

Pala di San Martino
South-West Pillar
"Gran Pilaster"

10 minutes
to summit

diagram continues
on lower right

35 m, II

30 m, III

top of
pillar

35 m, II - III

20 m, I

55 m, IV-

35 m, II - III

yellow wall

20 m, IV-

50 m, III

25 m, II

45 m, IV-

grey wall

50 m, IV-

40 m, III+

40 m, III

SU

50 m, IV-

SU

35 m, IV-

snow gully

edge of pillar

40 m, II - III

35 m, IV-

50 m, II

SU

contination of route
(from top left)

40 m, III+

50 m, II

600 mH
IV-   20 pitches
5-6 hours

1 hour

Rif. Rosetta

start

2-3 hours

K/M

From Rifugio Rosetta, follow the Rifugio Pradidali path, crossing the high plateau to Passo di Roda. Cross the col and descend to traverse below the cliffs of Cima di Roda. Where the path to the Col Becchi branches off right, continue on the waymarked path to Passo di Ball until the path leads directly beneath the South-West Buttress of Pala di San Martino. Scramble up rubble for a few minutes to the start of the route. 1 hour from the Rosetta Hut.

Start about 50m left of an obvious, usually snow-filled gully. Climb the easier-angled initial rocks to gain a niche at the foot of a chimney.

Follow the prominent chimney system to the left of the snow-filled gully to its end. Go up and diagonally left to the broad spur of the pillar and climb this to the summit, staying left of the ill-defined arête.

Descent is by the North-East Ridge, with its many pinnacles. From the summit (bivouac box), follow the cairns to the east to a ledge above the East Ridge. From here the descent is marked in red. In general, the five pinnacles on the ridge are climbed or descended on their left (north) sides, until the Pala high plateau is reached. The five pinnacles are numbered from the bottom up.

Down-climb (II) into the notch between the summit and the 5th pinnacle. Turn it on the left along ledges to reach a notch. Traverse left around the 4th pinnacle to an abseil piton. Make two 20m abseils and traverse into the notch between the 4th and 3rd pinnacle (or, instead of the abseil and traverse, continue for a further 40m to a cemented-in abseil peg and abseil from this directly into the notch). Go left round the little pinnacle in the notch. Left again, round the flank of the 3rd pinnacle. Descend into a gully and scramble up this to the next notch. Climb over the 2nd pinnacle (II) and turn the 1st pinnacle on the left. Bear left over rounded knolls then head rightwards over fields to Rifugio Rosetta and the funicular station.

81 PALA DEL RIFUGIO   2394m

North-West Ridge, "Castiglioni/Detassis" V

The North-West Ridge is without doubt the most compelling line on Pala del Rifugio. Although a little chossy on the lower pitches up to the shoulder on the ridge, it gets steeper and more solid the higher up you go – pure pleasure. For those who are fully capable of mastering the difficulties and the length of the route – and who, in addition, are capable of getting out of bed early – we would recommend combining this route with the West Ridge of Sasso d'Ortiga (Route 83). When viewed in profile from Val Canali the ridge, a combination of two arêtes, is a veritable Jacob's Ladder that will

elevate you from one climbers' Seventh Heaven to the next (once the aforementioned initial scrappy part is out of the way). But do note that with over 1000 metres of climbing (8–11 hours of climbing), stamina is the prerequisite for complete enjoyment of the climb.

🍴 Ettore Castiglioni, Bruno Detassis. 18 July 1934.

📷 Some belay and protection pegs in situ. Many possible thread placements.

🏠 Rifugio Treviso (1630m). From the Fiera di Primiero/Passo Cereda road, branch off along a little road to Val Canali. At the Cant del Gal guesthouse, turn right and park. Follow an easy path to the hut (45 minutes).

↗ From Rifugio Treviso, walk in the direction of Passo Canali until you reach the edge of the trees. Turn right off the path here and head straight up (no path) to the foot of the ridge.

E Start on the west side of the ridge.

R Stay to the right of the edge of the ridge as far as the shoulder and thereafter mostly on its left side. Topo p.189.

↘ Descent marked in red. Go down to the east and traverse ledges onto the NW side until below the West Ridge of Sasso d'Ortiga. Cross the gap at the foot of the ridge (tunnel) and traverse across the SW side to a gully with cables. Scramble down the gully using the cables, climb up a short way and traverse over to Forcella delle Mughe. Follow the path back to the hut.

82 PALA DEL RIFUGIO 2394m

North-West Face, "Frisch/Corradini" V+

For many years, the "Frisch/Corradini" was rated as one of the best and most difficult routes in the area. With the exception of the rather scrappy and grassy first few pitches, the climb is on absolutely sound rock with few signs of wear and tear. Although most of the difficulty is below grade V, it is well to remember that the route is still an alpine undertaking in terms of route-finding and requires competence on demanding terrain, since the protection pegs are sparse.

Hans Frisch, P. Corradini. 16 July 1967.

Some belay and protection pegs in-situ. Nuts and slings – many thread and flake placements necessary.

Rifugio Treviso (1630m). From the Fiera di Primiero/Passo Cereda road, branch off along a little road to Val Canali. At the Cant del Gal guesthouse, turn right and park. Follow a path to the hut (45 minutes)

From Rifugio Treviso, walk in the direction of Passo Canali until you reach the edge of the trees. Leave the path here and head right, straight up (no path), through pine trees to the foot of the face.

An obvious cairn marks the start.

Stay mainly just to the left of a vague arête bounding the West Face. Higher up, the arête of the pillar joins the North-West Ridge. Follow this to the summit.

Descent marked in red. Go down to the east and traverse ledges onto the NW side until below the West Ridge of Sasso d'Ortiga. Cross the gap at the foot of the ridge (tunnel) and traverse across the SW side to a gully with cables. Scramble down the gully (cables), climb up a short way and traverse over to Forcella delle Mughe. Follow the path back to the hut.

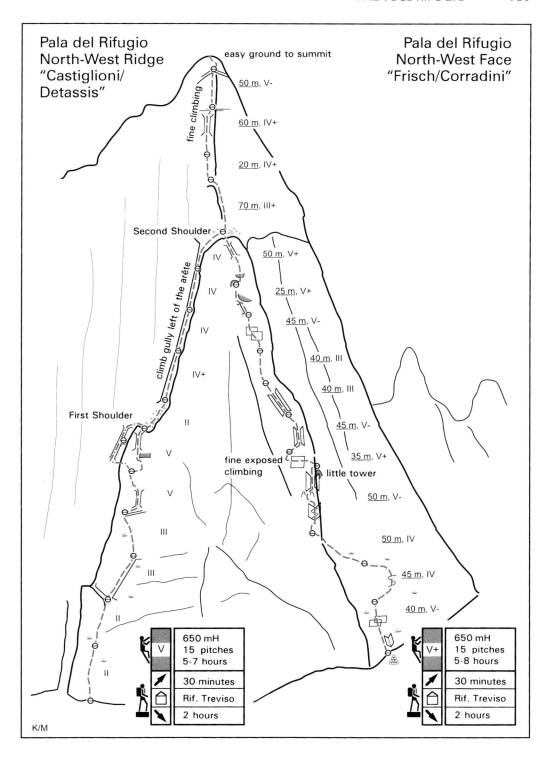

Pala del Rifugio
North-West Ridge
"Castiglioni/
Detassis"

Pala del Rifugio
North-West Face
"Frisch/Corradini"

easy ground to summit

fine climbing

50 m, V-

60 m, IV+

20 m, IV+

70 m, III+

Second Shoulder

IV

IV

IV

IV+

climb gully left of the arête

First Shoulder

II

V

V

III

III

II

II

50 m, V+

25 m, V+

45 m, V-

40 m, III

40 m, III

45 m, V-

35 m, V+

fine exposed
climbing

little tower

50 m, V-

50 m, IV

45 m, IV

40 m, V-

V	650 mH
	15 pitches
	5-7 hours
	30 minutes
	Rif. Treviso
	2 hours

V+	650 mH
	15 pitches
	5-8 hours
	30 minutes
	Rif. Treviso
	2 hours

K/M

83 SASSO D'ORTIGA   2361m

West Arête, "Wiessner/Kees" VI–

One of the finest climbs around! A more than obvious line, the rock steep, solid and extravagantly juggy, and, for all this, not even a little bit polished. This route is just as good as the famous "Schleier-kante" – yet far less crowded. This arête is positioned to be the logical continua-tion of the North-West Ridge of Pala del Rifugio and when combined with the latter is certainly one of the longest and most beautiful middle-grade outings in the Dolomites. But note that the combi-nation of the two routes as a one-day climb does involve over 1000 metres of sustained rock-climbing, demanding speed, skill and stamina to succeed. Those wanting to do just the Ortiga Arete will need to take the long and tiresome approach into account, but as recompense for the hassle the Gods have created a true miracle of a climb!

Fritz Wiessner, Hans Kees. 20 August 1928.

Some belay and protection pegs in situ. Countless thread placements.

Rifugio Treviso (1630m) – by a path from upper Val Canali (45 minutes, see p. 188).

Either descend from Pala del Rifugio to the start of the route or, from Rifugio Treviso, follow Path 720 to Forcella delle Mughe. From here, take an unmarked path to the left, traversing over to the lower crags of the Sasso d'Ortiga. Walk below the South-West Face to reach the West Arête; see p 192.

E Start to the right of the arête, in the fall-line of a chimney.

R A massive pillar, joined to the summit area by a huge jammed block forms the West Arête. Climb straight up, staying always slightly right of the edge of the arête, to gain the top of the pillar. Descend to the chockstone and climb the summit wall to the top.

Descend the South Ridge, crossing several little steps, to a steep, craggy slope which leads down to Forcella delle Mughe (II); marked in places, about an hour to the gap. Follow the path back to the hut.

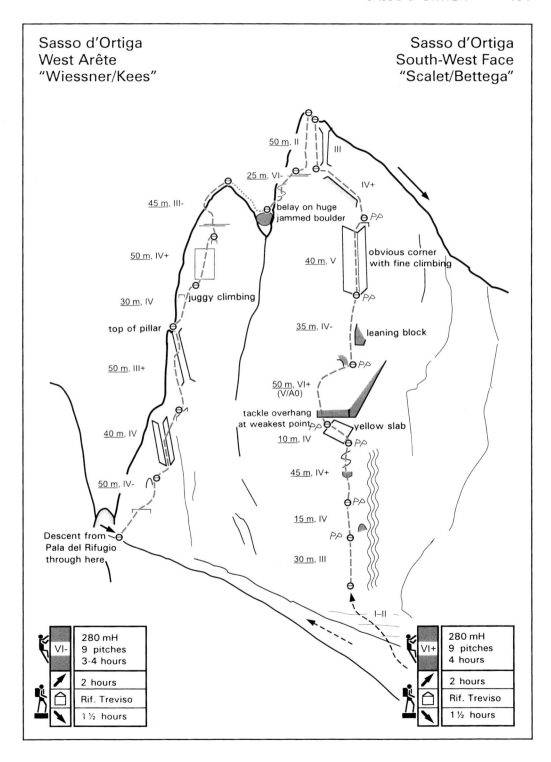

Sasso d'Ortiga
West Arête
"Wiessner/Kees"

Sasso d'Ortiga
South-West Face
"Scalet/Bettega"

50 m, II

III

25 m, VI-

IV+

45 m, III-

belay on huge
jammed boulder

PP

obvious corner
with fine climbing

50 m, IV+

40 m, V

PP

30 m, IV

juggy climbing

35 m, IV-

leaning block

top of pillar

PP

50 m, III+

50 m, VI+
(V/A0)

tackle overhang
at weakest point

yellow slab

40 m, IV

PP

10 m, IV

PP

45 m, IV+

50 m, IV-

PP

Descent from
Pala del Rifugio
through here

15 m, IV

PP

30 m, III

I–II

	280 mH
VI-	9 pitches
	3-4 hours
	2 hours
	Rif. Treviso
	1½ hours

	280 mH
VI+	9 pitches
	4 hours
	2 hours
	Rif. Treviso
	1½ hours

84 SASSO D'ORTIGA   2361m

South-West Face, "Scalet/Bettega" VI+

Climber-statisticians take note – if it were only a matter of balancing metres of approach with metres climbed, the South-West Face of Sasso d'Ortiga would be little frequented. The path up to the start of the route is long and strenuous and in descent it punishes the knees. But the climbing is good and the pitches after the big belt of roofs are superb – in particular the long and sustained corner high on the wall. The crux, at the left edge of the line of roofs in the middle of the face, is usually graded V/A0. Do not get annoyed with it, just be patient, scratch your head in wonder and try this unfriendly bulge free. You will feel very pleased with yourselves if you manage it without aid

Samuele Scalet, Aldo Bettega. 1961.

Sufficient belay and protection pegs in-situ; thread placements.

Rif. Treviso (1630m). Reached by a path from the upper Val Canali (¾ hour, see p.188).

From Rifugio Treviso, follow Path 720 up to Forcella delle Mughe. From here, take an unmarked path to the left, traversing over to the lower crags of Sasso d'Ortiga. Descend an exposed gully (II) with cable protection to a rocky corner and continue along a vague climbers' path to below the South-West Face of Sasso d'Ortiga. Scramble up easy ground (II) to the start of the route.

Start to the left of a prominent black water streak.

The route climbs the face to the left of the black streaks, as far as a prominent belt of roofs. This is breached on the left, at its weakest point. Climb up, trending right, towards the obvious corner on the upper part of the wall. Climb the corner and a ramp leading left to finish (topo p. 191).

Descend the South Ridge, crossing several little steps, to a steep, craggy slope which leads down to Forcella delle Mughe (II); marked in places, about 60 minutes to the gap. Follow the path back to the hut.

85 CIMA DEL CORO 2699m

South-West Face, "Gadenz" (Gadenz/Scalet) V–

In the uppermost Val Canali, Cima del Coro rises to block the head of the valley. The "Gadenz" threads its way up the central wall left of the prominent South-West Buttress, cleverly selecting the easiest line up this steep wall, on solid, hold-covered rock. The route offers several lovely pitches but also covers a relatively large amount of easy ground and here the cliff is sometimes covered in loose rubble. The route-finding

is not always straightforward, since the remoteness of the climb does not exactly encourage many ascents. Those who view the approach and descent not as irritating necessities but as a part of the whole mountain experience will enjoy the tranquility of this friendly face.

⌧ Michele and Lallo Gadenz, Quinto Scalet. 26 April 1953.

🗝 Some belay and protection pegs in-situ. Initiative required!

⌂ Rifugio Treviso (1630 m) – by a path from upper Val Canali (45 minutes, see p. 188).

↗ From Rifugio Treviso, follow Path 707 in towards Passo Canali to a point below the SW Face of Cima del Coro. Strike straight up the hillside to the big scree basin beneath the wall. At the highest point of this basin, a ramp line leads out left.

E Follow the ramp to its end (I and II). From here, the first pitch (hard) leads directly up onto the wall (pitons visible).

R The route takes a rising line to the right of the black/yellow zone located to the right of a big corner, cleverly seeking out the weaknesses of the wall. Topo p. 194.

↘ The route ends on the broad terrace below the summit. Go along this terrace to the right and through a tunnel to gain the grimly beautiful North Side. Either follow the red markers up and left to the summit (15 minutes) or descend directly down to the right (red markers). From a thread, abseil (20m) or down-climb (II–III, exposed), and make an exposed traverse (II–III) for a few metres into the notch between Cima del Coro and Torre Giubileo. Make three 20m abseils down chimneys to the East. Leave the gully (go left) and scramble down rock steps (I and II), bearing left, to join the "Reali Via Ferrata". Descend this to below the South-West Face (2 hours) and retrace your steps to the hut.

Cima del Coro
South-West Face
"Gadenz"

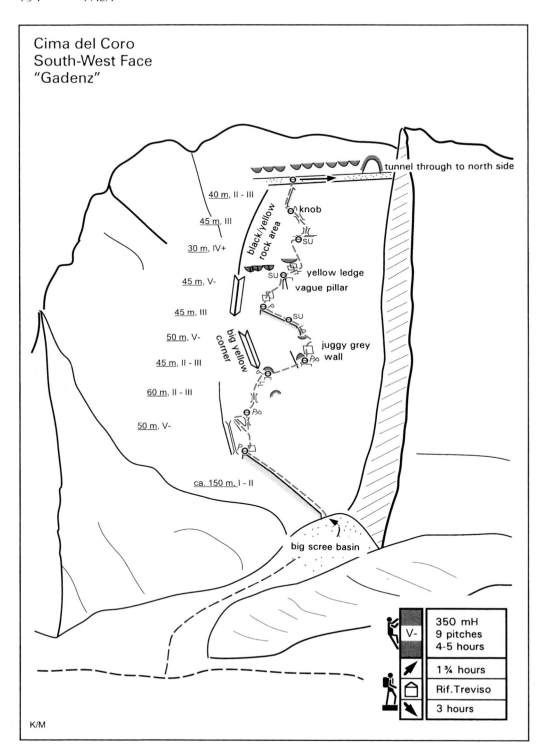

tunnel through to north side

40 m, II - III

45 m, III

black/yellow rock area

knob

SU

30 m, IV+

yellow ledge

45 m, V-

SU

vague pillar

45 m, III

SU

50 m, V-

big yellow corner

juggy grey wall

45 m, II - III

60 m, II - III

P

50 m, V-

P

ca. 150 m, I - II

big scree basin

	350 mH 9 pitches 4-5 hours
V-	
	1¾ hours
	Rif. Treviso
	3 hours

K/M

BRENTA

Lengthy and at times highly academic discussions have been conducted about whether or not the Brenta region, located to the west of the Etschtal and to the north of Lake Garda, ought to be officially included in the Dolomites. If the final judgement were to be based upon the rock beneath your fingertips, the answer to the problem is very simple, since that consists of best quality Dolomitic limestone. And one thing is certain: even if, geographically, the Brenta lies a little way off the mark, its character is as closely bound to the Dolomites as any other area. The walls and towers grow abruptly straight up out of the scree and are often breathtakingly steep and high, a rocky desert of savage, elemental beauty.

In general, Brenta rock is solid and well endowed with holds – and very steep. The latter fact does take some getting used to, especially on the easier routes, but the increased adrenaline production certainly invests climbing

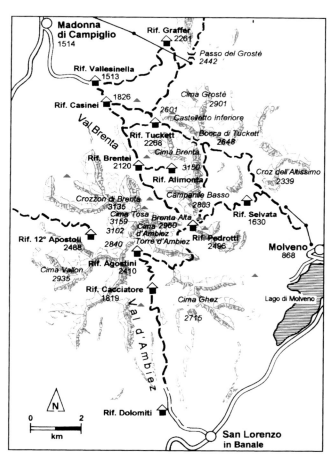

experiences with lasting value. The rock quality has a tendency to deteriorate as the angle eases and you approach the summit and this can sometimes sour the enjoyment of the exit pitches.

The mountains of the Brenta are high – several of them even exceed the 3000 metre mark – and some still wear the remnants of once larger glaciers. The climbing, particularly on Crozzon di Brenta, can soon acquire a singularly alpine tone.

The valley base for the routes in the area around the Tuckett, Pedrotti and Brentei Huts (routes 87 to 91) is the hotel village of Madonna di Campiglio (1522m). The central point of departure for several excursions in the group is certainly the Brentei Hut, with excellent camping nearby. As an additional bonus, during the summer here one can often admire in person that great character and past master Bruno Detassis, a pursuit that lends a particular quality to the ascent of one of his climbs on Crozzon di Brenta or Brenta Alta.

86 CASTELLETTO INFERIORE 2601m

South Face, "Kiene" V

The Castelletto Inferiore rises directly behind Rifugio Tuckett. The south-facing aspect of the cliff, the solid rock, the short approach from the hut and the relatively low height of the face make this an ideal climbing objective. The "Kiene", which traces a line directly up the South Face, is one of the most-loved routes on this mountain. The climbing is not very continuous but it does give several really outstanding pitches on very sound rock, especially those on the central section and on the steep summit wall. Unfortunately, entry to the really enjoyable rope lengths has to be hard earned in the initial two chimney pitches.

Erich and Kurt Kiene. 22 August 1910.

Numerous belay and protection pegs in-situ.

Rifugio Tuckett (2268m). Signposted path from Rifugio Vallesinella (reached by driving along a track from the centre of Madonna di Campiglio; car-park). Allow 2 hours.

From the hut, follow the climbers' path to the foot of the South Face.

Start in the direct fall line from the summit, at the foot of a big, obvious chimney leading to a terrace which runs right across the South Face.

Climb the chimney to the terrace. Up right and back left to a shallow corner system leading to a further terrace. Go diagonally left up chimneys to the shoulder beneath the steep summit wall. Climb the arête or the wall direct to the summit plateau.

Cross the summit plateau along a ridge to the east. There are then two options:
(a) Climb down into a notch (cairn) and descend a few metres more to a hidden abseil ring; make three 20m abseils to a ledge.
(b) Abseil 25m from two pitons to a ledge. Go up diagonally rightwards under a nose-shaped roof. Traverse round to a ledge on the N. side.
Both options now traverse left to an abseil point. Abseil 15m to the foot of the cliff. Descend to the path between the Rif. Tuckett and the Rif. Grafner and return to Rif. Tuckett..

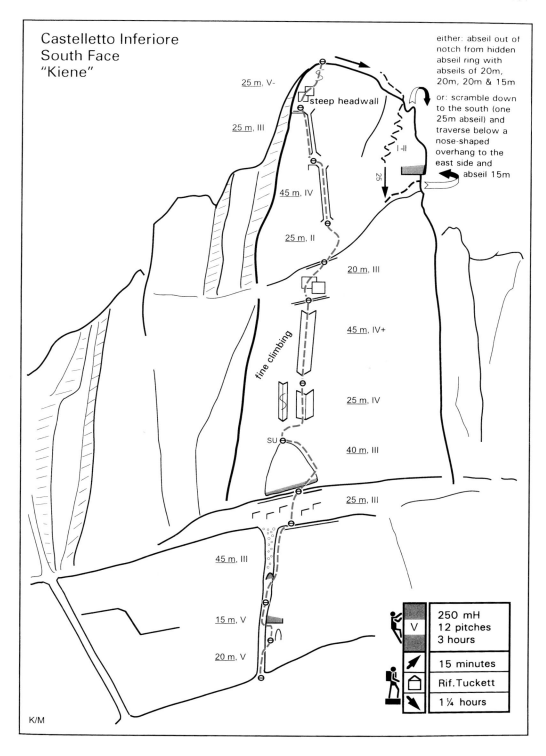

Castelletto Inferiore
South Face
"Kiene"

either: abseil out of
notch from hidden
abseil ring with
abseils of 20m,
20m, 20m & 15m

or: scramble down
to the south (one
25m abseil) and
traverse below a
nose-shaped
overhang to the
east side and
abseil 15m

25 m, V-

steep headwall

25 m, III

I -II

45 m, IV

25

25 m, II

20 m, III

45 m, IV+

fine climbing

25 m, IV

SU

40 m, III

25 m, III

45 m, III

15 m, V

20 m, V

V   250 mH
     12 pitches
     3 hours

     15 minutes

     Rif. Tuckett

     1 ¼ hours

K/M

87 CAMPANILE BASSO 2883m
GUGLIA DI BRENTA (original name)

"Normal Route" (Ampferer/Berger) V

The Ampferer/Berger Route is the ingenious first-ascent solution to what Walter Pause called 'this puzzle of stone'. For a "Normal Route" it is pretty hard.* The demanding face-climbing starts early with the now heavily polished "Pooli Wall". The pitch is actually named after Nino Pooli who, as early as 1897 dared to attempt the first ascent of this, the boldest of all the Brenta rock towers. Pooli's companions were Carlo Garbari and Antonio Tavernaro and the trio got as far as the stance below the intimidatingly vertical summit wall. Here, on a ledge, Garbari left a note in which he wished successive parties more luck with the continuation of the climb than they had had. The note had a calming effect on Otto Ampferer and Karl Berger two years later, when the sight of rusting pitons and empty wine bottles had caused them to begin to fear for their own fame as the first ascentionists of the tower. Their fears were groundless and everyone who nowadays stands on the summit – with safe belays and friction rubber shoes – having cracked that exposed final wall, would be prepared to doff their caps (or helmets) to Ampferer and his achievement in leading that pitch in 1898.

Viewed in a modern context, it is quite simply a most beautiful climb. It has bomb-proof rock, varied and, at times, very exposed climbing, bolt belays (albeit often shared with abseiling parties in descent) and interesting route-finding on a spiralling line opening up constantly changing vistas. In Ampferer's words 'It is a strange and lonely mountain. Most of the others disintegrate towards the top and allow easier movements. Not so the Guglia, which wears a stern demeanour and upon which the climbing, too, finds its most noble and sublime expression. Free, open walls decide everything here. Thus the form of this distinguished tower stands in perfect, harmonious accord with the ascent.'

* The continental habit of referring to the first ascent routes, or the easiest way up peaks as "Normal Routes" is a misnomer as such climbs (as in this case) can be the antithesis of 'normal' or 'ordinary' – 'original' is a more respectful adjective.

⚔ Otto Ampferer, Karl Berger. 18 August 1899. The Trento group of Nino Pooli, Carlo Garbari and Antonio Tavernaro had climbed to just below the summit wall two years previously.

⚒ Belays equipped with solid ring bolts. Beware of descending abseilers – if you start later to avoid the early morning rush you risk being caught in the contraflow! Plenty of reliable protection pegs on the difficult pitches.

🏠 Rifugio Pedrotti (2496m). Roughly in the centre of Madonna di Campiglio is the turn-off of the road up to Rifugio Vallesinella and car-park, which lies to the south-east of the town. From there, follow a pleasant path for 2 hours to Rifugio Brentei (2120m) and continue via Bocca di Brenta to Rifugio Pedrotti (3½ hours in total).

↗ From Rifugio Pedrotti via Bocca di Brenta, descend to the start of the Bocchette Route (about 100 m below the gap; ladders clearly visible). Alternatively, ascend to the same point from the Rifugio Brentei. Follow the Bocchette Route into the notch between Campanile Basso and Cima Brenta Alta (Bocchetta del Campanile Basso). From Rifugio Pedrotti, 45 minutes; from Rifugio Brentei, 1½ hours.

E Traverse left out of the notch onto Campanile Basso's South Face. The start of the route is located to the left of an obvious chimney system on the wall, which is crossed by ledges.

R Start by choosing your own line, more or less, to the prominent terrace beneath the "Pooli Wall". Climb this and move right to join the South-East Arête. Go round the arête and climb the East and North Faces up and diagonally right to reach a chimney system. Climb this to the big ledge ("Stradone Provinciale"). This is followed to the right, round the North-East Arête to a crack system leading up to a pulpit below the "Ampferer Wall". Climb the wall to the summit (topos on p.200 and 201).

↘ Abseil back down the approximate line of the route (ring bolts). Use double ropes! Allow up to 1½ hours to regain the Bocchetta del Campanile Basso.

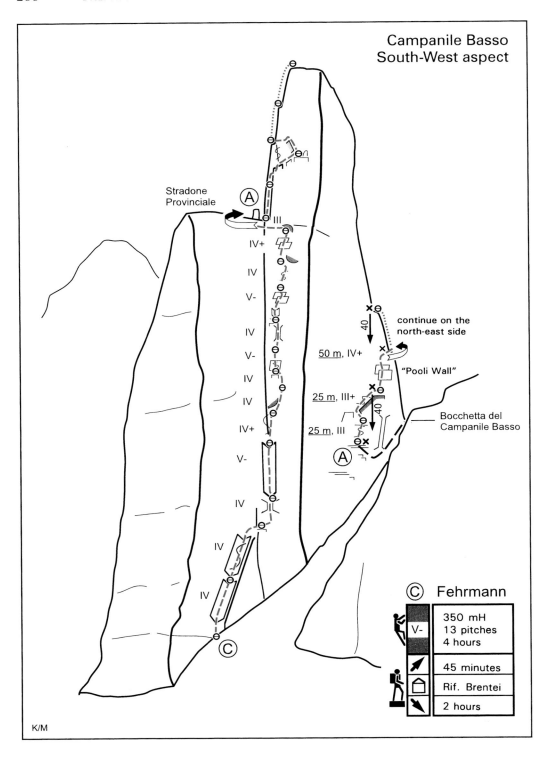

Campanile Basso
South-West aspect

Stradone
Provinciale

Ⓐ

III

IV+

IV

V-

IV

V-

IV

IV

IV+

V-

IV

IV

IV

Ⓒ

continue on the
north-east side

40

50 m, IV+

"Pooli Wall"

25 m, III+

40

25 m, III

Ⓐ

Bocchetta del
Campanile Basso

Ⓒ Fehrmann

V-

350 mH
13 pitches
4 hours

45 minutes

Rif. Brentei

2 hours

K/M

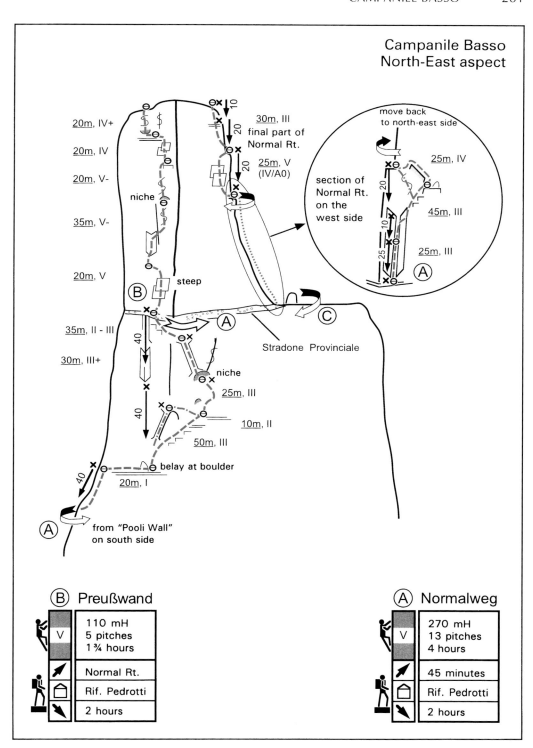

Campanile Basso
North-East aspect

20m, IV+

20m, IV

20m, V-

niche

35m, V-

20m, V

B

steep

35m, II - III

40

30m, III+

40

niche

25m, III

10m, II

50m, III

40

belay at boulder

20m, I

A

from "Pooli Wall"
on south side

30m, III
final part of
Normal Rt.

25m, V
(IV/A0)

10

20

20

section of
Normal Rt.
on the
west side

A

Stradone Provinciale

C

move back
to north-east side

25m, IV

20

10

25

25m, IV

45m, III

25m, III

A

B Preußwand

V	110 mH 5 pitches 1¾ hours
	Normal Rt.
	Rif. Pedrotti
	2 hours

A Normalweg

V	270 mH 13 pitches 4 hours
	45 minutes
	Rif. Pedrotti
	2 hours

88 CAMPANILE BASSO   2883m

East Face, "Preuss Wall" V

From the big terrace of the "Stradone Provinciale" there is a direct and more demanding alternative to the Normal Route – the "Preuss Wall". In July 1911, in a typically uncompromising display, that master of free-climbing Paul Preuss soloed straight up the vertical summit wall of Campanile Basso. Then, true to his own strict set of climbing rules, he soloed back down the same line – one of the very greatest of all the early rock climbing achievements. It was a remarkable performance, that becomes obvious as one happily clips into the pitons that protect the route today. The line is by no means obvious at first glance and thus requires both thought and forward planning. The climbing is also quite steep in places and there are few real resting places. The rock is sound but on certain sections there is a suspicion that this may not always have been the case.

- Paul Preuss. 28 July 1911.
- Many normal pitons, of distinctly variable quality.
- Rifugio Pedrotti (2496m). Approach see route 87, p. 199.
- Follow the Normal Route (route 87) to "Stradone Provinciale". Or climb the "Fehrmann Corner" to the same point.
- Start on "Stradone Provinciale", where the Normal Route comes in and the abseil piste starts (belay on a ring bolt).
- The route takes a slightly curving line up the wall to a corner. Climb the corner and move right around an ill-defined arête. More or less straight up now to a ledge. Go left and up to the summit (topo p. 200 and 201).
- Abseil piste, back down the approximate line of the normal route (drilled abseil rings); see topo. Double ropes! The first abseil ring is situated close to the North-West Arête. To find it from the summit, climb down approx. 10m in the direction of the Crozzon; Allow at least an hour to regain Bocchetta del Campanile Basso (topo p. 200 and 201).

89 CAMPANILE BASSO   2883m

South-West Corner, "Fehrmann" (Fehrmann/Perry Smith) V

With their ascent of the obvious S.W. Corner, Rudolf Fehrmann and Oliver Perry-Smith, carved their names for all time on the rock of the Campanile Basso. Fehrmann was the great Elbe sandstone pioneer and, with Paul Preuss, was one of the two great free-climbing apostles of the early days of rock-climbing. The "Fehrmann Corner" is the most obvious and classic line on the Campanile. The climbing is all on best quality rock, on a route with a marvellous singularity of line. Its only defect is that it finishes at the shoulder from where the final part of the Normal Route forms the logical topographic continuation of the climb. More logical in historic terms is to move round and reach the top via the "Preuss Wall", thereby paying homage to two great free-climbing pioneeers in one wonderful climb.

Rudolf Fehrmann, Oliver Perry-Smith. 27 August 1908.

All necessary belay and protection pegs in-situ. The corner is very 'nut-friendly'.

Rifugio Brentei (2120m). Waymarked path from Rifugio Vallesina (reached along the road from the centre of Madonna di Campiglio; car-park); 2 hours.

From Rifugio Brentei, take the path to Bocca di Brenta until below the West Face of Campanile Basso. Go right, past the SW Arête, to the foot of the wall, directly below the corner.

Start at a narrow ledge leading across to the South-West Arête ("Graffer Arête"), below a steep, diagonal ramp going up and right.

Climb for two pitches up and right to the start of the corner (terrace). Follow the general line of the corner all the way. Below the big shoulder, the corner widens to an unpleasant chimney but this can be avoided by climbing the wonderful slabs on the right. A traverse finally leads onto the shoulder. See topo p. 200 and 201.

If not continuing to the summit, abseil down the Normal Route (drilled abseil rings, double ropes)! From the shoulder, traverse round the "Stradone Provinciale" to the east flank to gain the first abseil ring above the chimney/gully right of the South-East Arête (at the start of the "Preuss Wall"). Allow 1 hour (topo p. 200 and 201).

90 CROZZON DI BRENTA   3135m

North-East Face, "Via delle Guide" (Detassis/Giordani) V+

The massive bulk of Crozzon di Brenta, with the seemingly endless and elegant line of its North Arête piercing the skies, is the mightiest and most alpine of all the giants in the Brenta Group – rising from the valley as a powerful monolith of stone. Its North-East Face is marked by two obvious water streaks. Along the right-hand streak runs the line of one of the most beautiful routes in the Dolomites, the "Via delle Guide", the most precious pearl of the great Brenta master Bruno Detassis and his fellow guide Enrico Giordani. A dream climb on steep, water-worn, compact limestone. Though the north-facing, the climb does get the sun for quite a long spell. The crux sections – the surprisingly 'unthrutchy' crack through the overhang after the second terrace and the compact, black slab beneath the prominent roof – are technically quite demanding. Yet on this impressively steep terrain even the easier pitches require careful climbing. But there must also be a sense of urgency as there is 800 metres of climbing to gain the summit! The bitter pill comes only after you have topped out, for the descent is long, delicate in places and again requires 100% concentration. The nice little summit bivouac shelter is sometimes quite a comforting thought. All in all, a big and serious undertaking.

⚔ Bruno Detassis, Enrico Giordani. 2 August 1935.

⚒ All necessary belay and protection pegs in-situ. Protection pegs on the crux pitches are not numerous. Slings for threads (some thread belays) and nuts indispensable.

⌂ Rifugio Brentei (2120m). From the centre of Madonna di Campiglio take the road up to Rifugio Vallesinella (car-park). From there, follow a pleasantly varied path for to the hut (2 hours).

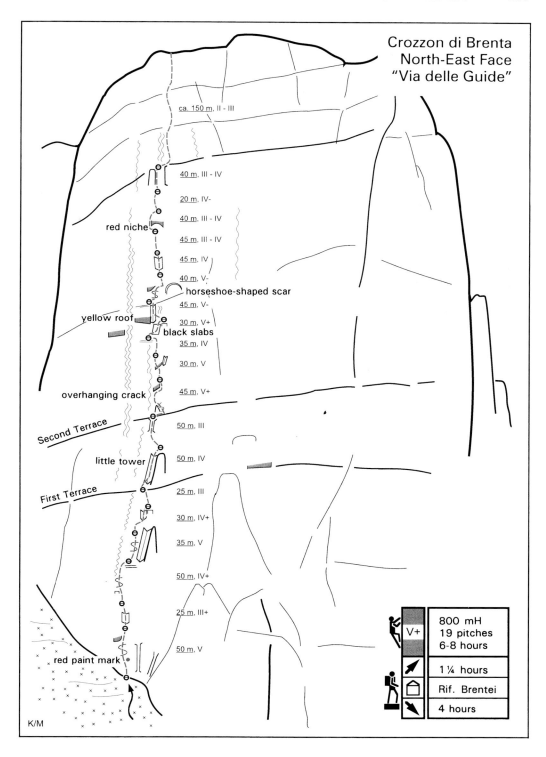

Crozzon di Brenta
North-East Face
"Via delle Guide"

ca. 150 m, II - III

40 m, III - IV

20 m, IV-

40 m, III - IV

red niche

45 m, III - IV

45 m, IV

40 m, V-

horseshoe-shaped scar

45 m, V-

yellow roof

30 m, V+

black slabs

35 m, IV

30 m, V

overhanging crack

45 m, V+

Second Terrace

50 m, III

little tower

50 m, IV

First Terrace

25 m, III

30 m, IV+

35 m, V

50 m, IV+

25 m, III+

50 m, V

red paint mark

V+

800 mH
19 pitches
6-8 hours

1 ¼ hours

Rif. Brentei

4 hours

K/M

↗ From Rifugio Brentei, take the Rifugio 12 Apostoli path down past the campsite below the hut and into Val Brenta. Follow the now rising path and turn off left below the Crozzon's North-East Face to follow a less well-defined path to the Tosa Gully. Climb a little way up the gully (depending on the time of year, this will hold either snow or large lumps of scree) until you can see the marked start of the route out right on the Face.

E The start is marked in red (faded lettering: "Via delle Guide" and a rather unfortunate portrait of the first ascentionists), to the left of two obvious chimneys, at the foot of a steep crack.

R The route follows the right-hand water streak on the left sector of the North-East Face. On the lower section, where the water streak is less clearly defined, the line of the route stays close to its right-hand edge. The left-hand edge of the streak is gained at the prominent yellow roof by trending up and left over several pitches from the second terrace. After the difficulties end, approximately 200m of easier-angled (II) climbing remain to the summit. The route is rather vague here. There is an emergency bivouac shelter (4 people) on the summit.

↘ The most complicated (alpine) part of the descent is the cairned traverse to Cima Tosa (see sketch), during which one has to circumvent and cross the Middle and South Summits of the Crozzon on occasionally unpleasantly loose terrain (sections of II and III). Surefootedness on steep ground is a prerequisite here (allow 2 hours to reach Cima Tosa). Traverse the summit plateau of the Tosa, heading north-west, and descend the Normal Route in an easterly direction to a basin-shaped hollow. Bear right at a steep crag and abseil down the steep section (chimney, in-situ abseil piton). Continue on down to the clearly marked path which is followed east to below Cima Margherita and Brenta Bassa, and thence to Rifugio Pedrotti (90 minutes). From Rifugio Pedrotti, cross Bocca di Brenta and return to Rifugio Brentei (45 minutes).

! Note: Depending on conditions, it is worth carrying in-step crampons on this route, both for the approach (Crozzon Glacier/Tosa Gully) and for the traverse across to Cima Tosa, where the small and compact summit snowfield has to be crossed.

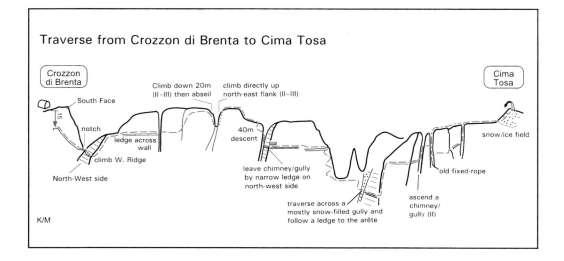

Traverse from Crozzon di Brenta to Cima Tosa

91 **BRENTA ALTA** 2960m

North-East Face, "Detassis" (Detassis/Battistata/Giordani) VI–

On the North-East Face of Brenta Alta is the first of the two great classic Brenta routes inspired by Bruno Detassis. The fact that he dared to climb this smooth and featureless wall as early as 1934 shows not only the extraordinarrily high standards at which he operated but also bears testimony to his self-belief and his sure instinct for what was then possible. The route-finding is anything but straightforward and one needs to have considerable faith in one's reserves of strength to carry on up the steep, sometimes blind sections of the wall. Face climbing on very solid and compact slabby limestone predominates and at times it can all get pretty strenuous. Even judged on modern sport-climbing criteria, this is a first rate climb. On the

upper third, the route is criss-crossed by ledges and here the rock quality and the aesthetic appeal deteriorate noticeably – the line becoming correspondingly less precise.

Bruno Detassis, Ulisse Battistata, Enrico Giordani. 14–15 August 1934.

To the end of the main difficulties, all necessary belay and protection pegs (average quality) are in place. Things get a bit thinner on the upper third of the route. Slings for threads and an assortment of nuts an absolute necessity.

Rifugio Pedrotti (2496m). Roughly in the centre of Madonna di Campiglio is the turn-off to Rifugio Vallesinella (car-park), which lies to the south-east of the town. From there, follow a pleasantly varied path to Rifugio Brentei (2120m – 2 hours) and continue via Bocca di Brenta to Rifugio Pedrotti (3½ hours in total).

From Rif. Pedrotti, descend the Orsi Path (branches off left at the Rif. Tosa) and walk along the east side of Brenta Alta (lots of up and down) to reach a corrie. Follow a faint path over scree and boulders up the corrie to beneath the North-East Face. The face is bounded on each side by the prominent lines of the "Oggioni Corner"(left) and the "Gogna Arête" (right).

E Start about 50m to the left of the fall line of the "Gogna Arête". There is a shallow, 'bathtub' of a groove up on the wall to the left of the arête. About 15m left of this groove is a crack leading to a corner below an obvious horizontal belt of roofs. This crack is the first pitch. The line of pitons leading out right from below the roof is a false line!

R The route takes quite a complicated line up the slabs to the left of the blunt, bathtub groove. The groove itself is joined briefly just before the big traverse left. After the end of the difficulties (and the good rock), the line of the route is no longer prescribed – several possibilities exist, all of a similar standard of difficulty and quality (follow the tracks!). The summit is reached by the East Arête.

↘ From the summit, descend the Normal Route to the south-east (rock steps and rubble) to the loose rocks of the upper terrace; follow the tracks and the cairns. On reaching the steep step dividing the upper and lower rubble terraces, traverse right and either down-climb to the lower terrace (I and II) or abseil. Scramble down scree and boulders to the steeper chimney which forms the entry pitch to the Normal Route. Abseil 20m (pegs in-situ) and traverse round the ledge to Bocca di Brenta (about 1 hour). A ten-minute walk leads back to Rifugio Pedrotti.

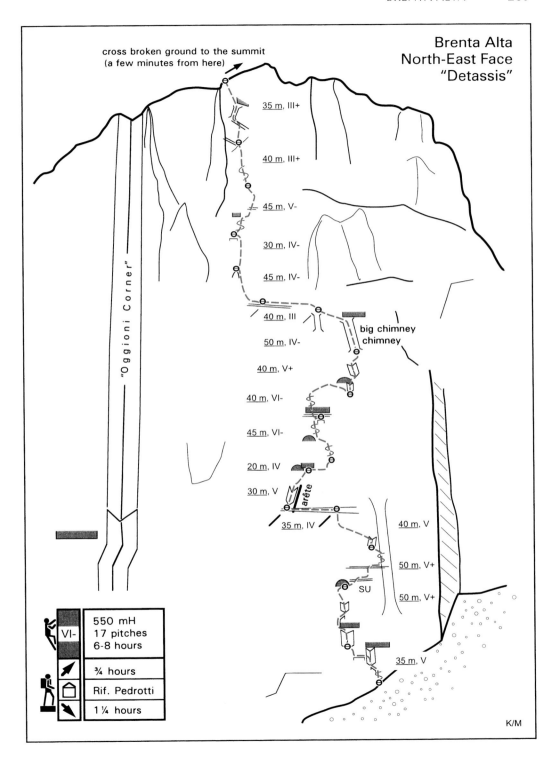

Brenta Alta
North-East Face
"Detassis"

cross broken ground to the summit
(a few minutes from here)

35 m, III+

40 m, III+

45 m, V-

30 m, IV-

45 m, IV-

"Oggioni Corner"

40 m, III

big chimney
chimney

50 m, IV-

40 m, V+

40 m, VI-

45 m, VI-

20 m, IV

30 m, V   arête

35 m, IV

40 m, V

50 m, V+

SU

50 m, V+

35 m, V

VI-   550 mH
       17 pitches
       6-8 hours

¾ hours

Rif. Pedrotti

1 ¼ hours

K/M

92 TORRE D'AMBIEZ   2840m

East Dièdre (Armani/Gasperini) IV+

The many summits of Denti d'Ambiez, of which that of Torre d'Ambiez is the largest and most important, do rather hide themselves in the shadow of the mighty South-East Face of Cima d'Ambiez. Yet Torre d'Ambiez has a fine natural line on offer. The entire East Face is marked by a single dièdre/groove composed of sound rock. It gives steep climbing right up the angle of the dièdre itself. It is not quite as elegant as the "Fehrmann Corner" on Campanile Basso but then again it is not half as crowded either. And that is far from the only reason why you should pay this climb a visit. The short approach from the hut, the east-facing aspect, the logical route-finding and the sustained standard of difficulty make this a route which can be thoroughly recommended.

🕱 Matteo Armani, Ettore Gasperini. 11 July 1938.

🔖 Some pegs in-situ but take a full collection of nuts and slings!

🏠 Rif. Agostini (2410m). Drive up the little road from San Lorenzo in Banale to the Rif. Dolomiti (parking). A three-hour walk leads up to Rif. Cacciatori (1819 m). Alternatively a jeep taxi can be booked at Rif. Dolomiti. Continue along the road on foot to Rif. Agostini (1 hour).

↗ Follow the Brentari Path to beneath the face.

E Start to the left of the bottom of the prominent East Dièdre, at an ill-defined arête just right of a little gully.

R Climb up and right to gain the dièdre. Follow it to the summit.

↘ Descend slightly to the notch between the Torre and the 4th Dente. Move down to the east to a ledge between the 4th and 3rd 'teeth'. Traverse around the 3rd Dente on ledges on the west side to the notch of the 3rd and 2nd Dente. Head west to the next notch. Continue on the west side, finally descending to the notch of the Denti and Cima d'Ambiez. Descend east to the ledge on the SE Face of the Ambiez. Traverse to regain the Brentari Path.

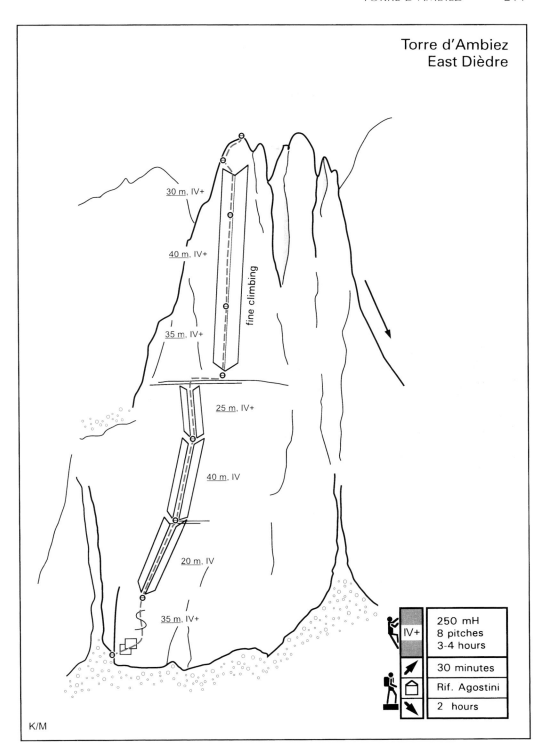

Torre d'Ambiez
East Dièdre

30 m, IV+

40 m, IV+

fine climbing

35 m, IV+

25 m, IV+

40 m, IV

20 m, IV

35 m, IV+

IV+ | 250 mH
8 pitches
3-4 hours

30 minutes

Rif. Agostini

2 hours

K/M

93 CIMA D'AMBIEZ   3102m

South-East Face, "Fox/Stenico" VI

Glowing golden in the morning sun, the South-East Face of Cima d'Ambiez is the paradigm, the idealist's Dolomite wall. A compact, featureless shield of rock, rising vertically as if formed from a single cast. The routes that climb this steep wall are all correspondingly difficult. The "Fox/ Stenico" was the first, and easiest route to be found on the face. It runs up to the left of the central section, alongside the two parallel black water streaks which stem from the twin 'ears' of rock high up on the wall. The climb is not too long but it is continuously difficult. Right from the first belay, things begin in earnest and those wishing to climb this first pitch totally free (the pitons are seductively close) will have to make a determined effort. The solid rock and the warming morning sun will, however, make even the loftiest climbing ambitions seem possible.

🍴	Pino Fox, Marino Stenico. 1939.
⚒	All necessary belay and protection pegs in-situ, but it is still worth taking nuts!
🏠	Rifugio Agostini (2410m). Approach, see route 92, p.210.
↗	Follow the Brentari Path from Rifugio Agostini. On reaching the start of the glacier, turn left onto the wide ledge crossing the entire Ambiez South Face. Go along the ledge, traversing below face and duck round a vague arête. Scramble up rock steps in the direct fall line of the left-hand of the two parallel water streaks to the start of the route.

🇪	Start at the foot of a corner to the left of a shattered slab.
🇷	Follow the two parallel black water streaks that stem from the obvious twin 'ears' of rock.

↘	Start down the Normal Route (cairned) on the South Ridge. Descend a gully in the West Face and continue down, scrambling and climbing (II), bearing right, over ledges and steep, rubble-strewn steps. Finally descend, keeping left, to the notch between the Denti and Cima d'Ambiez. Go down the gully to the starting ledge (1 hour).

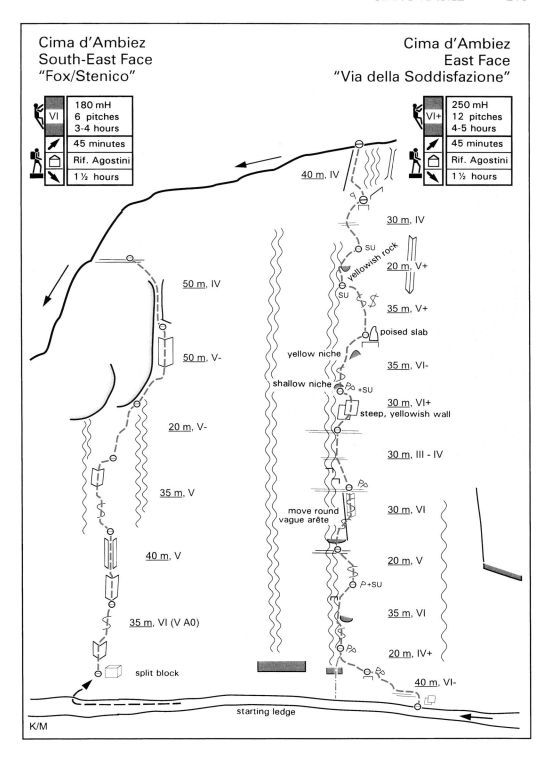

Cima d'Ambiez
South-East Face
"Fox/Stenico"

VI	180 mH 6 pitches 3-4 hours
	45 minutes
Rif. Agostini	
	1 ½ hours

Cima d'Ambiez
East Face
"Via della Soddisfazione"

VI+	250 mH 12 pitches 4-5 hours
	45 minutes
Rif. Agostini	
	1 ½ hours

40 m, IV

30 m, IV

SU   yellowish rock

20 m, V+

SU

35 m, V+

poised slab

yellow niche

35 m, VI-

shallow niche   +SU

30 m, VI+
steep, yellowish wall

30 m, III - IV

move round
vague arête

30 m, VI

20 m, V

P+SU

35 m, VI

20 m, IV+

40 m, VI-

50 m, IV

50 m, V-

20 m, V-

35 m, V

40 m, V

35 m, VI (V A0)

split block

starting ledge

K/M

94 CIMA D'AMBIEZ   3102m

East Face, "Soddisfazione" (Bosetti/Orlandi/Rigotti/Salvaterra) VI+

The "Via della Soddisfazione" is considered the most beautiful route on the
East Face of Cima d'Ambiez. The route is
strikingly clear and bold in concept,
tracing a direct line up the right-hand edge
of the central big black water streak. On
first acquaintance it is barely believable
that this modern dream-climb goes at a
'mere' grade VI. It does, however, require
all-round competence at this grade over its
entire length. There are cracks, traverses,
overhangs and face climbing so the whole
repertoire of techniques is required. The
climb is in a sunny position and on mostly
finest quality, water-worn rock – occasionally as rough as a porcupine and lavishly
well-endowed with threads, sharp little
finger edges and pockets. This is a fine
modern route that might only be improved
by holding its character a little longer
rather than declining into mediocrity on
the last couple of pitches.

⊠ Andrea Bosetti, Elio Orlandi, Livio Rigotti, Ermanno Salvaterra. 7 July 1982.

⚒ Sufficient belay and protection pegs in-situ. Some belays can be backed up with threads.

⌂ Rifugio Agostini (2410m). Approach, see route 92, p. 210.

↗ Follow the Brentari Path from Rifugio Agostini. On reaching the start of the glacier, turn left
onto the wide ledge that crosses the entire Ambiez South Face.

E The Direct Start begins in the direct fall line of the black water streak, to the right of a
prominent roof. A piton can be seen up on the very steep wall indicating the direct start
(VII–/VII)! This very difficult and bold start is not recommended here. Instead, start a good
50m further right, gaining the black water streak by a rising leftwards traverse.

R Follow the right-hand edge of the black water streak.

↘ Start down the Normal Route along the South Ridge (cairns). Then descend the West Face
to the notch between the Denti and Cima d'Ambiez. (See route 93, p.212. 1 hour.)

BIBLIOGRAPHY

Dolomite guidebooks and maps currently available are:

Ron James *Dolomites, Selected Climbs* Alpine Club, London 1988 offers an overview of the main mountain groups with 340 routes described in all grades. Available from climbing shops or from Cordee, 3a De Montfort Street, Leicester LE1 7HD. U.S.A.: Adventurous Traveler Bookstore (http://www.adventuroustraveler.com) or Chessler Books, P.O. Box 4359, Evergreen, Colorado 80437.

Gillian Price *Walking in the Dolomites* Cicerone Press, Milnthorpe. Also Dolomite scrambling and climbing guides and Dolomites Alte Via 1 & 2, the main long-distance paths. Available from: Cicerone Press, Harmony Hall, Milnthorpe, Cumbria, LA7 7PY, U.K.

Edizioni Dolomiti Cartografische Casa Editrice Tabacco, Udine (40 maps at 1:25,000 – the best maps for detailed navigation). Also the 1:50,000 maps of Kompass (Munich) and Freytag and Berndt (Vienna). Available from specialist shops and Cordee, and in some cases from Chessler Books and Adventurous Traveller Bookstore (see addresses above)

Other books/journals with chapters or total coverage on Dolomite climbing:

Chris Bonington *I Chose to Climb* Gollancz, London. 1966
John Brailsford *Dolomites East and West* Alpine Club, London. 1970 (earlier guidebooks)
Edward A. Broome "The Rosengarten Dolomites" *Alpine Journal* Vol 14, pp 459–472 A.C., London. 1909
Hermann Buhl *Nanga Parbat Pilgrimage* Hodder & Stoughton, London / Dutton, New York, 1956; Bâton Wicks, London / The Mountaineers, Seattle. 1998
Riccardo Cassin *50 Years of Alpinism* Diadem, London / The Mountaineers, Seattle. 1980
Peter Crew *Selected Climbs in the Dolomites* Alpine Club, London. 1963 (earlier guidebook)
L. Marion Davidson *Things Seen in the Dolomites* Seeley Service, London. 1928
Rev. J Sanger Davies *Dolomite Strongholds* George Bell, London 1894
Kurt Diemberger *Summits and Secrets* George Allen and Unwin, London. 1971 and in **The Kurt Diemberger Omnibus**, Bâton Wicks, London / Mountaineers, Seattle. 1999.
Amelia B.Edwards *Untrodden Peaks and Unfrequented Valleys* Longmans, London. 1873
Reginald Farrer *The Dolomites* A & C Black, London 1913 (25 paintings by E.T.Compton)
Hermann Frass *Dolomites, Mountains of Magic* Athesia, Bolzano. 1977 (pictures/history)
Giusto Gervasutti *Gervasutti's Climbs* Hart-Davis, London 1957; Diadem, London / The Mountaineers, Seattle. 1979
Josiah Gilbert / George C. Churchill *The Dolomite Mountains* Longmans, London 1864
Dougal Haston *In High Places* Cassell, London/Macmillan, New York. 1972/73
Roger Hubank *The North Wall* Hutchinson, London / Viking, New York. 1977. Also collected in **One Step in the Clouds** Diadem, London / Sierra Club Books, San Francisco. 1990. A powerful novel about hard Dolomite climbing
C.F. Meade *Approach to the Hills* John Murray, London. 1940
Reinhold Messner *The Seventh Grade* Kaye and Ward, London. 1974
C. Douglas Milner *Rock for Climbing* Chapman and Hall, London. 1950 (pictures)
C. Douglas Milner *The Dolomites* Robert Hale, London. 1951 (pictures/history)
Ludwig Norman-Neruda *The Climbs of Norman-Neruda* Fisher Unwin, London. 1899
Walter Pause / Wolf Jürgen Winkler *Extreme Alpine Rock* Granada, London. 1979
Gaston Rèbuffat *Starlight and Storm* Dent, London. 1956
Guido Rey *Peaks and Precipices* Fisher Unwin, London / Dodd Mead, New York 1914
Doug Scott *Big Wall Climbing* Kaye and Ward, London. 1974 (history)
Leone Sinigaglia *Climbing Reminiscences of the Dolomites* Fisher Unwin, London. 1896
Frank Smythe *The Adventures of a Mountaineer* Dent, London. 1940
Miriam Underhill *Give Me The Hills* Methuen, London. 1956, Chatham Press/Appalachain Mt. Club, Boston. 1971
Don Whillans / Alick Omerod *Portrait of a Mountaineer* Heinemann, London. 1971
Emil Zsigmondy *In the High Mountains* The Ernest Press, Holyhead. 1992

Films worth noting:

Hazard (a safety film made for British Steel) which features spectacular views of the Yellow Edge; *Abimes* recreates a gripping fall scene and recovery on the Swiss/Italian route on Cima Ovest and *Cliffhanger* with its magnificent big-screen scenes of Dolomite spires plus some very unrealistic but amusing climbing sequences.

NOTES FOR THE ENGLISH LANGUAGE EDITION

English-speaking climbers, more familiar with Italian titling for peaks and features, may find the German titling a little confusing. Prior to World War I most of the Dolomite range was within the boundaries of the Austro/Hungarian empire, but thereafter was Italian administered – leaving a certain historical and cultural ambiguity. The German mountain titling is retained (to preserve the character of the guidebook) with Italian translations added for cross-reference. Huts are given their Italian names which fits with the waymarking of their approach paths, though sometimes both Italian and German hut titles are given.

The gradings of the climbs are pitched at a slightly higher level than that found in the 1988 Alpine Club guide – this reflects the modern assumption that the pitches are led free whereas in the past a semi-aided alpine approach would have been the norm. Many of the routes have been given eponymous titles – "Comici", "Dibona", "Fehrmann" etc. Often this disguises the contributions of others on the first ascent party, so a full list of personel is appended to each title. In some of the official guidebooks these names are listed alphabetically, and in other cases with clients first and guides second etc – all of which serves to disguise where the true credit (for either climbing or concept) should lie.

The authors Memmel and Köhler, genuflect respectfully to the great free-climbing achievements of the pioneers: Winkler, Ampferer, Pruess, Detassis and many others. Conversely they seem happy to applaud the establishment of fixed belays and protection (pitons and bolts) on many of the classic climbs. This may seem to create an ethical contradiction for those accustomed to the clear cut deliniations of other areas. While idiot-proof rigging (often for commercial reasons) of the short classic easy climbs is to be deprecated, on this large and very challenging Dolomite stage the odd fixed piton or bolt on the longer climbs, though still unfortunate (with nuts etc now so good), make little difference to overall character of the climb – their main value being more for route-confirmation. Occasional 'caustic' publisher's notes are added in [ ] parentheses and additional historical footnotes are also included where necessary.

Climbers versed in the styles of smaller cliffs will have to make a rapid adjustment to the sterner demands of this unique region. Apart from a few training climbs, the other routes are long (ranging from big Scottish route length to major Yosemite scale). The climbs are consistently steep, set at around 3000 metres in altitude, exposed to changeable weather and ending on vertiginous summits often with a finale of a long and complex descent, frequently involving a series of committing abseils. In such an environment climbers will wish to give careful consideration the length of the climb, the weather, equipment, footwear, fitness, food, ability, stamina, time-available, route-finding skill and speed in order to ensure an epic-free ascent. Even the strongest parties might be well-advised to include some training climbs in their 'sports plans'. Stonefall at points during the ascent, and particularly on the usual couloir/gully located descents will suggest the wisdom of wearing helmets. The choice of footwear (lightweight boots versus climbing-shoes/trainers) will also be a matter for consideration with comfort and warmth (should bad weather arrive) being factored into the solution. Sound route-finding (on often anonymous terrain) combined with brisk climbing, long pitches, and rapid placing of well-spaced protection, is the big mountain style that needs to be perfected. On descent, precision in route-finding and abseil anchor selection, is important. Abseiling techniques also need care, with precautions against stonefall and rope retrieval high on the list of matters to be watched.

These peculiar Dolomite problems have 'intrigued' generations of climbers. It is one reason why this guide is particularly welcome as the authors have given attention to route location in both ascent and descent, using their topos to great effect.

ACKNOWLEDGEMENTS: The authors and the publisher are indebted to Tim Carruthers who made the original translation which is adapted to fit the straightjacket of the German layout. In addition a debt is owed to the following for sundry research and advice: Gabriela Cecchin, Paul Dèmogè, Margaret Ecclestone, Carlo Gandini, Sheila Harrison, Grant Jarvis, Reinhold Messner, Mike Mortimer, Giorgio Redaelli, Hermann Reisach, Audrey Salkeld, Anne Sauvy, Anna Stenico, Mirella and Luciano Tenderini and Klaus Wolfsperger.